Being Hungarian
in Cleveland

Endre Szentkiralyi

Being Hungarian in Cleveland

Maintaining Language, Culture, and Traditions

HHP

KKL Publications LLC, Helena History Press
Reno, Nevada USA

Publishing scholarship about and from Central and East Europe

H P
www.helenahistorypress.com

Distributed by IngramSpark and available through all major e-retail sites
info@helenahistorypress.com

Copy Editor: Jill Hannum, Krisztina Kós
Maps are courtesy of Maria Julia Honfi
Graphic Designer: Sebastian Stachowski

Dedication

To all my fellow Cleveland Hungarians, I dedicate this book to you, for it is your unseen work on an ongoing basis, day to day, week to week, year to year, decade to decade, that maintains these Hungarian-American traditions. This not only gives me something to write about but also provides an active social community in which my family and I can take part, passing our values and traditions on to the next generation.

But most of all, to my children Keve, Bendegúz, Vajk, and Enese, and to my wife Eszti: only you truly know what writing this book really meant – köszönöm!

Table of Contents

Foreword

Cleveland's Hungarian community holds an almost mythic status locally. When speaking of immigration to the city it is almost *de rigueur* to note that Cleveland's Hungarian population was the second largest in the world—so Cleveland becomes analogous to Debrecen. Then too, there is the lament that what was, is no more. For some, the empty storefronts in the old neighborhoods define an endpoint for the community. Yet, both statements obscure essential historical truths, and this volume by Endre Szentkiralyi serves as a much-needed corrective and an important update to our knowledge of the Magyars of Cleveland. He clearly shows us that the Cleveland Magyar community is neither Debrecen nor dead.

More importantly, *Being Hungarian in Cleveland: Maintaining Language, Culture, and Traditions* is a significant update to the existing secondary literature on the city's Hungarian community. The last major published work on the community was Julianna Puskas's "The Magyars of Cleveland, 1880–1930" published in 2002 in *Identity, Conflict, & Cooperation: Central Europeans in Cleveland, 1850–1930*. Prior to that, Susan Papp's *The Hungarian Americans and their Communities in Cleveland*, published in 1981, was the critical singular source. Based on a variety of sources, including oral histories, surveys, and local publications, *Being Hungarian in Cleveland* not only updates the existing literature but also expands it with important new details about the organizations and agencies that defined and continue to define the community. Indeed, the sections on organizational cultural infrastructure are encyclopedic, and thus very useful to researchers looking for dates and other historical details.

Beyond this factual cornucopia, the book's focus on what might be called the "post-Ellis Island" Magyar migration to the city is particularly important as it opens up new vistas on the persistence of culture and memory within the community. Although different from the earliest large-scale migration in terms of educational background and political awareness, the most recent Hungarian migrations to Cleveland have served to perpetuate a sense of community despite their geographic residential dispersion. Szentkiralyi shows us that a community is no longer defined by a physical neighborhood, but rather by a shared set of cultural values. Language schools and scouting movements are, in many ways, as important to "seeing" a Hungarian community as were the Magyar signs that once adorned streetscapes in the Buckeye neighborhood. And while the declining attendance at older, inner city Hungarian Roman Catholic parishes seems a harbinger of a communal end point, the broader activist movement to keep those parishes open suggests a significant cultural vibrancy.

In many ways, what occurred in Cleveland, "the American Debrecen," in the years since the 1920s is a model for testing the experiences of other European migration streams to the United States. While the numbers of immigrants have substantially diminished and pioneer neighborhood infrastructures have been lost in Cleveland and elsewhere, there are still important continuities that can be seen—continuities that challenge the myths of the past and argue for new ways to see and understand cultural affinities in the present. This book prompts us to look beyond the somewhat clichéd "streetscape view" of ethnicity and to search for the virtual realities that shape and define memory and community in the twenty-first century.

John J. Grabowski, Ph.D.
Case Western Reserve University
Western Reserve Historical Society

Preface

This work intends to show what it means to be a Hungarian in Cleveland, examining the community's language and literature, culture, and traditions from 1950 to the present. It will do so with a variety of methodologies, looking at the community historically, sociologically, and from a literary and linguistic perspective. What does it really mean to be Hungarian in the greater Cleveland area?

Thanks to Dr. Tibor Glant at the University of Debrecen in Hungary, who initially sparked my interest in bringing aspects of Cleveland's Hungarian life to the scholarly community as my PhD advisor. He believed in me then, as did my current editor when I approached her several years ago with this manuscript. In fact, Katalin Kádár Lynn is one of the friendliest, most helpful, most supportive, and all-around best editors I have ever worked with.

Thanks also to those who read the manuscript in its final stages and provided helpful insights: Andrea Mészáros, Zsolt Dömötörffy, Walt Mahovlich, and István Szappanos. László Bőjtös and Ernie Mihály also provided their insights and extensive recollections about the community to me. Thanks to Anna Tabor for transcribing interview recordings, to Enese Pigniczky for survey data entry, to Maria Julia Honfi for the maps, to Laura Lakatos for assembling the index and cross-checking the bibliography, and to Zsolt Molnár and Mary Jane Molnár for tirelessly promoting the surveys among Cleveland Hungarians.

Introduction

My Big Fat Cleveland Hungarian Wedding

First, a disclaimer: my wedding was not really in Cleveland. It was actually near Philadelphia. But it was big, it was fat, it was definitely Hungarian, and about half the attendees were from Cleveland, so maybe that qualifies. Plenty of Hungarian food, about half of the 400 or so guests in traditional folk attire, live Hungarian folk music all through the night and finally ending from sheer exhaustion around 6:30 a.m. the next morning. So it was definitely a big fat Hungarian wedding, because I'm proud to say that I am a product of Cleveland's Hungarian community.

I was born in the Buckeye Road Hungarian neighborhood of Cleveland, and lived there until my parents had had enough of the neighborhood's decline and moved our family to the West Side, to the safer suburb of Lakewood. I was six years old when my parents took me to my first Hungarian scout meeting, I vaguely recall. Growing up in the 1970s and 1980s, my Hungarian identity revolved around the scouts, Hungarian school, church, and of course the language spoken in our home; speaking English in the family was just never an option.

Then at age 14 I joined the Hungarian Scout Folk Ensemble, known as the *Regös* group, and thus folk dancing, Hungarian traditions, and folk art also became a part of my identity. Dancing at church harvest festivals filled the autumns, and age 16 brought my participation in debutante balls, which were great elegant parties. Being in the *Regös* group also exposed me to other nationalities; performing with Serbs and Croats and Poles and Slovenians made me realize similarities among Eastern European cultures as well as bringing to the forefront of my consciousness what a treasure Cleveland's many nationalities bring to the city.

When I got married, I got to know the cities in which my wife had grown up. Thus I was exposed to Hungarian communities near Philadelphia, in New Brunswick, NJ, and in the San Francisco Bay area. When we started our family, the whole cycle started anew as I began taking my own children to scouts and to the Hungarian school so that they could also learn the language and take part in the richness that is Cleveland's Hungarian culture. And then I was asked to become the director of development for the Hungarian Scouts Association in Exteris,[1] to discover and map newer Hungarian communities and to try to initiate scouting in these fledgling communities. While traveling to and talking with Hungarians living in Orlando, Seattle, San Diego, and other nontraditional "Hungarian" cities, I realized that Hungarian communities are the same the world over: all have their older, entrenched members, their new arrivals, and their open-minded members of both younger and older generations who are able to bridge differences.

My university studies have always taken me into the fields of languages, literature, and linguistics. My close personal experience growing up Hungarian in Cleveland, coupled with a bird's eye view of my own and other Hungarian-American communities led me to this research and to this book. My original intent was to update and complement Susan Papp's excellent 1981 monograph about Cleveland Hungarians; in the course of my research, the guiding question morphed into: What does it really mean to be Hungarian in Cleveland? However, being a native ethnographer presents the dilemma of documenting one's own culture while also trying to step back and provide context. While trying to answer the core question, I will tread a very fine line between analysis and interpretation, which require objectivity and distance, and my own subjectivity stemming from living in the community I examine. It will be up to the reader to decide whether I have succeeded in this or not.

What is Meaning, Really?

This work arose from an attempt to answer the question, "What does it mean to be Hungarian in Cleveland?" When exploring such issues, it is helpful to analyze the basic definitions of the core concepts. "Meaning" is something conveyed or signified, an expressed intention, the content as opposed to linguistic expression. It may also help to examine what a concept is not: "meaningless" is without significance, purpose or value.

To answer the question of what it means to be Hungarian in Cleveland, one must explore questions of intention, hidden content, and conveyance. Intention means that persons or a group, or in this case, an ethnic community intentionally maintains its language, culture, and traditions; the way in which it does so is neither haphazard nor random, but rather it deliberately wants to maintain and propagate its ways of doing things. Hidden content means the unwritten, unofficial, and sometimes unintended lessons, values, and perspectives that a given community hands over to its successive members. Lastly, conveyance means how both overt and hidden content are intentionally transferred to individual members of a community, how members of a community pick up on and propagate its values and norms. The work views this question from three aspects: tradition, culture, and language.

Of these, language is the most recognizable and most easily definable: it is used to express and communicate thoughts and feelings. It implies a social context, and this work will address not only Hungarian language used and literature produced in the Cleveland area but will also examine the factors that impact language maintenance in the second and third generations after immigration.

Culture can be defined as the totality of socially transmitted behavior patterns, arts, beliefs, institutions, and other products of human work and thought, specifically intellectual and artistic activity and the works produced by it. Culture thus goes beyond language, yet nevertheless retains meaning in a social context.

Language is often viewed as a facet of personal expression, while culture shifts to a broader social context. The third aspect of the work adds another dimension to the question of meaning, that of time. For tradition is the passing down of elements of a culture from generation to generation, a mode of thought or behavior followed by a people continuously, viewed as a coherent body of precedents influencing the present. In its most distilled definition, tradition is a time-honored practice or set of practices, and this is what this work purports to explore. By seeing the language use, culture, and traditions of Cleveland Hungarians, the reader will hopefully better understand what it really means to be Hungarian in Cleveland.

However, one cannot even begin to understand what it means to be Hungarian in Cleveland without understanding the process of cultural and language assimilation. Assimilation into American culture is a phenomenon that every ethnic group faces. One can draw a continuum of assimilation, with complete assimilation at one end, followed by symbolic ethnicity, then segmented assimilation, and finally biculturalism and transnationalism.[2]

Complete assimilation	Symbolic ethnicity	Segmented assimilation	Biculturalism	Trans-nationalism
Americanization and rejection or loss of ethnic identity and culture The melting pot *Traditional prevailing view*	Nostalgic allegiance, pride and food, historical interest, but no time or effort Leisure-time activity that does not interfere with everyday life *(theory by Gans)*	Hold values of native culture while maintaining solidarity within the ethnic community Living on an island but visiting the mainland *(theory by Portes & Zhou)*	Retaining ethnic identity while integrating into American society Feel at home in both cultures; preserve and fit in *(theory by Barkan, Diner, & Kraut)*	Maintaining ethnic connections in an age of globalism; the mainstream expands to accommodate Vigorous ethnic pluralism *(theory by Alba & Nee)*

Continuum of Assimilation

However, assimilation on one end of the spectrum and transnationalism at the other end are not merely theories, but rather dynamic social processes, and they are inextricably intertwined. Furthermore, four generations of at least five different waves of immigration are present in one community of Cleveland Hungarians, and thus it is hard to apply one theory across all members of a community, especially to members who have varying intensity in the strength and proximity of their ties to the community. Some consider themselves Hungarian and take part in the community's life once a year or less frequently, while for others their Cleveland Hungarian identity entails taking part in social activities on an ongoing basis several times per week.

Having said that, despite the seemingly inevitable process of assimilation, i.e., that each succeeding generation tends to maintain its culture and language less and less, an ethnic community such as Cleveland's Hungarian community provides a social means of group identity and vigorous ethnic pluralism, one that enables even second and third generations to maintain their language, culture, and traditions. This adds to and enhances their city and the American mainstream. Indeed, the community offers an opportunity for language and identity maintenance for first generation immigrants, i.e., those who were born in Hungary or its surrounding countries. An additional yet separate issue is language and identity formation for the second and third generations, i.e., those who were born in the Cleveland area but whose parents or grandparents immigrated. This is the crucial difference: language and identity maintenance for the first generation, and (in addition to the maintenance) language and identity formation for the second and third generations.

The three most important theories for illuminating these two processes, identity maintenance and identity formation, are the communication theory of identity of Ewa Urban and Mark Orbe, the microcosm of inherited values by Attila Z. Papp, and the spiritual homeland theory of László Bőjtös. Urban and Orbe developed a theory that everyday communication builds, sustains, and transforms identity, while at the same time identity is expressed through communication. This holds especially true in ethnic communities, where the language of communication is closely tied to personal and group identity. Papp's theory, on the other hand, states that Hungarian-American communities are diaspora micro-universes, unique community cultures that are built upon inherited values from the old country. Founded by immigrants but sustained by ongoing generations, these communities bring their culture from Hungary but then preserve it their unique Hungarian-American way. Unlike Urban, Ore, and Papp, Bőjtös is not an outside observer; rather, he is an integral part of the Cleveland Hungarian community. He observed that Cleveland's Hungarian neighborhoods in the 1950s shifted from geographical entities to purely social entities, communities kept alive by suburban Hungarian commuters who attend shared events in the evenings or on weekends.[3]

Recent scholars of Hungarian-American communities, including Gábor Tarján, Ágnes Fülemile, and Balázs Balogh, have temporarily lived in those communities and documented their ethnographic and folk traditions. This study uses a similar ethnographic methodology but offers the additional advantage of a researcher who is intimately familiar with the community. It tries to document the patterns among Hungarian-Americans, specifically those living in Cleveland, as a distinct ethnographic group. Ethnographers and folk-musicologists, including Zoltán Kodály, Béla Bartók, and their contemporaries in the early twentieth century, have long studied Hungarian communities in and near the Carpathian basin, documenting Hungarian village life in detail. Hungarian-Americans also have a tradition of bringing folk culture with them and nurturing it in their newfound homelands. These and other traditions, derivatives of culture and language use, as well as the intellectual products of the community are the subject of this study.

Indeed, some Cleveland Hungarian traditions date back over a hundred years, brought with immigrants from the Carpathian basin and maintained through several succeeding generations, passed on from grandparent and parent throughout the last and current century, whether in ethnic dress or in customs. Hungarian immigrants to Cleveland are not homogenous however, since they came from many different enclaves in Hungary and the Carpathian Basin. Furthermore, they also revived certain Hungarian folk and cultural traditions, often relearning them from books, and over time they passed these traditions on to each successive generation, not necessarily in their original incarnation or in the way in which they were regarded in the land of origin, but rather as markers and simultaneously generators of identity. But much as Hungarian villages in Hungary and its surrounding countries maintain folk traditions, and much as Hungarian-American communities in other states, or Hungarian communities on other continents such as South America or Australia or Western Europe maintain their traditions, so too do Cleveland's Hungarians.

Research Methodology

The purpose of this research was not only to document Cleveland Hungarians' current culture, values, language use, and traditions, but also to analyze how and why these traditions serve to perpetuate the community and slow their assimilation.

My methodology for this study was qualitative, comparative, and interdisciplinary in order to provide the academic scholar familiarity with what it is like and what it means to be Hungarian in Cleveland and how that meaning has changed over the years. Research entailed mostly primary sources and personal interviews, with the use of some secondary sources. The research was mostly carried out from 2008 to 2017, but the author has been drawing on insights and personal contacts gained from 47 years of living in Cleveland and taking an active part in its ethnic Hungarian community. The state of Hungarians in Cleveland in 2018 is that of a shrinking yet still thriving community with extended roots significantly shaped by succeeding generations, a community that continues to maintain its Hungarian language, culture, and traditions. To sharpen this examination, occasional historical flashbacks are used to provide a broader view. The ethnic Hungarians in Cleveland, who add to and enhance the American mainstream and the vibrancy of their community, with its literature and language use, its culture, and its traditions – these Hungarians are the focus of this study.

In order to shed light on what it means to be Hungarian in Cleveland in 2018, slightly different methods of research were used in each of the topics of interest. Thus each section has a somewhat different focus and uses varying methodologies. The chapter on background dispels some myths about Cleveland's Hungarian community and uses mostly historical and comparative analysis to understand the broader context, although the section on population seeks to provide a fresh, new approach to ascertaining how many Hungarians live in Cleveland, going beyond mere Census figures. The chapter on traditions is factual but with a personal slant, offered with the insights gained from living among Cleveland's Hungarians for over four decades. The chapter on culture offers analysis of the social groups, the interactions, and the artistic products of the community, as well as a political analysis, while the chapter on language and literature offers an overview of Hungarian publishing and language instruction in Cleveland. The last chapter takes a case study approach to analyzing Hungarian language use, both quantitatively as well as qualitatively, looking at the factors that impact language maintenance in the second and third generations.

In addition to hundreds of personal interviews conducted, some of them quite extended, two anonymous survey instruments were used to accumulate data. One was a sociological overview of participation in Cleveland's Hungarian community, and the other attempted to ascertain the level of political involvement of Cleveland Hungarians. Both surveys were available online for about three months from early February to early May 2017 at two separate websites, that of the United Hungarian Societies and of the Bocskai Rádió, but were advertised multiple times on all three Hungarian radio programs, in Hungarian church bulletins and in the newsletters and several email blasts of the various Hungarian organizations in the greater Cleveland area. Three hundred copies of each survey were distributed at the annual meeting of the United Hungarian Societies in February 2017 (25–50 copies to each church and to each organization represented at the annual meeting), with PDF files emailed to organization presidents and church pastors on two separate occasions with requests for distribution. The Hungarian Cultural Center of Northeast Ohio mailed an additional 350 copies to each of its members as well, all scout families received emailed notices of the survey in April, and the online links were shared with the Cleveland Hungarian Facebook group.

Of these two anonymous surveys, the sociological survey had 288 responses (183 submitted online and 105 paper copies mailed or given to the author), with almost half of the respondents born in and living most of their lives in the greater Cleveland area (47 percent), while the political survey had 223 responses (126 submitted online and 97 paper copies mailed or given to the author), with about half of the respondents born in the US and almost half born in Hungary or outside the USA. Although the online survey software enabled numerous submissions in order to allow for several entries per household, the individual IP addresses were collected and examined for results skewing, and no discrepancies were found.[4]

Sociological survey: 288 total responses

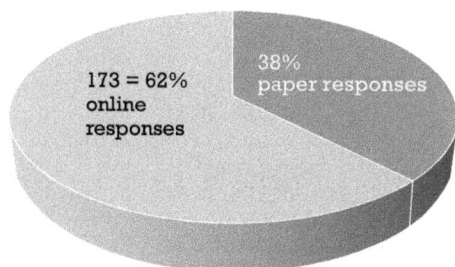

173 = 62% online responses

38% paper responses

Political survey: 233 total responses

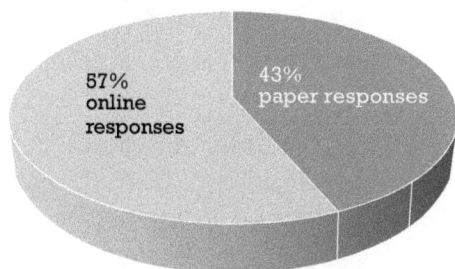

57% online responses

43% paper responses

These disparate methodologies, although differing in focus, all serve to show the state of Hungarians in Cleveland, while at the same time unearthing the extended roots of the community, especially the impact of the various generations of immigration. Finally, the conclusion provides an overview of the legacies of each wave of immigration to Cleveland, addresses recent developments including the current communication strategies of its organizations, and provides an outlook for the future.

CHAPTER ONE
Background, the Evolution
of Today's Cleveland

How, then, did Cleveland's Hungarian community become what it is today? How does one measure an ethnic community when "being Hungarian" has different meanings for different people?

Mythology

Let us begin by dispelling a common myth about the "American Debrecen," i.e., that it was once the second largest Hungarian city, second only to Budapest. This statistic entered the popular mythology sometime early in the twentieth century and has been falsely perpetuated ever since. The facts do not quite justify the myth. According to the 1910 edition of the *Révai Encyclopedia*, the order of Hungarian cities by population was Budapest (881,604), Szeged (118,328), Debrecen (92,729), Pozsony (78,038, today known as Bratislava, Slovakia), Temesvár (72,555, Timisoara, Romania), Nagyvárad (64,169, Oradea, Romania), and Kolozsvár (60,808, Cluj, Romania). Steven Béla Várdy's research shows that at the same time Cleveland had a gross population of 364,463, with a little over 60,000 of the population being Hungarian. Thus Cleveland should be seventh or eighth on the list, or if one discounts Pozsony, Temesvár, Nagyvárad, and Kolozsvár as having other nationalities reflected in the population figures in addition to Hungarians, Cleveland still ranks only fourth on the list in 1910. However, 60,000 is still a significant number, and the myth did not evolve accidentally. But the facts show that Cleveland was never the second largest Hungarian city outside Budapest, despite common lore.

The Context of Cleveland

Cleveland is a rust-belt city, once known for its heavy industry, that in the late twentieth century saw economic decline and loss of population. Divided in two by the Cuyahoga river, its East Side tends to be slightly hilly, with the foothills of the Appalachian mountains not too far to the east, while the western side tends to be more flat, with the Great Plains stretching westward all the way to the Rocky Mountains. Its downtown, like many similar industrial northern cities, is mainly skyscrapers, office buildings, and stadiums, surrounded by a ring of working class neighborhoods and desolate ghettos, albeit with pockets of recent re-gentrification, and with mostly middle class suburbs in the outer rings. Places of significance to Hungarians are scattered throughout its downtown, inner city, and suburbs, reflecting the history and migration of its Hungarian population.

Like the Hungarians, other ethnic groups living in Cleveland also maintain their own traditions and culture. As a city of heavy industry such as steel and auto production, Cleveland attracted many blue collar workers throughout the years, not only from Eastern Europe but more recently from all over the world. Africans, Chinese, Croatians, Germans, Greeks, Indians, Irish, Italians, Japanese, Jews, Latvians, Lithuanians, Mexicans, Palestinians, Poles, Romanians, Russians, Serbs, Slovaks, and Ukrainians all maintain ethnic communities in and around Cleveland.

Immigrants from Ireland are by far the largest group. Their annual downtown parade on St. Patrick's Day, March 17, draws hundreds of thousands of participants and onlookers. Italians are the next largest in number—a neighborhood called Little Italy near University Circle has quaint cafes, restaurants, art galleries, bakeries, and an annual Columbus Day parade. For most members of these two groups, identity is mainly symbolic, as defined by sociologist Herbert Gans. The Germans have at least three cultural centers, with the Deutsche Zentrale park in the suburb of Parma, the Donauschwaben Kulturverein in Lenau Park in suburban Olmsted Falls, and the Sachsenheim in Cleveland proper. Another of the neighborhoods of Cleveland is known as Slavic Village and is home to numerous Polish, Slovak, and Czech churches, businesses and residents.

Most of Cleveland's ethnic groups, among them the Hungarians, no longer live in distinctly ethnic neighborhoods, but in the suburbs. Although some suburbs tend to contain higher concentrations of ethnic populations than others, such as Ukrainians in Seven Hills, Poles in Parma, Russians and Italians in Mayfield Heights, and Palestinians on the West Side, most nationalities are dispersed around the greater Cleveland area. Like the Hungarians, their churches also function as repositories of social traditions, and many of them house ethnic dance groups or weekend language schools, such as in the Greek, Serbian, Romanian and Ukrainian orthodox churches, or in Indian temples and Jewish synagogues.[5]

Recent collaboration among Cleveland's ethnic groups is also occurring, including *www.ClevelandPeople.com*, a website dedicated to the customs, cultural events, and various nationalities of Cleveland and northeast Ohio. This website lists recent events, with over 80 local ethnicities represented. On the business side, GlobalCleveland is an initiative with the goal of regional economic development through actively attracting talented immigrants and other newcomers, hoping to welcome and connect them both professionally as well as socially.

The politician Dennis Kucinich, former mayor of Cleveland, former Congressional Representative, and a candidate for governor of Ohio in 2018, saw Cleveland's Hungarian population as one of the best organized, with its strengths being the number of organizations and its programs for children. He observed that Hungarians had a great influence on local politics up until the 1960s and 1970s, serving as a strong influence in local elections.

Geographically close to Cleveland lie several other communities with larger concentrations of Hungarians, including Fairport Harbor to the east, Lorain and Elyria to the west, Akron to the south, and Youngstown to the southeast. By and large these communities are self-sufficient, having mostly their own local traditions and events, though their members occasionally go to Cleveland to take part in social events. And while only a small minority of the population of these neighboring Hungarian communities understands and speaks the Hungarian language, they are nevertheless fiercely proud of their heritage. For them, Hungarian identity provides a sense of belonging to a local community that shares its Hungarian traditions worldwide.

The city of Cleveland, with a population of almost 400,000,[6] is located in Cuyahoga County, named after the Cuyahoga River that flows into Lake Erie and divides the city east to west. Cuyahoga County also includes all the contiguous suburbs of Cleveland. Surrounding Cuyahoga County are five additional counties: Lorain County to the west, Lake County to the east, Medina County to the southwest, and Summit and Geauga counties to the southeast.[7] Due to urban sprawl, these adjacent counties also include residents who identify with Cleveland (fans of Cleveland professional sports teams, workplaces downtown, etc.). Thus the entire Cleveland metropolitan area encompasses over 2 million residents, with approximately 1.2 million in Cuyahoga County (Cleveland and its adjacent suburbs).

Other Hungarian-American Cities

To a certain extent, Cleveland's Hungarian community bears resemblance to communities of Hungarians all across North America. Furthermore, its community shares characteristics of other émigré Hungarian communities worldwide. Visitors to established Hungarian communities most anywhere in the diaspora will find many parallels: in the midst of various other local foreign (Anglo-Saxon, or Latin American, or German) cultures and environments, language is maintained, culture is propagated through literature, lectures, music, folk dance, and often scouting, and culinary and holiday traditions are preserved and passed along to successive generations. These communities must work hard at promoting active participation and make an effort to maintain their ethnic origins, and their members spend countless volunteer hours, donating their time, labor, and money to ensure the success of their community institutions.

As an example, the city of New Brunswick, New Jersey, is the home of the corporate headquarters of Johnson & Johnson, the healthcare giant. Early in the twentieth century, New Brunswick's Hungarian population constituted two-thirds of the employees of Johnson & Johnson, and one third of all city residents. Today, a walkable neighborhood encompassing several city blocks is home to Catholic and Protestant Hungarian churches, a Hungarian Athletic Club, a scout center, and the American Hungarian Foundation, all of which own buildings and organize cultural activities for New Brunswick's Hungarian community. New Jersey had a total of 102,004 persons listing Hungarian ancestry and 6,167 persons speaking Hungarian in the home in the 2015 American Community Survey.

In New York City, Manhattan has a Hungarian church and a cultural center, the Magyar Ház on East 82nd Street. New York State had a total of 147,111 persons listing Hungarian ancestry and 11,641 persons speaking Hungarian at home in the 2015 American Community Survey. Chicago also has several Hungarian churches, a Hungarian scout troop, a weekend Hungarian school taught by volunteers, and numerous cultural activities held on an ongoing basis. Going further westward, California had a total of 119,209 persons listing Hungarian ancestry and 12,444 speaking Hungarian at home in the 2015 American Community Survey.

New Brunswick, New York City (191,592 of Hungarian ancestry and 15,348 speaking Hungarian in the household), Chicago (49,146 ancestry and 2,809 speakers), Los Angeles (46,807 ancestry and 5,851 speakers), and San Francisco (15,758 ancestry and 2,190 speakers), as well as older or smaller Hungarian communities such as in Buffalo, Detroit, Sarasota, Passaic (NJ), Portland, Seattle, or Washington, DC, and countless other North American cities, all have significant Hungarian communities, sharing similar characteristics, often with a Hungarian church in a crumbling neighborhood, and dinners and picnics and dances and language instruction. A newly vibrant community is in Boston, which in the last 15 years has seen a blossoming and expansion of its volunteer Hungarian cultural institutions that include a weekend language school, scout troop, lecture club, and other social events and groups. Indeed, its Metropolitan Statistical Area shows 15,155 people reporting Hungarian ancestry, with 1,240 speaking Hungarian in the house-

	State of New Jersey	State of New York	New York (NY-NJ-PA Metro area)	Chicago (Chicago-Naper-ville-El-gin-IL-IN-WI Metro area)	State of California	Los Angeles (Los Angeles-Long Beach-Anaheim Metro area)	San Francisco (San Fran-cisco-Oakland-Hayward Metro area)	Boston
Hun-garian ancestry	102 004	147 111	191 592	49 146	119 209	46 807	15 758	15 155
Speak Hungar-ian in the household	6 167	11 641	15 348	2 809	12 444	5 851	2 190	1 240

Other Hungarian-American Cities
Source: 2015 American Community Survey

hold. But whether in Boston or Los Angeles, San Francisco or Chicago, New York, New Brunswick or Cleveland, for that matter, North American diaspora Hungarian communities have greater similarities than differences.

Waves of Hungarian Immigration

There have been six major waves of Hungarian immigration to Cleveland. The first arrived in the mid-1800s but did not have significant impact on the city. A much larger second wave, the *óamerikás* [old-timer] generation, built most of the physical landmarks of Hungarian Cleveland today, including establishing and actually building most of the Hungarian churches. The third wave arrived shortly after the Second World War and brought an intellectual bent to the cultural life. Émigrés of the 1956 Revolution comprised the fourth wave; their descendants either assimilated into American life or eased into existing Hungarian institutions. The fifth wave was comprised of economic refugees of the 1960s, 1970s, and 1980s, and the final wave of Hungarian immigrants to Cleveland was part of the so-called brain drain: professionals arriving in the late 1990s through the present day. But how did it all start?

The first wave of Hungarian immigrants to Cleveland started even before the visit on January 31, 1852, of the great nineteenth century Hungarian statesman Lajos Kossuth. Two organizations requested his visit, the Hungarian Society of Cleveland and the Ladies Hungarian Society of Cleveland, and this relatively small wave of immigrants consisted mostly of freedom fighters from the 1848 Revolution. Thereafter came the first businessmen and entrepreneurs. Not many traces of these earliest Hungarian immigrants can now be seen in Cleveland, although their accomplishments and businesses were famous in their time. One of the most notable was Theodor Kundtz, born in 1852 in Metzenseifen (then in Hungary but due to shifting borders is now in Slovakia, and is called Medzev), who came to Cleveland as a penniless immigrant in 1873. He started his own manufacturing businesses specializing in wood products and by 1915 owned five large factories. In his hometown a descriptive phrase even originated because of Theodor Kundtz, known to his family as Tori: *"Er hat es so gut wie Tori in Amerika"* [It's going well for him, just like for Tori in America].

The next wave of immigrants, coming in the latter part of the nineteenth century and the beginning of the twentieth century, built most of the Hungarian churches still standing today. They came primarily for economic reasons to escape the grinding poverty of the landless social strata of the Austro-Hungarian Empire. Julianna Puskás estimated one half million emigrants from Hungary to the United States before the First World War; according to one estimate, 23 percent of those were people who had been to the United States before, staying for several years, earning money and then going back to Hungary. They found hardship in America as well, living in boarding houses and sharing a bed by sleeping in alternating shifts, but over half ended up staying and bettering their lives.[8] They congregated around churches and built social institutions. Hungarians kept coming to America and to Cleveland up until the First World War. This group and their descendants are often referred to locally as *öregamerikások* or *óamerikások* [old timers].

The end of the First World War left Hungary dismembered from the treaty of Trianon, with 71.4 percent of historic Hungary's territory and 63.6 percent of its population suddenly under the jurisdiction of new countries.[9] This upheaval in Hungary and its surrounding states caused a shift in attitude of many Hungarian-Americans: instead of viewing their stay in the United States as temporary and economic, many decided not to return home and began a transition to permanent residence, changing their lifestyles, attitudes, and value system. The percentage of Hungarian immigrants who became naturalized citizens virtually doubled from 28 percent in 1920 to 55.7 percent in 1930.[10]

A small group of political immigrants left Hungary after its short-lived communist dictatorship under Béla Kun in 1919, and a few Hungarian immigrants also arrived in America between 1933–1941. However, the restrictive immigration laws imposed after WWI set a miniscule quota for Hungarian emigrants, and compared to prior waves of immigration the numbers were small, but included some Hungarians of note, many of whom were of Jewish extraction, including physicists Tódor Kálmán, János Neumann, Leó Szilárd, and Jenő Wigner, as well as the authors Arthur Koestler and Sándor Márai. Because of the quota laws and the economic turmoil caused by the Great Depression, very few Hungarians succeeded in emigrating to America. In Cleveland no traces of this tiny emigration remain, if in fact any ever made it to Cleveland.

The next, larger wave of Hungarian immigrants fled the advancing invasion of the Soviet army near the end of the Second World War. Members of the Hungarian government and the military were evacuated into Germany, and hundreds of thousands of civilians also fled westward.[11] Hearing of the atrocities of the Russian onslaught, as well as recalling the short-lived communist rule in Hungary in 1919, many members of the educated and propertied upper middle class, professionals and leaders of industry and commerce decided to leave Hungary. When the war concluded in 1945, around 62,000 Hungarian refugees found themselves awaiting their fate in displaced person (DP) camps in Western Europe set up by the Allied forces. The various countries from Australia to Argentina, Canada to the United States, took up to four years to decide to accept these refugees, decisions expedited only after it became evident that the countries of Central and East Europe were permanently occupied by the Soviet Army.

At the end of the Second World War, refugee camps in the following locations had large Hungarian populations: Heidelberg, Landshut, Metten, Münzingen, Osterode, Piding, Pocking/Plattling, Polling (Weilheim), Prüfening (Regensburg), Rosenheim, Simmens Schule (Munich), Mittenwald, and Waldwerke (Passau) in Germany, and Kellerberg (Villach)/Spittal an der Drau, Kufstein, Wörgl, and Innsbruck in Austria. During these years, not knowing how long they would stay in the DP camps, the Hungarian refugees established cultural activities and impromptu schools for their children within the camps, and some also continued boy and girl scouting traditions, especially after news filtered out of the banning of scouting in communist Hungary in 1948. Limited publishing took place in these refugee camps, with the exception of mimeographed newsletters, but the Hungarian refugees formed societies and organizations to mitigate the misery of daily life in the camps.

An executive order issued by President Harry Truman in 1945 called for the admission of 40,000 displaced persons to the United States under the regular quota system, which was followed up by the Displaced Person Act of June 25, 1948, which provided for the permanent settlement of over 220,000 people over a two-year period. Two years later, a revised Displaced Persons Act was passed, with a new ceiling of 415,000 participants, followed by the Refugee Relief Act of 1953, which admitted 205,000 refugees as non-quota immigrants. Between 1945 and 1956 26,532 Hungarians entered the United States as Displaced Persons. From May 1946 to June 1952, 446,616 Displaced Persons entered the United States. Of those, approximately 4–6 percent, or 17,000–25,000 were Hungarian. Half were Roman Catholic, 35 percent Protestant and Orthodox, and 15 percent Jewish. At about the same time, Canada also accepted about 200,000 Displaced Persons, including about 12,000 Hungarians.[12] Ferenc Somogyi wrote of more than 6,000 Displaced Persons arriving in Cleveland, sponsored by *óamerikás* immigrants between 1947 and 1953.[13] (The Displaced Person label, in the strict legal sense of the word, is actually a misnomer in this case, but for practical purposes, everyone has come to refer to this wave as the DP generation.)

The new arrivals to Cleveland did not immediately integrate into existing Cleveland Hungarian *óamerikás* life. István Szappanos, himself a DP, delineates why:

There were several sociologically unavoidable reasons. There was the clash of cultures (village vs. city), and the cultural divide that separated these two groups not only by decades of fast-moving history, but also ide-ological differences of the two worlds. While the old-timers had come to the New World seeking a better life, leaving behind a homeland shroud-ed in bittersweet memories, the newcomers felt that they were evicted from their homeland by forces of evil, not the least of which was per-ceived to be the very United States they had now arrived in. The old-time Hungarian print media that had formed the political views of their read-ers, such as *Szabadság, Népszava*, and others, were rather left-leaning and not at all understanding of the wartime predicament of the Old Country [faced with a fateful choice between two evils, allying with Soviet Russia or Hitler's Germany, with neutrality an impossibility], and could not rid themselves even by the early 1950s, of the notion that those who left their homeland at this time were mostly nazi collaborators and war criminals, or at least members of that 'feudal' society whose oppression and exploi-tation was perceived to have caused the emigration of the poverty-strick-en masses during the first half of the twentieth century. This created an undercurrent of suppressed resentment on both sides, and prevented the new and the old generations from forming closer personal or organiza-tional relationships, with one notable exception: Hungarian churches.[14]

Not knowing the language, these DPs found menial labor jobs in facto-ries. Missing the intellectual life they had left behind in Hungary, and cer-tainly not finding it in their weekday American factory jobs, they immediate-ly started a Hungarian social scene of their own, founding literary circles and other social organizations, including Hungarian scouting, which they pro-ceeded to impart to the next generation. Because most of them came from the upper-middle class and viewed their American sojourn as merely tempo-rary, intending to return as soon as the Soviets left Hungary, they had a hard time fitting into the öregamerikás social circles as well as into American soci-ety. Furthermore, because many were already middle-aged, their English lan-guage skills were either nonexistent or practically so, with not much hope of betterment, limiting their possibilities professionally and socially. Thus their active social life, with its customs, greetings, titles, and rituals, reflected the pre-war Hungarian gentry life that they had been forced to leave behind or that they aspired to. Their formal and literary modes of communication expressed their Hungarian identity: they considered themselves Hungarian gentry, not American factory workers.

The 1956 Revolution in Hungary brought another influx of Hungarian refugees to the United States, about 40,000 around 1956 and 1957. Of those, Susan Papp estimated that 6,500 to 10,000 came to Cleveland.[15] Broader in scope in terms of social class but substantially younger than the previous DP wave, this group assimilated more seamlessly into American society than the DP generation. Because many of the 1956 refugees shared the anticommunist leanings of the DP generation, some fit into the organizations and newly founded institutions, continuing their work. The 1956 refugees, if not at first, eventually found a shared heritage and had more in common with the DP generation than with the second and third generation Hungarians already in Cleveland.[16] However, many of the '56 refugees, being of a younger generation found the language and customs of the DP generation Hungarians archaic and reminiscent of the pre-WWII Hungarian society and did not at first join Cleveland's Hungarian community.

The 1960s, 1970s, and 1980s did not see a large influx of Hungarians coming to Cleveland, but during this period smaller numbers of economic refugees sporadically settled in the Cleveland area. Some assimilated immediately into American culture and did not take part in any of Cleveland's Hungarian communities, while others did. Most of these arrivals came to America simply for a better life and were economic refugees, although a few did come because of political or religious reasons; under the Kádár government in Hungary, religious and political persecution was much less overt than during the Rákosi government's era. This wave of economic immigrants was characterized by educated professional and technical workers with higher education levels than the óamerikás generation. In a 2016 lecture given at the American Hungarian Educators Association, independent researcher George Lázár dubbed this group the "Forgotten Generation," because immigration research has focused on the postwar DPs and the 1956-ers, but scholarship has virtually ignored those who left Hungary between 1959 and 1989. Few of the Forgotten Generation left Hungary legally—most defected to the West. To cite just one example, Lázár estimates the number of defectors in 1964 to be

896, and 1,366 defectors in 1965, or 0.5 percent and 0.8 percent of permitted travelers to capitalist countries. All in all, Lázár estimates 130,000 people left Hungary between 1959 and 1989, with an average of 4,000 Hungarians defecting to the West yearly in the 1980s.[17] An estimated 500 Hungarians entered the United States annually during the thirty-year period, with only a small fraction of those ending up in the Cleveland area.

The 1990s and the early twenty-first century saw a new development in the immigration of Hungarians to Cleveland: brain drain from Hungary and its surrounding countries. Young professionals, many of them doctors, scientists, or engineers with advanced degrees, saw few opportunities in their native Hungary or Hungarian areas of Romania and Serbia after Communism fell. These educated immigrants arrived in Cleveland as well as other American cities such as Boston, Phoenix, Pittsburgh, Portland, Seattle, and Sarasota, and immediately found work in their fields. Although not as many in sheer numbers as the 1956 and DP waves of immigration, this newest group, much like any immigrant group, is hard-working and motivated. Some found their niche in existing Hungarian organizations in Cleveland, whether at a church or cultural group, but most tend to gravitate to informal social groups with their peers. In the first years of immigration, building one's personal life and career is paramount, and following Abraham Maslow's pyramid of needs, shelter and security are the concerns first addressed; only when living circumstances are established do people advance to the social ladder sections of Maslow's pyramid, with self-actualization at the top.[18] Only after the passage of several years, frequently when their children no longer speak Hungarian as easily as when they first arrived, do immigrants start showing an interest in working within existing community entities such as museums, scouting, or a Hungarian school. The post-communist wave of immigrants, however, has fewer financial and political constraints on travel, is more mobile and often spends longer periods of time traveling back to Hungary, and thus may prove to be different in their pace of assimilation than previous generations. George Lázár's research estimates that approximately 1,000 Hungarians were admitted legally to the United States each year between 1989 and 2002. In 2008, Hungary entered the Visa Waiver program, and based on overstay rates, Lázár estimates there are

Fiscal year	EXPECTED DEPARTURES	OUT-OF-COUNTRY OVERSTAYS	SUSPECTED IN-COUNTRY OVERSTAYS	TOTAL OVERSTAYS
2016	82 533	431	1 841	2 272
2015	75 904	356	1 860	2 216
2014	71 335	376	2 320	2 696

Overstay rates from Hungary[20]

Source: U.S. Department of Homeland Security

about 12,000 undocumented Hungarians currently in the United States.[19] Around 2,000 Hungarians overstay their US visas yearly (at 70,000 visitors annually, a rate of 2 percent), some of whom end up in the Cleveland area and gravitate to personal contacts.

Each successive wave of immigrants eventually assimilates into American life, earning their living and spending their working days among Americans. Although the continuum of assimilation can range from complete assimilation to symbolic ethnicity to segmented assimilation to biculturalism and transnationalism, three major trends exist for the rate, or speed of the assimilation process: quick and complete assimilation, progressive assimilation of succeeding generations, or retarded assimilation due to involvement in the Hungarian community. In the first, the members of the immigration can completely assimilate and forego contact with Cleveland's Hungarian communities, blending into their American neighborhood. In the second, the emigrating generation can establish contact with the existing community of Cleveland's Hungarians, but their children and grandchildren assimilate into American life and forego contact with the Hungarian community, usually due to language difficulties. The third group, by far the smallest but significant nevertheless, finds the immigrants establishing contact with the Hungarian community, with their identities being actively formed by the community, continuing their language maintenance and holding onto their Hungarian traditions. Their social communicative processes are built upon shared values of the community.

As time passes, each successive wave of Hungarian immigration has blended and possibly will continue to blend into the pre-existing Hungarian community, resulting in greater homogeneity. Living together in the United States and being Hungarian serves to unite them, and over time the differing reasons for emigrating become less important than their contemporary social interactions, thus forming the present dynamic Hungarian community of Cleveland.

Population: How Many Hungarians Are There in Cleveland?

Historical Census data from 1940 through 2010 show the effects of assimilation and also the sudden influx of two major waves of Hungarian immigration, the DP generation and the 1956 refugees, followed by another recurring albeit slow assimilation process. Although the question regarding ancestry has been phrased in different ways through the years of the census, the meaning of the numbers remained the same from 1940 to 1960; they reflected immigrants to the Cleveland area from Hungary. Missing from the 1940–1960 data is the number of ethnic Hungarians arriving from Romania, Czechoslovakia, or other countries bordering Hungary, even though those countries also had and have an extensive Hungarian population, but these details could not easily be ascertained from US census figures, which only kept track of country of origin, not nationality. The most recent United States Census in 2010 did not ask about ethnicity or ancestral heritage, as had previous ones. The 2010 United States Census data delineated ancestry or ethnic heritage only among the Hispanic population, while other groups remained non-specific in broad categories like Asian, Black, and White.

However, the Census Bureau, in addition to conducting its detailed census as mandated by the US Constitution every ten years, also conducts an ongoing statistical survey that samples a small percentage of the population every year. This process is called the American Community Survey, and it samples 3 million addresses yearly, using three modes of data collection: mail, telephone, and personal visits. Its five-year estimates include 60 months of collected data and are the most reliable, while its one-year estimates are the most recent, albeit with slightly less reliability. In the case of ancestry,

Hungarian Ancestry Through the Years

	1940 CENSUS Whites born in Hungary	1950 CENSUS White persons born in Hungary	1960 CENSUS Persons of foreign stock reporting Hungary as country of origin	2000 CENSUS Persons listing Hungarian ancestry	2010 AMERICAN COMMUNITY SURVEY Total persons listing Hungarian ancestry	2010 AMERICAN COMMUNITY SURVEY Persons listing Hungarian ancestry as first choice
USA				1 398 724	1 501 736	930 994
Ohio	49 185	43 410	106 307	193 951	193 512	133 462
City of Cleveland				8 400	6 822	4 521
Cuyahoga County	23 833	20 223	47 477	47 392	44 605	27 607
Summit County	4 388	4 002	8 602	10 706	19 645	11 809
Lorain County	3 178	2 524	6 347	14 042	15 474	10 351
Lake County	913	981	3 740	11 356	12 343	8 562
Medina County	430	401	895	6 443	7 887	5 344
Geauga County	248	322	1 195	4 507	5 137	3 553
Cuyahoga and adjoining counties	32 990	71 863	68 256	94 446	105 091	67 226

both the 2000 Census and the American Community Survey used the same phraseology to ask respondents: "What is your ancestry or ethnic origin?" The table below shows the Cleveland area's number of persons with Hungarian ancestry; the 2010 data include both the number of persons listing Hungarian first as their ancestry, as well as those who may have listed it second or third (included in the totals). Indeed, the table shows a shifting of persons of Hungarian ancestry from Cleveland and Cuyahoga County to adjoining counties, reflecting suburban sprawl.

A 2012 map of the United States reflecting Hungarian ancestry as a percentage of county population also shows that northeast Ohio figures prominently.[21] But in the last ten years, the Cleveland area's population listing Hungarian ancestry has not changed much. When comparing the 2010 American Community Survey data of around 44,000 people to the 2011–2015 five-year estimate of around 38,000 with the 2016 one-year estimate of around 41,000, one can safely say that in Cuyahoga County, which includes Cleveland and its adjacent suburbs, about 40,000 people claim Hungarian ancestry. Factoring urban sprawl and outlying suburbs into the equation, the same number span ranges from 90,000 to 105,000 claiming Hungarian ancestry.

	2011-2015 ACS 5 YR ESTIMATE Total people reporting Hungarian ancestry	2016 ACS 1 YR ESTIMATE Total people reporting Hungarian ancestry
USA	1 411 132	1 424 423
Ohio	187 684	183 534
Cuyahoga County	**37 853**	**41 161**
Summit County	15 793	N / A
Lorain County	13 748	N / A
Lake County	10 878	N / A
Medina County	7 525	N / A
Geauga County	4 204	N / A
Cuyahoga and adjoining counties	90 001	90 779[1]

Hungarian Ancestry
Source: American Community Survey

	2000 CENSUS Hungarian spoken at home	2010 AMERICAN COM-MUNITY SURVEY Hungarian spoken at home	2009–2013 AMERICAN COM-MUNITY SURVEY 5 YR ESTIMATES Hungarian spoken at home	2011–2015 AMERICAN COM-MUNITY SURVEY 5 YR ESTIMATES Hungarian spoken at home
USA	117 785	91 445	N / A	82 819
Ohio	11 859	8 496	N / A	6 399
City of Cleveland	890	621	N / A	342
Cuyahoga County	4 830	3 440	**2 870**	**2 656**
Summit County	1 050	730	638	547
Lorain County	875	827	634	470
Lake County	720	430	257	220
Medina County	175	283	328	420
Geauga County	365	364	449	132
Cuyahoga and adjoining counties	**8 015**	6 074	5 176	4 445

**Persons Speaking Hungarian in the Household, number of persons
aged 5 and above**

But ancestry alone does not fully describe Hungarian identity, for it entails the entire spectrum from symbolic ethnicity (as exemplified by "My grandmother was Hungarian, and I like goulash") to the transnational immigrant who just arrived from Hungary. However, an easy marker for Hungarian identity, because it entails quantifiable effort, is the number of people who report speaking Hungarian in the household. These numbers show a decline, and further analysis of the data also reveals the current status of Hungarians in the greater Cleveland area, a shrinking community.

Data from the most recent American Community Surveys show that of about 1.4 million Americans who listed Hungarian ancestry, only 82,000 spoke Hungarian in the family, which is almost 6 percent. Of approximately 183,000 Ohioans who listed Hungarian ancestry, about 6,000 spoke Hungarian in the family, almost 4 percent. Narrowing it to Cleveland, it is important to note that in local parlance "Cleveland" includes the surrounding suburbs as well. Indeed, the Cleveland–Elyria Metropolitan Statistical Area

	Hungarian ancestry	Hungarian spoken in household	
USA	1 411 132	82 819	5.8%
California	119 209	12 444	10.4%
New York state	147 111	11 641	7.9%
Ohio	187 684	6 399	3.4%
Cuyahoga County	37 853	2 656	7%
Cuyahoga + adjoining counties	90 001	4 445	4.9%

Ancestry vs Household Language Comparison

as defined by the United States Census Bureau includes Cuyahoga and its adjoining counties, but not Summit County.

Cuyahoga County census tracts (Cuyahoga County contains Cleveland and all of its contiguous suburbs), using five-year estimates from 2011 to 2015, indicate that 2,656 people spoke Hungarian within the family, and 37,853 people listed Hungarian ancestry. Due to suburban sprawl into the adjoining counties of Lorain, Summit, Medina, Geauga, and Lake, the number of Hungarians almost doubles. The American Community Survey data for Cuyahoga and its adjoining counties (the greater Cleveland area) shows a total of 4,445 census respondents reporting speaking Hungarian in their households and 90,001 residents listing Hungarian ancestry. Thus, while Ohio and nationwide statistics show that 3–6 percent of those who report Hungarian ancestry speak Hungarian in the household, that number is 5–7 percent in Cleveland and its adjoining suburbs. These results can be attributed to the area's vibrant community, which will be shown in later chapters.

Comparing these numbers to the detailed data of the 2000 Census, the number of people in Ohio, in the United States, and in the greater Cleveland area who reported speaking Hungarian in their homes saw a decline both in their overall numbers as well as in their percentages compared to totals reporting Hungarian ancestry. However, other measures of Hungarians in Cleveland, such as enrollment in its Hungarian school and participation in its cultural activities, show less of a decline.

With minor exceptions, Cleveland's various ethnicities tend not to overlap much, and each ethnic community conducts its own activities primarily

Total population	1 198 635
Speak only English	1 063 114
Spanish	41 840
Arabic	10 917
Chinese	8 806
Hindi, Gujarati, Urdu, & other Indic languages	8 686
Russian	6 101
Italian	5 212
Ukranian	5 170
German	5 125
Serbo-Croatian	4 997
Polish	4 433
Romanian	3 820
French	3 210
Hungarian	**2 870** (margin of error is +/- 412 with 90% accuracy)
Greek	2 085
Albanian	2 015

Languages Spoken in Cuyahoga County Households

Source: American Community Survey 2009-2013 estimates, released 2015

among its own members. Still, one can compare the Hungarian community to other nationalities by looking at the number of households reporting languages other than English spoken in the household, as sampled by the latest American Community Survey, a five-year estimate released in 2015. The margin of error is +/- 412, which means that there is a 90 percent chance that the number of Hungarian speakers in Cuyahoga County is between 2,458 and 3,282 persons, according to Census Bureau methodology.

Another way to shed light on the size of the Hungarian community in the Cleveland area is to look at the number of Hungarian funerals. Instead of relying on Census statistics alone, it is possible to look at the issue from various angles, one of them being trying to ascertain approximately how many families bury their loved ones using the Hungarian language. Although the research findings are imprecise because not all Hungarians in Cleveland frequent the same funeral parlors, examining the records of several of the prominently Hungarian funeral homes does shed light on aspects of Hungarian social life in Cleveland. Indeed, those who conduct a funeral service in Hungarian despite knowing and being surrounded by everyday English language, show that a Hungarian identity as manifested in language was important to the deceased and his or her family and by extension to the community. A funeral reflects values held and gives meaning to lives lived.

A spot-check of the Hungarian funerals held by the Bodnar-Mahoney Funeral Home shows a decline in Hungarian funerals on the West Side but nevertheless is one way to show the extent of current Hungarian language use. According to Lajos Bodnár, whose father started the business in 1929, 2010 saw 34 Hungarian funerals at his business. Ten years earlier his Hungarian funerals numbered 42, 1990 saw 47 Hungarian funerals, while 1980 saw 64 Hungarian funerals.

Also revealing are the statistics from the funeral homes serving the Hungarian and Slovak immigrants in the Buckeye Road neighborhood, especially in terms of a shrinking Hungarian population, or rather, of a population that fled to the suburbs during the late 1960s and early 1970s. Hartman Funeral Home was the business that most Lutherans and Reformed Hungarians of the Buckeye neighborhood frequented. In business since 1953, they averaged about 70 funerals per year, of which about 90 percent were Hungarian. They have since moved, but even today hold 20–25 Hungarian funerals per year.

Several funeral homes served other religious denominations of the Hungarians in the Buckeye Road neighborhood, but they have since closed or they left the neighborhood in the 1980s, much like Hartman. Cheroszky Funeral Home predominantly served the Hungarian Greek Catholic population, while Riczo Funeral Home had the biggest volume in its heyday, holding about 200–225 funerals per year, about 90 percent of which were Hungarian. Now out of business, the Jakob and Toth Funeral Home also catered to Hungarians in the Buckeye Road neighborhood, holding about 100 funerals per year at two locations.

One cannot draw valid statistical conclusions about these numbers, but as anecdotal evidence they show the use of the Hungarian language in an ongoing ritual, the tradition all humanity partakes in, joining together in community to remember the life and values of the decedent. And communicating in the chosen language of Hungarian is a choice laden with symbolism.

Aggregating the Hungarian funeral market, we can see that up until the 1980s, hundreds of Hungarian funerals were held in Cleveland every year. Indeed, the above-mentioned funeral parlors advertised extensively in the Cleveland Hungarian daily newspaper *Szabadság*. In the late twentieth century, seventy-five to a hundred were held yearly, and even today fifty to seventy-five Hungarian funerals are held yearly in the Cleveland area. Hungarian funerals are social occasions, which is why funeral statistics help to give an overall picture of Hungarian life in the Cleveland area. These numbers do not reflect those Hungarian families who choose to hold funerals at a funeral home that is not Hungarian, but the businesses that cater to an established Hungarian market nevertheless show a steady percentage of Hungarian funerals.

Another way to ascertain the number of Hungarians active in Cleveland is to examine the membership lists of the major Hungarian organizations. Churches are the easiest place to start. Assuming that most people do not regularly attend more than one religious denomination's services, although some do, my aggregation of weekly attendance figures indicates that on any given Sunday about 400 people attend various Hungarian-language church services in Cleveland and its suburbs, with about 800 attending on major holidays such as Christmas or Easter. These are the people who are active in Cleveland Hungarian churches.

For secular organizations, the total membership numbers are somewhat misleading because a significant number of Cleveland Hungarians belong to multiple organizations. But looking at the total membership numbers and discounting for overlap, a reasonable number can be attributed for Hungarians in Cleveland that are connected in a verifiable way to their community. These numbers do not reflect those Hungarians who do not belong to Cleveland Hungarian organizations, and their Hungarian identity may not depend on associating with an organization; in fact, some do not wish to have anything to do with what they see as politics and posturing among the organizations. Informal house parties at private residences among Hungarians in the Cleveland area, in fact, also provide a sense of community to their participants, but can be problematic for the scholar to research. Nevertheless, paying yearly dues or getting onto the mailing list of an organization shows a certain level of measurable commitment, which is why this method is a useful way to characterize Cleveland's Hungarians, in addition to using Census figures, church attendance, and funeral estimates.

Of the membership lists of the major Hungarian secular organizations in Cleveland, that of the American Hungarian Friends of Scouting is the largest with 1,197 total households as of 2011 (Cuyahoga and its adjoining counties only). The rest range from 45 to 520 paid members, with the Hungarian Association, the Hungarian Cultural Garden, the Hungarian Cultural Center of Northeast Ohio, and the Cleveland Hungarian Heritage Society averaging 387 members.[22]

Each list was examined, checking for overlap; the scouting list was by far the largest and most comprehensive, so that was used as a master list to verify the others, and the results show that six Cleveland Hungarian organizations collectively have 2,756 names on their mailing lists, with 799 of those 2,756 who hold various memberships or are on several mailing lists.[23] An additional 400 to 800 are involved in Hungarian churches, albeit with some overlap between the religious and the secular. Therefore the number of people actively associated in some tangible way with Cleveland's Hungarian organizations and churches can be estimated at around two to three thousand in 2017.

The geographical dispersion of two representative mailing lists shows that the suburbs of Lakewood, North Olmsted, Parma, Rocky River, and Westlake contain the most Hungarian families involved in Cleveland's Hungarian community.[24] To cite some examples of common Hungarian family names in the Cleveland area, the scout mailing list has 12 separate families named Horvath, 7 unique Kiss families, 12 Kovacs families with a thirteenth spelled Kovats, 7 families with the last name of Meszaros, 20 named Nagy, 11 named Szabo, 15 families named Takacs and a sixteenth spelled Takats, 14 households that bear the last name Toth, and 11 that carry the name Varga.

Worth mentioning is the extended reach of two of these Cleveland Hungarian organizations. The Hungarian Association has worldwide members in addition to its 416 households in the greater Cleveland area; its complete mailing list totals about 1,100 addresses. The scout mailing list has 1,197 in the Cleveland area, but around 1,850 total. An important feature of these two Cleveland organizations is their outreach and communication with Hungarians internationally; this extended reach shows a view of identity as being Hungarian, and what is important about that identity is solidarity with other Hungarians, a sense of belonging along the lines of the spiritual homeland theory. Other Hungarian organizations and churches in Cleveland also share this characteristic; the scout and Hungarian Association mailing lists merely quantify it in large-scale numbers.

Indeed, the sociological surveys filled out online and on paper for the purposes of this study support this: 57 percent of the respondents, or 163 of 286, reported meeting other Hungarians from the Cleveland area not including family weekly or more often; 75 of 286, or 26 percent reported meeting other Hungarians almost or at least monthly, while 45 of 286, or 16 percent reported meeting others yearly or less frequently; 31 of 286 (11 percent) attend Cleveland Hungarian events but do not belong to any organizations. These data show that those who are involved in community activities are deeply involved.

The survey responses also reflect the proportion of involvement in the major organizations: 84 percent reported being involved with the Hungarian scouts in Cleveland in one way or another, 30 percent were dues-paying members of the Cleveland Hungarian Heritage Society, and 28 percent members of the Hungarian Cultural Center of Northeast Ohio. Organizations with a lesser reach, polling in the 10 percent range, included the Hungarian Business and Tradesmen's Club, the Cleveland chapter of the William Penn Association, former athletes of the Cleveland Magyar Athletic Club, and the Hungarian Cultural Gardens. Of the 285 respondents, 197 were from the 50 and above age category (69 percent), from which can be surmised that older people feel more ties to the community or attribute more to the importance of filling out a survey, and 149 of 285 (52 percent) reported having a spouse, partner, or significant other who was also Hungarian.

To summarize the findings about the Hungarian population of the greater Cleveland area: approximately 90,000 people listed Hungarian ancestry in the 2016 American Community Survey, with about 4,500 of those speaking

Hungarian in the household. Over 2,000 are active in one or more of Cleveland's secular Hungarian organizations as of 2017, and about 400–800 attend a Hungarian church, with 50–75 Hungarian funerals yearly.[25]

Organization	Addresses from the Cleveland area	Total on mailing list	Number of unique names	Members who belong to other organizations as well
American Hungarian Friends of Scouting (CsBK)	1,197	1,798	736	461
Hungarian Association	416	455	65	390
Hungarian Cultural Gardens	328	385	171	157
Hungarian Cultural Center of Northeast Ohio	342	520 from 5 previous years	426	94
Cleveland Hungarian Heritage Society	187	1,301	45	142
Hungarian Genealogical Society of Cleveland	45	45	29	16

Membership and Mailing Lists of Cleveland Hungarian Organizations, as of 2011

Households	American Hungarian Friends of Scouting	Hungarian Association
Total on mailing list:	1,197	416
in Cleveland	256	
in Lakewood	70	38
in North Olmsted	57	
in Rocky River	55	33
in Parma	55	
in Westlake	43	21

Geographical Breakdown of Two Representative Mailing Lists, as of 2011

CHAPTER TWO
Cleveland's Hungarian Traditions

Traditions are those ongoing cultural events that are repeated year after year, providing a recurring expectation and a continuity to social groups. Brought over from Hungary and transplanted into American soil, these traditions provide consistency to the community but can change as the geography and the make-up of the community changes. What it means to be Hungarian in Cleveland was once tied to living in particular neighborhoods, but has now become a social construct based on the time and effort expended on participation in Cleveland's Hungarian community.

Hungarian Neighborhoods Since the 1950s: A Shrinking Community

Second and third generation Hungarians, descendants of the öregamerikás generation, as well as newly-arriving immigrants of the DP generation, found themselves in Cleveland of the early 1950s in an almost completely Hungarian world. The most famous Hungarian neighborhood was the area around Buckeye Road, which enjoyed the heyday of Hungarian culture and social life in the 1920s with the construction of ten Hungarian churches, eight clubhouses for Hungarian organizations, and countless businesses and office buildings. This was the age of expansion of the Hungarian community in Cleveland. The Buckeye neighborhood did not include the Lorain Avenue neighborhood on the West Side, which alone saw the building of four

Hungarian churches, but there was significant overlap in terms of social contacts and migration. From 1930 to about 1965 the Buckeye neighborhood was fairly stable, with an area population (not including other neighborhoods of Cleveland) of approximately 40,000, 87 percent of which was Hungarian, as recorded in the 1930 census. This meant that Hungarians in Cleveland in the middle part of the twentieth century lived in an extremely concentrated neighborhood where most aspects of life were Hungarian.

The Buckeye neighborhood's social calendar, as compiled by John Palasics and published by Karl Bonutti,[26] had regular events annually, including 12 grape harvest festivals, 11 New Year's Eve dances, 14 picnics, 12 plays, 20 banquets, and over 100 Hungarian weddings. Over 300 Hungarian-owned businesses and 81 Hungarian organizations were noted already in 1920. This same bustling atmosphere prevailed and was visibly evident in 1951, as many firsthand participants observed in interviews with the author. Ernő and Ibolya Sárosi, for example, recalled harvest festivals, a *debreceni vásár* [market as in Debrecen] that lasted a week, Hungarian picnics, walking around the neighborhood to go caroling around Christmastime and being offered food and drink at many a house, and numerous plays including famed actor Pál Jávor from Budapest. János Palasics recalled ten halls for dances and Hungarian theater productions, and five cinemas showing English and Hungarian films. He also remembered Hungarian synagogues, two Roman Catholic churches, a Greek Catholic church, a Reformed church, a Presbyterian, Baptist, and Adventist church, all conducting services in Hungarian. Ernest Mihály recalled choir and dance groups in each church, and summer Hungarian language classes three times per week, organized by the various Hungarian churches in the neighborhood. Ernő and Ibolya Sárosi also spoke of over 300 Hungarian stores, including butchers, a baker, a candy store, dentists, dress shops, restaurants, taverns, florists, hat stores, drugstores, bowling alleys, and a locksmith. Mihály, Palasics, and the Sárosi couple were all born in Cleveland and grew up in the Buckeye neighborhood. Audio and visual evidence from 1953 substantiates their recollections: a Lutheran church harvest festival photo shows hundreds of people in Hungarian folk costume, and film footage from *The Last Hungarian on Buckeye* shows street parades and the St. Margaret parking lot filled with hundreds dancing in Hungarian folk costume.[27] Even non-Hungarians learned Hungarian in the neighborhood. Indeed, numerous Cleveland Hungarians remember dropping off guests at downtown hotels in the mid-1990s, where the parking lot attendants, elderly African-American gentlemen, asked, "*Hogy vagy?*" [how are you?]. It turned out that they were retired mailmen or bus drivers from the Buckeye Road neighborhood who had learned basic Hungarian expressions in the 1950s and 1960s. Others reminisced about arriving to the Buckeye Road neighborhood in the early 1950s and hearing everyone on the street speaking Hungarian.

The area also boasted Hungarian music companies such as B & F Record Company, owned and operated by Barb and Frank Szappanos, at 3046 East 123rd Street, which issued phonograph records such as, among others, "Azt mondják hogy tavasz nyílik [They say spring blooms]," featuring Apollónia Kovács, László Szalai, Jolán Boross, and the Lajos Boros orchestra.

Also a part of Cleveland's artistic life was a successful amateur Hungarian theater group called *Déryné Színház* [Mrs. Déry Theater], which was formed around 1963 and led by Sándor Szabadkai and Sándor Marady. It staged successful popular Hungarian plays for almost a decade, with audiences of 300–400 people, taking some of its productions to Toledo and Pittsbugh as well. In its waning years, a competitor arose: *Clevelandi Magyar Színház* [Cleveland Hungarian Theater], under the leadership of the poet and NASA scientist Dr. György Gyékényesi. This theater was formed and staged its first play, "Mit ér az ember, ha magyar?" [What good is someone who's Hungarian?] in 1968. In addition to staging scenes from famous literary works by József Katona and Imre Madách, the theater group held yearly shows and later invited noted Hungarian writers such as Sándor Kányádi, András Sütő, and Sándor Csoóri. Its director's sudden death in 1973 contributed to this theater group's demise.

The Buckeye Road neighborhood also boasted three movie theaters that showed Hungarian films—the Moreland, Regent, and Sun theaters. Presentations and lectures were often organized by author Fréda B. Kovács, Gábor Papp, József Kondor, and helped by Lajos Szőke. Numerous Hungarian radio programs included the Szappanos, Kállay, Hudák, and Krasznay programs. Cleveland's Hungarian community built and sustained the Hungarian identity of its residents, and they belonged to this community by simple virtue of living in the neighborhood. Numerous statues and a park also attested to Cleveland's Hungarian character in 1951. In the Buckeye neighborhood, about seven blocks west of Shaker Square, on the corner of East Shaker Boulevard and East 121st Street, is Kossuth Park. A small park with a playground, it has a tidy city sign clearly labeling it.

In the late 1960s, however, the Buckeye neighborhood changed precipitously. A similar change happened in the Lorain Road neighborhood. Second and third generation Hungarians began moving outward to the suburbs, although they still came back to the old neighborhood to shop for Hungarian delicacies and for festivals and social events. As the Hungarian population of the Buckeye neighborhood decreased, more African-Americans moved in. Drawing on contemporary newspaper accounts of the time, Susan Papp found that between 1966 and 1970, the number of homicides, robberies, assaults, and breaking and entering doubled, the number of stolen cars tripled, and in 1974, over half the neighborhood population had been victims of crime. Blockbusting was a technique practiced by unscrupulous real estate agents in which they sowed fear of the incoming African-American population to white homeowners. In a documentary film produced by one of Cleveland's television stations, Cleveland council member Jane Muir Zborowsky, who represented Ward 29, the Buckeye neighborhood, mentioned 20 real estate companies that in 1970 went door to door, waging a campaign to get people to sell their homes. She said that her office received many calls asking why so many real estate companies were operating in the neighborhood. She said, "What stabilizes any community is the business community, and as the crime rate is increasing, the business community gets scared and goes." Ralph Rosenbluth, a merchant in the same film, attributed the businesses leaving to a lack of police protection and a lack of city interest. Jóska Rab, violin player and owner of the Gypsy Cellar, a Buckeye neighborhood tavern, related how his son urged him for years to go, "because [the Hungarian clientele] were scared to cross the suburbs [to return to Buckeye]," how he did not know where to relocate to, did not want to forsake the neighborhood.[28] His tavern eventually did close.

Fear of crime and of the changing population, sinking home values, and predatory and unscrupulous real estate agents, coupled with the prospect of a better, safer life in the suburbs led to the Buckeye neighborhood's fast demise. Most Hungarians moved out in the 1970s, leaving behind a scattering of older people and once grand buildings. St. Elizabeth's church and several Hungarian-owned businesses still remain, and some beautiful, traditional tulip-carved signs in English, Slovak, and Hungarian welcome the visitor to the Buckeye neighborhood. However, most Hungarian residents, businesses, and churches are long gone, having moved to the suburbs. Not as dangerous as in the late 1970s, 1980s, and 1990s, the city has designated it part of the Opportunity Corridor, hoping for a rebirth of new construction and development, but the houses are still run-down, and the neighborhood is a shell of what it once was.

The Lorain Avenue Hungarian neighborhood also changed in the 1970s and 1980s. The Kundtz mansion on Lake Avenue in Lakewood, torn down long ago, is now the site of the Winton Place condominiums. Most of the West Side Hungarian residents, like their Buckeye counterparts, moved out to the suburbs in the 1970s and 1980s. St. Emeric's Catholic Church closed in 2010, much to the dismay of its parishioners, but its congregation appealed to the Vatican, and it has since reopened and seen a rebirth. Some businesses on Lorain Avenue such as Menyhart Plumbing, Fodor Realty, Farkas Pastry and Csatary CPA remain, but the neighborhood has shifted from a geographic entity to a mostly social entity, kept alive by suburban "Hungarian commuters."

Cleveland's Hungarian life has definitely been shrinking. Several organizations, once vigorous, are now closed or have ceased to exist. These include religious congregations, cultural organizations, and smaller groups. Although they may have had hundreds of members at one time, their dissolutions show Hungarian life in Cleveland is significantly less than what it once was.

Several Hungarian religious congregations no longer exist, but at one time were active parts of Cleveland Hungarian communal life. These include Shomre Hadath, a Jewish minion established in 1922 with a synagogue built at East 123rd Street and Parkhill Avenue in 1926; the building was sold in the early 1970s. Sherith Jacob was an Orthodox Jewish congregation founded by Hungarian immigrants to Cleveland in 1899; its records from 1905 and 1932–1971 can be found in the library of the Western Reserve Historical Society. St. Michael's Hungarian Byzantine Catholic church was already standing in 1925 on the West Side of Cleveland at 4505 Bridge Avenue, but in 1986 was no longer in Hungarian possession. The list of disbanded Hungarian churches in Cleveland also includes St. Margaret Roman Catholic church, the Kegyelem Baptist congregation, and the First Hungarian Lutheran church, which up until 2016 still had a half dozen steadfast member gathering every two weeks for Hungarian services.

The Magyar Club of Cleveland was founded in 1924 and was comprised mostly of successful businessmen and educated professionals. Its purpose was to encourage the preservation and continuation of Hungarian art, literature, music, science, and drama, and it provided a forum for lectures, exhibits, and performances. The club invited guests such as Zoltán Kodály, Béla Bartók and Prime Minister József Antall (in 1990), and in its heyday had hundreds of members. As the DP generation and the refugees from 1956 started other cultural organizations, interest waned in the Magyar Club, and it disbanded on May 28, 2009, donating its treasury to other Hungarian organizations in Cleveland.

A staple of Cleveland's Hungarian scene was radio and TV broadcasting. Kalman Novak had a long running but now canceled Hungarian radio program on WZAK and Miklós and Mária Kossányi had their NBN Broadcasting Corporation. Located in the suburb of Lakewood, they purchased an AM radio station in 1991, hosting live programming on WKTX 830 AM, and also streamed Kossuth Rádió from Hungary. Their TV studio streamed reports about local Cleveland Hungarian events and also programs from Hungary through the SCOLA cable television channel. After the Kossányis' deaths, the stations and studio were eventually sold. For many decades Frank Borisz, who had his own Hungarian dance band, also hosted the Popular Second Generation Hungarian Radio Program on Sunday mornings on WSLR in nearby Akron, streaming throughout northeast Ohio, but that is also no more.

The World Federation of Hungarian Veterans [*Magyar Harcosok Bajtársi Köre: MHBK*], was formed in 1946 in Germany as a fraternal association for exiled Hungarian military officers. It published and still publishes today a military history newspaper entitled *Hadak Útján—Bajtársi Híradó*.[29] The

Cleveland chapter was started in the early fifties and long organized social activities for its members and their descendants; although the Hungarian veterans from the Second World War still living today are few and far between, the Cleveland chapter of the MHBK organized its yearly debutante ball (a significant social event with hundreds attending) up until 2014, with proceeds going to Hungarian charities mostly in the Cleveland area. In keeping with the military traditions of the organization, local US military Reserve Officer Training Corps (ROTC) cadets provided an honor guard and presented the colors at the ball, as they had for many decades. At the end of December 2017, the Cleveland chapter officially ceased operations and distributed its remaining funds to the Cleveland Hungarian Heritage Society and to the American Hungarian Friends of Scouting.

CMAC, the Cleveland Magyar Athletic Club, had its start in 1957 at the Woodland Recreation Club on the East Side, and throughout its history sponsored soccer teams and other sports leagues, fencing, boxing, and tennis instruction, and owned its own social hall and training facility at 4125 Lorain Road on the near West Side. Its membership once numbered near a thousand; it had Olympic-caliber coaching, especially in fencing under coaches János Szentkirályi (sometimes spelled Szent Kiraly) and Ferenc Áprily, and trained some Golden Gloves boxing finalists in the late 1950s. The early 1990s saw its demise. American suburban soccer became popular, and parents no longer had to support nationality teams to find quality sports, because every community suddenly had their own teams. The club organized yearly dances called the Athletic Ball, but in the mid-1980s it sold its social hall. Although just a shadow of its glorious past, the CMAC did play a significant role in the attempt to establish a Hungarian Cultural Center in 2003. No other Cleveland Hungarian organization supported the venture as much as the CMAC; it was willing to front the initial costs in the hope of mobilizing Cleveland Hungarians to invest in and establish the center. Although the attempt was unsuccessful, CMAC committed a significant portion of its assets in the endeavor. Its former members still play informal soccer games, but the organization effectively dissolved after its 50th anniversary sport ball in 2007.

From 1975 to the mid-1980s CMAC members endeavored to establish a Hungarian sports and recreation club on Lake Plata in Twinsburg, an outlying suburb of Cleveland. Lake Plata started when younger families wanted to find a Hungarian place to congregate that was not in a dangerous neighborhood. A group of local Hungarians[30] purchased the property with soccer fields and a large pondlike swimming pool. Many Hungarian teens got summer jobs as grounds crew or lifeguards there. The group went bankrupt in the mid 1980s, and the property was razed and developed into new housing.

Several organizations used to propagate Hungarian culture in Cleveland. One once-active group was the Hungarian Theatre and Dance Company of Cleveland. Its beginnings trace back to 1969 and 1970, when István Soltay taught the scouts the opening court dance for their debutante ball and folkdance for performances. In 1970 or 1971 Magdi Bíró suggested forming a Hungarian dance group. Dr. György Gyékényesi, the director of the waning Hungarian Theater of Cleveland, helped start the new theater and dance ensemble by buying folk costumes and donating funds from his own dwindling theater troupe. Under the direction of Soltay, the Company soon grew to eight couples and in addition to performing Hungarian dance for Cleveland audiences, also toured the USA. The group tried organizing a children's dance club, but lack of interest derailed that attempt. By 1982 the Company had dissipated, and it dispersed its folk costumes among its members, eventually donating the remainder to the scouts' folk ensemble. At its peak, however, the Hungarian Theatre and Dance Company of Cleveland boasted 16 female and 10 male members, and for many years was a proud addition to Cleveland's Hungarian culture.

The *Bocskai István Kultúrkör* [István Bocskai Cultural Club] originally started when the Hungarian leadership of the West Side Hungarian Reformed Church decided around 1980 that a group should be organized to support ministers and writers from Hungary and its surrounding countries. László Berta became the main catalyst for this organization, which later became independent and organized many cultural programs, inviting Hungarian lecturers and famous personalities to Cleveland, among them Olympic champion András Balczó and the Reverend László Tőkés, whose actions in Timișoara (Temesvár) sparked the Romanian Revolution of 1989 which toppled the dictator Nicolae Ceaușescu. The group organized cultural events throughout the 1980s and 1990s, usually four to eight per year, and also had an ongoing weekly or biweekly Hungarian film screening. The number of its members and attendees slowly waned throughout the years, and its last president was Erzsébet Nagy.

The Hungarian Communion of Friends, known in Hungarian circles as *Magyar Baráti Közösség* (MBK), began publishing its newsletter *Itt-Ott* in 1967 and formally incorporated in Oregon in 1974. The purpose of this national organization is to promote and support independent non-denominational religious life in the Magyar tradition, charitable work by and among people of Magyar extraction, and cultural-educational endeavors that further established Magyar values. It is best known, however, for its weeklong conference at Lake Hope State Park in central Ohio, also called *Itt-Ott*, with intellectual programming aimed at Hungarian families throughout the diaspora. The conference regularly invites guests, lecturers, and musicians from Hungary and its surrounding countries. The forty-sixth *Itt-Ott* conference was held in August 2017. A Cleveland chapter organized many cultural events in the late 1980s and early 1990s, including lectures by then-Hungarian member of Parliament Miklós Pálos, historian and later Minister of Defense Lajos Für, literary critic Mihály Czine, famed Hungarian priest György Bulányi, author László Dobos, and Transylvanian author András Sütő, among others. Most active in the Cleveland chapter were László Bőjtös, István Hargitai, and István Csíszár. Although MBK members still live in Cleveland and take part in the national organization's work, the Cleveland chapter no longer organizes cultural events on an ongoing basis.

The two East Side Hungarian scout troops, numbered 22 and 33, no longer conduct programs on a weekly basis, with Troop 22 having ceased scouting operations with children in 1993, and Troop 33 in the late 1990s. Their alumni members do, however, support and help Cleveland's Hungarian scouting activities in important ways. These include fundraising and helping the existing two scout troops with programs and background work, whether with dinners, debutante balls, scout park maintenance, collecting clothes for Hungarian villages in the Ukraine, or helping staff the yearly Labor Day festival called *Cserkésznap* [Scout Day]. Thus a shrinking community has been transformed to a certain extent, as its members fulfill other roles in the community as they age.

Relatively recently formed but lasting exactly 20 years, *Csárdás* was a nonprofit dance ensemble that celebrated traditional as well as contemporary works stemming from Hungarian tradition. The company had ongoing weekly rehearsals and performed regularly. It was founded in 1994 by Richard Graber, a native Clevelander who was a member of the Hungarian Scout Folk Ensemble. Graber later majored in dance performance at the Ohio State University. The ensemble consisted of 15–20 members, predominantly youth, and it had been the recipient of numerous grants, awards, and proclamations. Notable performances included a collaboration with the world-renowned Cleveland Orchestra at Severance Hall, as well as several performances in Budapest, Hungary, and for hundreds of children throughout the years in many schools regionally. It suspended operations and then dissolved after 20 successful years, selling and donating its costumes.[31]

A smaller organization, no longer active but with a history spanning many decades, is the *Csendőr Családi Közösség* [Family of Hungarian Gendarmes]. The Hungarian gendarmes were a military unit that provided law-enforcement duties in rural areas of Hungary, but were mobilized for combat duty during the last months of the Second World War, earning the post-war hatred of the communist authorities. Many were imprisoned and executed because they were not willing to adjust ideologically to the communist system. In Cleveland, the organization's chapter was founded by János Borgoy, then was led by István Molnár from 1978 until his death in 2011; he organized a yearly benefit dinner that attracted hundreds of Cleveland Hungarians. In the 1960s–1980s, original gendarmes who fled Hungary attended these dinners, formal balls, and New Year's Eve parties held by the organization. But at the last dinner in 2010 only two living gendarmes were in attendance, Molnár and László Kemes. However, over a hundred family members and friends of former gendarmes still did attend the event, as the author personally observed.

A group formed in 1956 called *Magyar Felszabadító Bizottság* [Committee for Hungarian Liberation] was a political organization formed to protest Soviet occupation of Hungary, and its lobbying and publications were quite extensive. It had a Canadian chapter as well; its Cleveland headquarters were led by former Hungarian general Gyula Kovács, and its secretary was Dr. Elemér Hommonay.[32] Similar political committees were established shortly thereafter to represent the rights of Hungarians living outside the borders of Hungary: the *Délvidék Felszabadító Tanácsa* [Yugoslavia Freedom Committee] led by Dr. Antal Lelbach, the *Csehszlovákiai Magyarok Nemzeti Bizottmánya* [Czechoslovakian Hungarians National Committee] led by Dr. László Sirsich, a committee for Transcarpathia led by Károly Hokky and Mihály Pánczélos, and a committee for Romania led by Lajos Lőte. All of these were eventually dissolved.

Another organization which did not meet frequently but still impacted Hungarian culture was the Hungarian Relief Agency [*Magyar Segély Egyesület*], founded in 1950 as a charity organization. Every year the organization held a silent ball, which meant that instead of donning a tuxedo or an evening gown, participants sent in a donation in lieu of buying ball entrance tickets. Each year the "ball invitation" showed the previous year's donors and their donation amounts, which functioned as an indicator of local social standing. Retirees contributed a little, wealthier persons contributed more, and with overhead costs staying minimal, the organization distributed $10,000–20,000 in aid every year to Hungarian schools, universities, kindergartens, and churches of various denominations in Romania, Serbia, Slovakia, and Carpatho-Ruthenia in Ukraine. For example, donors sent in $15,596.11 for the 2011 ball, printing and postage costs came to $799.93, and thus $15,001.78 was distributed in aid, mostly through personal contacts. The list of donors was mostly Hungarians living in the Cleveland area. Donating financially also shows the vibrancy of the community, inasmuch as doing so concretely displays a sense of common purpose, and by helping other Hungarians, the donors' own Hungarian identity is strengthened.

Another Hungarian organization with close Cleveland ties was the American Hungarian Friendship and International Care Association. Originally incorporated in Alabama in 1968, it was transferred to Ohio in 1986, and was once the umbrella organization for ten subsidiary organizations with charitable missions. Its recent Cleveland subsidiaries included the Hungarian Relief Agency, the Hungarian School Care Club, and the United Hungarian Fund. Around 2012 its activities ceased and the organization dissolved.

The World Federation of Hungarian Engineers and Architects, which no longer exists, was a subset of the Hungarian Association, which still exists, and is vibrant. With the founding leadership of Dr. István Tuba from Pittsburgh, who was its president from 1968 to 1978, this autonomous group met annually for well over 30 years as a part of the Hungarian Congress in Cleveland, with their own series of lectures and presentations given by distinguished engineers, scientists, and architects from around the world.

The West Side Hungarian Retiree Club gathered three times per month at the West Side Hungarian Reformed Church, meeting on Thursdays and alternating Hungarian film screenings with card games. Started by Gábor Papp in the late 1980s, it had a peak membership of about 80, and the last leader of the club was Ildikó Szénásy. There was once an active Hungarian stamp collecting club, active in the 1960s and 1970s, but no longer. Other smaller groups also no longer exist, such as an informal group that called itself simply "the Hungarian group." About a dozen people met once a month at the Bay Village senior center, to speak a mixture of English and Hungarian and to enjoy Hungarian food.

The Physical Landscape:
Statues, Gardens, Memorials

A shrinking community is by no means an antiquated or dead community, and despite suburban flight, the demise of dense ethnic neighborhoods, numerous church closings, and defunct organizations, Cleveland's Hungarian community remains vibrant, with a long history of traditions. Transformed from a geographic entity, the social community carries many traditions both from the old Buckeye neighborhood, as well as transplanted from Hungary and the Carpathian basin.[33] Take, for example, the manifestations of tradition expressed in the physical landscape: statues, gardens, and memorials.

Places in and of themselves are merely geographic features, inanimate stone or asphalt. What gives places significance is the sense of community that shared historical experiences generate for any particular place, which in turn evoke emotions. In the case of statues and memorials, they are communal creations, built for others, and their conceptions are inherently based on common values and shared cultural traditions. Social agreement has to be eked out, with political maneuverings to establish geographic places, and then fundraising to allow construction, which fundamentally shows the material commitment of any community of individuals with shared goals. Finally come dedications, which are also extremely social events, with people gathering together to listen to ideas expressed by the prominent personalities of any given generation, and to reflect upon the values they as a community share. As the years go by, some places are revisited on important anniversaries, adding to the emotional significance of the place, and others are neglected but nevertheless signify important principles, in retrospect being given historical value by those who are aware of the past. Cleveland's Hungarians have many such places; although not all are sacred, all do have communal significance, whether historically or ideologically. These places materially express ideas and ideals, shared common values of groups of Hungarians, expressions of a historical tradition.

If the Buckeye neighborhood was the largest manifestation of Cleveland's Hungarian community, then the statue of Lajos Kossuth is one of the oldest, together with the churches. Still standing almost two miles from Kossuth Park, in a small parklike area on Euclid Avenue at Martin Luther King, Jr. Boulevard, near University Circle, one can see the Cleveland Art Museum from the base of the statue. Dedicated in 1902 with 26,000 people in attendance, the base of the statue contains earth sent in 1902 from various historical places in greater Hungary, including the straits of Verecke, where Árpád's Hungarian tribes first entered the Carpathian basin in 896 AD; the battlefields at Mohács and Majtény; Kossuth's and Áron Gábor's gravesites; forts at Eger, Drégely, Komárom, Szigetvár, and Trencsén; the castles of King Mathias and his father, János Hunyadi; as well as cities such as Debrecen, Esztergom, and Szolnok, among others.

Kossuth's contemporary, the poet Sándor Petőfi, also has a marble bust downtown in the Cleveland Public Library on Superior Avenue, on the third floor of the old building. The plaque below the bust reads "SÁNDOR PETŐFI MAGYAR POET 1823–1849," while the marble bust itself is engraved "Finta 1929." The sculptor was born in the Hungarian village of Túrkeve in 1881 and spent his boyhood years as a shepherd, then became a sculptor, with works in the Hungarian National Museum, the New York

47

Metropolitan Museum of Art, and in various cities throughout Hungary and the United States. The idea for a bust of Petőfi was proposed in 1923 at a meeting of the Cleveland United Hungarian Societies [*Egyesült Magyar Egyletek*] and organized in 1924; the project was postponed in 1925 due to donor capacity limitations (constant donations to charities in Hungary left no room for collecting for a Petőfi bust). In 1926, 10,000 numbered donation fliers were printed and distributed, and by 1929 over $2,000 had been collected. On February 30, 1930, with the sponsorship of the *Plain Dealer* and *Szabadság* [Liberty] Cleveland newspapers, a performance of Petőfi's "János Vitéz" was staged at Cleveland's Public Auditorium, where 3,000 Cleveland Hungarians filled the audience, and 1,500 were turned away.[34] On May 25, 1930, the finished bust was presented to the Cleveland Public Library, where it still stands today.

The Hungarian Cultural Garden is one of a series of ethnic gardens along East Boulevard and Martin Luther King, Jr. Boulevard (formerly Liberty Boulevard) in Rockefeller Park, among them German, Italian, Polish, Czech, Yugoslav, Rusin, Greek, Syrian, Chinese, Hebrew, Ukranian, and Irish, reflecting some of the many immigrant groups settling in Cleveland. The origin of the cultural gardens lies in the Shakespeare Garden of 1916, which is now named the British Garden. The Hungarian Garden was dedicated in 1934, with 25,000 in attendance. Its first president was Judge Louis Petrash, and its longest-serving president Lily P. Volosin. In 1951 the garden had relief sculptures of Ferenc Liszt, Imre Madách, Endre Ady, and the local writer József Reményi, as well as an ornate wrought-iron gate with traditional Hungarian motifs. The iron gate was commissioned by the Verhovay Aid Association, which later became the William Penn Association. After a period of neglect in the 1980s and 1990s, the Hungarian Cultural Garden has seen somewhat of a rebirth, with several fundraisers held yearly and clean-up activities held at the gardens. In 2011 a Liszt concert was held in the garden to commemorate the composer's 200th birthday, and yearly summer Liszt concerts are now held there, the latest, in June 2017, attracting over 250 guests. In 2013 the Legacy Wall was added to the lower garden, a wall which is dedicated to famous Hungarians in the fields of music, art, science, mathematics, and technology. An endowment fund for landscape maintenance was established by Ernest Mihaly, and the overall organization is led by Carolyn Balogh, with yearly golf outings attracting 40–70 people, wine tastings also attracting about 70 people, and of course the summer concerts, recently with performances by Cleveland Hungarian Vera Holczer and students and faculty from the Aurora School of Music. The Hungarian Garden also participates in the annual One World Day, a celebration of Cleveland's many ethnicities.

A bust of Joseph Cardinal Mindszenty was erected in 1977 at Lakeside Avenue and East 12th Street, at the southern end of the plaza between the Doubletree Hotel and the Cleveland Department of Water. The plaza had been named Cardinal Mindszenty Plaza a year earlier through the assistance of then-mayor Ralph Perk, and a street sign stating such is still posted. The bust was sculpted by Gyuri E. Hollóssy. Occasional commemorations are still held at the site of the statue, especially around October 23 or on major anniversaries of Mindszenty's 1974 visit to Cleveland.

The most recent statue commemorates an anonymous Hungarian freedom fighter of 1956, placed directly behind the statue of Mindszenty on Cardinal Mindszenty Plaza. The figure has an anguished look on his face and holds a Hungarian flag with a hole torn from the middle. The statue was commissioned and dedicated in 2006 for the 50th anniversary of the Hungarian Revolution of 1956.

For their final resting places, Hungarians in Cleveland have chosen various cemeteries throughout the general area. One cemetery, though, has a particular concentration of Hungarian graves and is the site of a memorial to Hungarian soldiers who lost their lives during the Second World War. Located in North Olmsted's Sunset Memorial Park on Columbia Road, the memorial and Hungarian section of the cemetery were dedicated on June 1, 1986. Sculpted by Gyuri E. Hollósy, the memorial depicts the Hungarian coat of arms, a mythical Hungarian eagle called the *turul*, a bust of St. Stephen, first king of Hungary, and a bust of Árpád, who led the ancient Hungarians into the Carpathian basin. Initiated and organized by Árpád Dobolyi and a committee of seven, the memorial was supported by Cleveland's Hungarian Association, the Cleveland chapter of the World Federation of Hungarian Veterans (*Magyar Harcosok Bajtársi Közössége*, or MHBK) as well as the entire Cleveland Hungarian community. The memorial has also frequently been the site of annual commemorations on the last Sunday of May, on the day before Memorial Day. The names of some of those Cleveland Hungarians who lost their lives during the Vietnam War are also listed on the memorial, and the surrounding graves contain the remains of many former officers of the pre-world war Hungarian army.

Churches and Social Life

For many, being Hungarian in Cleveland means attending a Hungarian church, if not every Sunday, at least on important holidays or when church dinners are held. For churches, like statues, gardens, and memorials, are lasting physical presences that host social events. And although church traditions are first and foremost religious, in émigré communities the ethnic churches, in addition to their religious pastoral work, also take on a role of ethnic identity promulgation, as can be seen by the social events organized by the churches. And although Cleveland's Hungarian community is shrinking, seven Hungarian church communities do still remain in the greater Cleveland area. They are microcosms of the larger Cleveland Hungarian community, each with its own traditions, social fabric, and history. Each holds Hungarian-language services on Sunday mornings (or Saturdays for the Adventists), hosts various dinners, festivals, and dances throughout the year, and most still hold annual harvest festivals. All of these church communities show the vibrancy of Cleveland's Hungarians, because they are in fact living and vibrant entities. Thousands of miles away from Hungary, these churches reflect a culture built upon inherited values, as Attila Z. Papp described, a definite spiritual homeland of sorts.

The churches in Cleveland's Hungarian neighborhoods were built by the öregamerikás generation of the early twentieth century and even before. Indeed, scarcely one hundred years after the founder of Cleveland, General Moses Cleaveland, set foot upon the banks of the Cuyahoga river, the first Hungarian churches were established in Cleveland in the early 1890s. The first Roman Catholic, Greek Catholic, Reformed, and Lutheran churches were the first Hungarian churches built in all of North America. All four were built by Hungarians on lower Buckeye Road. By the early 1900s, eight Hungarian churches of six denominations were established all around Cleveland, along with three Hungarian Jewish temples.

Of those Hungarian churches remaining in Cleveland today, three were established in 1892. The early 1800s and the 1920s saw the founding of two more, while two churches were built in 1936 and two more in the 1950s. The two largest congregations were the two oldest: the First Hungarian Reformed Church, established in 1891, and St. Elizabeth of Hungary, established in 1892. Both churches' Buckeye Road locations seated 1,200 people.

Although not as large and not nearly as famous as the Buckeye neighborhood, the near West Side area around Lorain Avenue was also a significant neighborhood, once home to four Hungarian churches, numerous Hungarian-owned businesses, the Cleveland Magyar Athletic Club hall on Lorain Avenue, and the massive Hungaria Hall on Clark Avenue.

Worth mentioning is the recent closing of several Hungarian churches as part of an overall downsizing effort by the Roman Catholic Diocese of Cleveland. By the end of a five-year program in 2010, 50 Catholic parishes in the greater Cleveland area had been closed. In the farther suburbs these included Sacred Heart church in Elyria, closed in the summer of 2009, a church with some Hungarian members but without a Hungarian priest for over 25 years. Also closed in September 2009 was Saint Ladislaus, a Hungarian church in Lorain with some Hungarian members but also without a Hungarian priest for a decade. Saint Margaret was closed in 2010, with about six families transferring to Saint Elizabeth. All of these examples show the traditional view of assimilation, the melting pot theory that immigrant communities eventually lose their heritage and become Americanized. But how do Hungarian churches in the Cleveland area function today?

The most vibrant congregations today include St. Emeric church, with about 370 registered households and average weekly attendance numbering around 150, swelling to 400 at Christmas and Easter. The church still hosts the scouts and the Hungarian school, as it has for decades, and serves also as a cultural center for many of Cleveland's Hungarians, with a full social calendar. In 2015 Fr. András Mezei arrived from Hungary to become the new parish administrator, and since then the parish has seen a resurgence of vibrancy, with increased attendance, the addition of a monthly youth Mass with contemporary music, and the addition of an August 20 St. Stephen festival that attracted over a thousand visitors.

Next is the Westlake Seventh-day Adventist Church, with a modern structure in the West Side suburb of Westlake. Led by Reverend Marius Marton, the congregation is one of the strongest Cleveland Hungarian churches; 80–100 members attend Hungarian-English bilingual services on any given Saturday, with multiple church choirs and an orchestra, children's and youth groups, Bible study groups, Pathfinder and Adventurer groups, a Vacation Bible School, a cooking school, and an active social calendar.

Probably the most close-knit and active Hungarian church community in Cleveland is the Hungarian Bethany Baptist Church. It was founded in 1958 and moved to its current location in 1989. Most of its members are Hungarians from Transylvania, and its pastor is the Reverend Sándor Kulcsár. Two Hungarian services are held on Sundays, at 10:00 am and 6:00 pm, with a Wednesday evening Bible study group. The average attendance on an ordinary Sunday is about 70 people, but for major holidays over 100 participate. The church has a strong children's ministry, a very active youth group, a high-quality choir, a 16-page Hungarian monthly newsletter entitled *Ébresztő* [Awake], and all events are conducted in Hungarian. According to József Szerencsy, who broadcast a Baptist missionary monthly local radio program in the Hungarian language from 1985 until 2010, there are also an additional 60 Hungarian Baptists in the Cleveland area who do not congregate in any one church, but rather conduct their Hungarian Sunday services at each other's houses.

With smaller numbers but nevertheless averaging 20–50 attendees each at weekly Hungarian church services are the First Hungarian Reformed Church, St. Elizabeth of Hungary (which has a Hungarian dance group), and the West Side Hungarian Reformed Church. Another congregation of 20–30 people is that of the West Side Hungarian Lutheran Church. Although without its own church building, this congregation under the leadership of Reverend Éva Tamásy probably organizes the most cultural activities, including musical concerts, literary evenings, its own Hungarian school, a monthly playdate for toddlers, and frequent church dinners. Ladies from the

First Hungarian Reformed Church still get together on Tuesday mornings to make *csiga tészta*, a spiral noodle for soups, by hand. St. Elizabeth of Hungary recently celebrated its 125th anniversary, and the West Side Hungarian Reformed Church also has a long and varied history.

Each of the active churches listed in Appendix III has its own somewhat autonomous community with separate social lives. Although significant numbers of church members cross into and socialize with other churches and community groups, the majority of each church tends to stay within the confines of its own group. Indeed, one can find all sorts of community events happening regularly at each location. In addition to their religious functions maintained every Sunday morning, the churches also fulfill important social roles, organizing harvest festivals with food, music, and dancing, holding dinners throughout the year including hog butchering dinners, Mother's Day, Father's Day, mock weddings, Valentine's Day dances, and the occasional literary evening or St. Nicholas festival. Traditional Hungarian food plays an important role in almost all of these social events, with stuffed cabbage, goulash, *lángos* (a fried bread similar to elephant ears), sausage stuffing, and other Hungarian specialties.

The physical appearance of most of these churches is typically Hungarian-American and resembles the exteriors and architecture of Hungarian churches in Youngstown, Toledo, Chicago, Buffalo, New Brunswick, Garfield, or any of several studied in Western Pennsylvania by the scholar Balázs Balogh:

> Invariably, church buildings were constructed with a large basement which then served as a community center. To this day, these basements constitute the scenes of Hungarian community life in Western Pennsylvania. National holidays are celebrated there, church picnics and bazaars are held there—this is where community sausage stuffing events are held, the women learn to make the so-called "spiral noodles" to be used in soups and the men while away the time playing cards. This sub-church community room was a phenomenon totally unknown in Hungary where it has neither meaning nor a tradition. "The church was everything. The biggest, largest community organizer. There was nothing else. Back then, if there was a Hungarian holiday celebration, you had to

fight for a seat in the community room. Now its [*sic*] all totally empty," an elderly widow from Duquesne remembers. The entrance to the church is adorned with the map of Greater Hungary and a picture of national hero Louis Kossuth. Down in the community room, there is a small stage and everything is painted in the national colors of red-white-green. The walls are decorated with folkloristic depictions and archive photographs from the life of the community.[35]

The portrayal above happens to be of Hungarian churches in western Pennsylvania, but the description fits Cleveland Hungarian churches almost exactly. As Mihály Hoppál observed about a South Bend, Indiana community:

The social dancing is the important thing in the dance, it is not the song or the text that is important in the singing but the fact of singing together and in the money-raising it is the gesture of giving and the contribution, the nostalgic feeling of strengthening the ethnic bonds that are important. All these factors together explain the participation in such activity. In reality, it is the being-there (Dasein) that is important and the presence is important, not the nature of their presence.[36]

Though not established churches per se, there are also several smaller organizations with a religious bent. The Hungarian Spiritual Society [*Magyar Szellemkutatók Társasága*] was founded on Buckeye Road by Julius Trombitás in 1916; its members engage in the study of evangelical spiritualism's philosophy. Moved to Northfield Road in Bedford in 1974, its weekly meetings are conducted in Hungarian, and membership is made up of first and second generation Hungarians.

Another is the Hungarian Lutheran Conference in America, the umbrella organization for Hungarian Lutheran churches throughout North America. A majority of its officers live in the Cleveland area and they publish a Hungarian-language periodical in Cleveland, *Erős Vár: Amerikai Magyar Evangélikusok Lapja* [Strong Fortress: American Hungarian Lutheran newspaper].

The St. László Association and Order [Szent László Társaság és Rend] is a worldwide organization of which the Cleveland chapter is comprised mostly of members of the DP generation. Formed by papal breve in Hungary in 1863, the society was disbanded by communist authorities in the early 1950s, reborn in West Germany in 1965, with Archduke Joseph of Habsburg as its leader, and since then has spread throughout the world, with chapters wherever larger groups of Hungarians emigrated. Its purpose is to recognize and express appreciation for those who serve and better the Hungarian community selflessly and tirelessly. It awards orders of merit to deserving individuals. The chapter's leaders over the recent past have been Reverend Béla Bernhardt and Viktor Falk.

Ongoing Events: Cleveland Hungarian Customs

Traditions give life a stable structure. Indeed, shared events repeated from year to year, decade to decade, century to century, are what ethnologists and folk culture experts study. In Cleveland the traditions were brought over from Hungarian villages and cities and then maintained, sometimes subtly or not so subtly modified to fit the new American surroundings, propagated, and finally passed on to the next generations. They became an important part of the social fabric of the community.

Wintertime brings many traditions to Cleveland Hungarians. Numerous families and friends get together to make their own sausage or butcher a hog, and some even distill their own *pálinka* [brandy], just like in the old country. At the beginning of December, the *Mikulás* [St. Nicholas] arrives to social gatherings. For some organizations such as the William Penn Association, this is the traditional American Santa Claus. But for most Cleveland Hungarian organizations, such as the scouts and some churches, the tradition is a remnant of prewar Hungary, a European tradition of the bishop Saint Nicholas arriving on or near December 6, dressed as a bishop, with his crooked shepherd's staff and his *Krampusz* servants, who are dressed in black, have horns or masks, carry chains or switches, and are the personification of just punishment. This Saint Nicholas is different from the American Santa Claus; he reads from an elegant book and confronts each child with the past year's good deeds and transgressions, then gives each a small package, usually containing fruit, nuts, and chocolate. Newer immigrant arrivals to Cleveland are more familiar with the *Télapó* [Father Winter] prevalent in the Hungary of 1945–1989, but most Cleveland Hungarian children are exposed to the childhood memories of the DP and 1956 generation, transposed and maintained through the decades.

December also brings *betlehemezés* [a nativity play], a tradition which the scouts have been maintaining in Cleveland at least since the 1960s. This tradition involves memorizing Hungarian scripts involving shepherds and the nativity story, often humorous, with teenagers playing the parts of an angel, Hungarian shepherds, and the three kings. An old Hungarian tradition in which actual shepherds went door-to-door in the villages, telling the nativity story in their own way with folk rhymes and verse, Cleveland Hungarian families nowadays also may get a knock at their doors, with up to a dozen teenagers standing outside wearing Hungarian folk garb. After entering the house, acting out the scene and singing Hungarian Christmas songs, the hosts provide refreshments and often *pálinka* [brandy], and the tradition turns into a social event, repeated in various homes a dozen times per day on December weekends.

Christmas traditions often involve the churches, where attendance swells from about 50 per week into the hundreds. Some of the churches offer candlelight services or midnight Masses on or shortly before Christmas Eve, and these are always well-attended. In addition to the churches, most secular Hungarian organizations also hold Christmas events, from an elaborate children's pageant put on by the scouts to simpler parties organized by other groups. For example, the Hungarian Heritage Society and Museum organizes children's Christmas programs directed primarily to non-Hungarian speakers as an alternative to the scouts' programs.

Winter is also the time of formal balls. The traditional age at which young girls are presented as debutantes is 16. It is customary to wear tuxedos and long gowns, and this is also a tradition carried over by the DP generation, a relic of prewar high society Hungary transplanted to modern American elegant surroundings. This tradition is a unique diaspora Hungarian phenomenon in which the community builds upon its inherited values, values it has brought from Hungary. The end of November starts off with the Hungarian Association's ball, known locally as the *Magyar Bál*. Coinciding with the American Thanksgiving holiday, the most important family event of the year, many young adults who are away at college return home, and the ball is a perfect opportunity to reconnect with old friends. Hundreds attend this ball, which is held at a downtown hotel. For over three decades young scout leaders have also held a tackle football game on the day of the ball; meeting at the Mastick Road picnic area of the Cleveland Metroparks, they call their informal event the Turkey Bowl. The football game serves as an alumni reunion of sorts, with almost everyone meeting later in the evening for the ball; this Turkey Bowl consistently attracts 25–40 younger Cleveland Hungarians, most of the second and third generations. In late February or early March is the Paprika Ball, organized by the Cleveland Hungarian Development Panel; this event is in a much higher price category, so fewer average Cleveland Hungarians and more high-end Cleveland socialites attend, but it is nevertheless an important social event from a Hungarian perspective.

February or March traditionally hosted the *Bőgőtemetés* (burial of the bass), a pre-Lenten party among Cleveland Hungarians for over a century. With origins in the Buckeye neighborhood, it used to be a street festival and large parade, with Gypsy musicians holding an extravagant funeral procession for the bass instrument of the band, to be put away for the forty days of Lent, with no music (and thus no income) until Easter. With the demise of the Buckeye neighborhood, parishioners of St. Margaret church maintained the tradition for decades, always learning the humorous script by heart and acting out the funeral procession in the context of a church dinner. Later, the Hungarian Cultural Center of Northeast Ohio held such an event, and most recently, St. Emeric church in 2018 revived this old Cleveland Hungarian tradition. Another Hungarian émigré community where this tradition survives is Melbourne, Australia.

Springtime shows the ongoing vibrancy of the community and brings with it another set of events. The United Hungarian Societies, an umbrella organization encompassing all of Cleveland's Hungarian churches and secular organizations, holds its commemoration of the Hungarian national holiday of March 15. The event is held at a local Hungarian church on a Sunday afternoon in mid-March, with recited poems, musical numbers, and a keynote address by a noted personality. These commemorations are usually attended by several hundred Hungarians and are always conducted in the Hungarian language. Easter is an event that for many people involves attendance at a Hungarian church service, just like Christmas. A folk tradition brought over from Hungary and maintained for over half a century in an organized fashion by the scouts and some families is the Easter sprinkling known as *locsolás*. In Hungarian villages, on the Monday immediately following Easter, boys would don traditional folk attire, find the girls in their village and sprinkle their hair with perfume, or in some places, douse them with buckets of water, in an act symbolic of fertility rituals. Scouts in Cleveland get together, wear their Easter best, and their *locsolás* ritual involves reciting lines of apropos folk verse, token amounts of perfume, beautifully hand-decorated eggs, and then a dance. Another folk tradition maintained by the Hungarian Scout Folk Ensemble, or *Regös* group, is the *májusfa* [May tree]. This tradition involves teenaged boys getting together on the eve of the first of May, decorating freshly-cut saplings with crepe paper, a small bottle of wine, and an appropriate poem, and driving around to all of the girls' houses and planting the *májusfa* in their front yards under cover of darkness, so that the girls discover them early in the morning on the first of May. This is a Hungarian village tradition still alive in rural areas of Hungary, and also among Cleveland Hungarians. Spring also features the American Memorial Day holiday at the end of May, and in Cleveland it means the scouts travelling to Fillmore, New York, for their annual *Akadályverseny* [obstacle course; often shortened locally as *Akiverseny*], a weekend camping competition measuring outdoorsmanship and scouting values along with fellow Hungarian scouts from other North American communities.

In summer many families still go on vacation to Lake Chautauqua, a pleasant lake almost the size of Lake Balaton in Hungary, that lies about a two and a half hour's drive from Cleveland. Numerous Cleveland Hungarian families have owned vacation houses around the lake, most of them in a community called Point Chautauqua between Dewittville and Mayville. At any given time beginning in 1958 and today, at least six families own or owned houses there. At least three boarding houses owned by Hungarians rented rooms to Cleveland's vacationing Hungarians in the 1970s and 1980s, including the Balaton Hotel, the *Halásztanya* [Fishing camp], and István Tábor's home, which also housed the local post office at one time. *Bagolyfészek* [Owl's nest] was the name of a house on the lake owned by a man known locally as Tóth ügyvéd [lawyer Tóth], and the large house called the Loon Lodge was also once owned by a Hungarian, as was the Monostory-Papp villa. Even today the Globits, Jálics, Kondray, Mészáros, Nádas, and Tábor families still own houses there, with the Bodor, Szánthó, and Torontáli families owning houses on the other side of the lake.

Summer is also the time that the scouts traditionally go for a one-week summer camp in June, often to their property in Ashtabula County, and attend a ten-day leadership training camp in Fillmore, NY, called *VK tábor* [acronym for *Vezetőképző tábor*, leadership training camp] in August. Some also attend a two- or three-week Hungarian summer school camp in July, also held in Fillmore, NY, every year since 1968. Other organizations, especially the Hungarian Cultural Center of Northeastern Ohio at its Hiram grounds, hold summer outdoor picnics, while the Hungarian Cultural Garden has organized an annual summer Liszt concert since 2009. A recent addition to the ongoing summer events for the Cleveland area is the Hungarian Heritage Night at Classic Park in Eastlake, organized by the Lake County Captains, a minor league Class A affiliate of the Cleveland Indians baseball team; hundreds of Hungarians attend a summer baseball game which includes their recognition as well as Hungarian food. Another recent addition is the Buckeye Road Nationality Reunion, comprised of Slovaks, Hungarians and others who grew up in the Buckeye neighborhood. First held in 2009, the afternoon dinner-dance event attracted 655 people, over 800 in 2011, and 450 people in 2012.

Fall is the time when the Hungarian schools start their instruction, and the beginning of September always means the scout festival, *Cserkésznap*, which regularly draws an attendance of over two thousand. This event is held on the Sunday before the American Labor Day holiday, and for most of its 62 years it has taken place at the *Deutsche Zentrale* [German central park], a German community park located in suburban Parma. The day always involves Hungarian food such as *lángos*, goulash, *laci pecsenye* [pork chops], stuffed cabbage, beer and wine, a Mass and Protestant church services, soccer games, carnival-like games and children's activities, public performances by the scouts and *Regös* dance group, and Hungarian music and dancing to the wee hours of the night. It is a reunion of sorts, and even Hungarians who have long moved away from Cleveland travel from far away to visit and meet old friends at this ongoing event.

Fall is also the time of church harvest festivals, with their origins in the grape harvests of Hungarian villages. Almost every Hungarian church in the Cleveland area organizes one, and has for decades, so that all through September and October, one can attend a harvest festival almost every weekend. They are very similar in nature; all involve live Hungarian music with dancing, Hungarian food, beer and wine, and are attended by hundreds of local Hungarians. Most also have decorations of grapes and fruit hanging from overhead, some with a guard called the *csősz*, and it is customary to try to steal the grapes without the *csősz* noticing. If he notices, he makes the person pay, or in the case of the Hungarian Cultural Center of Northeastern Ohio's festival, a barred enclosure clearly labeled *BÖRTÖN* [jail or prison] is the playful resting place until the person pays up. All of the harvest festivals usually include Hungarian dance performances either by the respective church groups, including St. Elizabeth's and the West Side Hungarian Reformed Church's, by the *Regös* scout group, or by the *Csárdás* dance group before its demise.

The church groups usually wear a uniquely Hungarian-American folk costume, which consists for the women of a white skirt with red, white, and green striping around the bottom edges, white hand-embroidered blouses, and a red vest with piping. Men wear dark slacks with white shirts and embroidered vests. These are no longer in use in Hungary proper, but were very much widely considered to be Hungarian folk dress in the late nineteenth century, with many a contemporary photograph from a hundred years ago showing their use throughout Hungary. Cleveland Hungarians' ancestors brought this tradition from Hungary over a hundred years ago, and have been wearing such dress at harvest festivals ever since, usually passing the clothing down within each family from one generation to the next. Community members look forward to these harvest festivals because it gives them a chance to interact socially in traditional, ritual-laden surroundings, consuming Hungarian food. They do not need to actually harvest grapes in Hungary; rather, it is a spiritual homeland. The first generation immigrants, according to Hoppál, had a "natural human reaction [in] that the individual, deprived of the everyday security of community existence, shifted the sense of belonging to the community from the everyday sphere to the festive sphere... [and] the ethnic identity manifested by the symbols is not a social stigma, but the source of a new kind of pride."[37] This concept of symbolic ethnicity is different from the formulation of Herbert Gans, however, because it involves much more emotion and a deeper symbolism; it is in the form of "intellectually experienced symbolical behavior patterns... particularly characteristic of second and even more of the third generation." Hoppál predicts that this emotionally experienced ethnic allegiance will continue to exist for a long while in this symbolic form, and the century-old tradition of the harvest festival with its folk costume seems to have survived quite a while.

Another regular event held every fall is the Vintner Dinner, a black-tie formal event organized by the Cleveland Hungarian Heritage Society to benefit its museum. Fall is also the time of the commemoration of the 1956 Revolution on October 23. Organized by the United Hungarian Societies, with a program provided by the scouts, the Hungarian school, a combined choir, and various literary and musical individuals, the commemoration is much like the one for March 15. With many local Cleveland Hungarians being refugees from the Revolution and having witnessed firsthand the 1956 events, however, this commemoration holds deeper significance. Indeed, when such commemorations were banned in the Hungary of 1957–1989, Cleveland Hungarians felt it their duty to honor and remember for the sake of those who could not, and the event has been held ever since the late 1950s, every year in late October.

Regular events also include musical concerts by various groups or individuals on North American tours stopping in Cleveland. Organized by various churches and private or public groups, these concerts vary in venue and in attendance, but every year Cleveland Hungarians can attend several concerts by notable artists, many of them who play Hungarian folk music. In the past these have included Kálmán Balogh, the Carpathian Quartet, Vilmos and Dániel Gryllus, Kabar, Düvő, Zsuzsa Koncz and János Bródy, Magos,

Rajkó, Szászcsávás, Tükrös, Gyímes, and Üsztürü. The Hungarian State Folk Ensemble also visited Cleveland in 1987, 1990, and 1994, with shows held at major downtown theaters and attracting audiences nearing a thousand. Also worthy of note are classical music concerts, sometimes held in the Hungarian Cultural Garden, other times at other venues, with local and guest artists playing Liszt or Brahms.

Another "tradition" seemingly unique to Cleveland Hungarians is the high percentage of American military service among the community's members. In an earlier study, the author found over 336 Cleveland Hungarians who served in the United States armed forces, including ten who made the ultimate sacrifice on the battlefields of Vietnam. Even after the military draft ended in 1975, scores of Cleveland Hungarians volunteered to serve, many out of a heightened sense of duty brought about by the community's strong anticommunist tendencies. Even today, over a dozen Cleveland Hungarians serve on active duty.[38]

These ongoing events show a merging of Hungarian traditions with American traditions, forming a uniquely Hungarian-American ethnic culture. For these Cleveland Hungarians, the American holidays Memorial Day and Thanksgiving, each with their own traditions and customs, are equally important as are harvest festivals, March 15, and October 23 commemorations. The merging of the two cultures builds on inherited values and serves to strengthen the bicultural identities of individuals. In addition, we can also see that being Hungarian in Cleveland means taking part in traditions, in the elements of a culture passed on from generation to generation over the course of time. Children take part in these traditions usually unknowingly until they grow up, after which participation becomes conscious, especially on the part of parents who wish to pass on certain values and experiences to their own children while themselves also taking part or promulgating the traditions. Finally, the oldest generation gets the most meaning from these traditions, for the repetitive nature of traditions coupled with social contact and friendships formed over many decades provides stability and something meaningful to which to look forward.

CHAPTER THREE
Culture

While traditions are elements of culture passed on to succeeding generations, e.g., a coherent body of past precedents influencing the present, culture itself is the totality of current socially transmitted behavior patterns, arts, beliefs, institutional and other products of human work and thought, intellectual and artistic endeavors. To understand what it means to be Hungarian in Cleveland, one must investigate the organizations and institutions that provide social environments for Cleveland Hungarians to meet and interact; these are primarily the churches, cultural organizations, and businesses. Foremost among the cultural organizations are the scouts.

The Hungarian Scouts in Cleveland

While all the churches and organizations are important in their own right, perhaps none of them has the clout or sheer numbers of the scouts. As far as breadth of membership and ongoing activities of Hungarian social organizations, Cleveland's Hungarian scouting movement is unarguably the most vibrant. While its main goal is to work with Hungarian-speaking youth, the movement's work also encompasses significant parental involvement, a folk dance group for teenagers known as the Hungarian Scout Folk Ensemble, a major yearly festival with over 2,000 attendees,[39] and an extensive alumni network with tentacles throughout Cleveland's Hungarian social institutions. At peak membership levels in the 1970s, four Hungarian scout troops in Cleveland worked with around 400 Hungarian-speaking youth on a weekly basis. Current levels are still around 100 children meeting almost every week of every year, many of them second and third generation Cleveland Hungarians. The prerequisite for joining the movement, as it has remained for over 66 years, is being able to understand and speak Hungarian on a basic level.

Hungarian scouting was introduced in Cleveland in 1951, brought over by refugees from the DP camps in Europe, where mostly upper and middle class refugees who had fled the Soviet invasion of Hungary at the end of the Second World War stayed for years. Hungarian scouting abroad was founded in German and Austria camps in 1946, with its most important center at the Waldwerke DP camp near Passau, in Bavaria. News of the banning of scouting in 1948 communist Hungary only strengthened the resolve to "rescue" or "carry over" the ideals of scouting to wherever they found refuge worldwide.

Ede Chászár and Ferenc Beodray, newly arrived from DP camps, first met in January 1951 in Cleveland's downtown Terminal Tower to discuss ways to start Hungarian scouting in Cleveland. Others soon joined them, and by March scouting activities were already taking place. The first overnight camping excursion was held in May 1951 at Camp Mather, located about an hour from Cleveland. The scouts were organized into troop Number 12, with the name of Ferenc Rákóczi, but after Ferenc Beodray left for his US military service, they were organized into two troops. Number 22, named after the Hungarian poet György Bessenyei, held meetings on the city's East Side, and troop Number 14, named after the 1848 general Arthur Görgey, held meetings on the city's West Side. In 1952 girl scout troop Number 34 was also formed on the West Side, taking the name of Ilona Zrínyi, and in 1957 another girl scout troop, Number 33 with the name of Erzsébet Szilágyi, was formed on the city's East Side.

The American Hungarian Friends of Scouting (AHFS), known locally as the *Cserkész Barátok Köre*, or CsBK, is a nonprofit organization formed to sustain the work of the scout troops financially. In 1960 it purchased a 180 acre parcel of undeveloped land in Ashtabula County, about an hour and a half's drive from Cleveland, for the use of scout camping. They named it Teleki Scout Park, after the scout leader and former prime minister of

Hungary. The road leading into the park still bears Teleki's name on county maps, and an iron sign at the park entrance, painted red, white, and green, albeit rusty, also proclaims "Teleki Scout Park." The scouts and their parents erected multiple buildings on the property, but only the pavilion still remains. In 2011 the AHFS sold a major portion of the park to its neighbor, the Nature Conservancy, a nonprofit organization purchasing wetlands to save them from development, but kept the five acre lake and all of the park's usable meadow area.

In the late 1980s, the pastor of St. Emeric, Father Sándor Siklódi, offered the scouts a 20-year lease on a small abandoned warehouse on the premises. The scouts signed the lease with the Catholic Diocese of Cleveland and proceeded to renovate the building. Steve Graber donated most of the building materials, and the Center remains a veritable hotbed for Hungarian activity that it has been since its inception in 1991, hosting the scouts, the Hungarian school and many meetings and events. The 100 or so members of scout troops 14 and 34 still meet every Friday evening at St. Emeric and at the Scout Center. They go on camping trips almost monthly, sometimes traveling far to meet other Hungarian scouts in North America, and also maintain Cleveland Hungarian traditions.

The Hungarian Scout Folk Ensemble, known locally as the *Regös Csoport*, is a subgroup of the scouts whose membership is comprised of teenaged scouts who must read and write fluent Hungarian and be willing to work with younger scouts. The precursor to the group was a yearly folk performance given by the scouts called *Gyöngyösbokréta* in the 1960s. Founded in 1973 by Magdi and András Temesváry, local scout leaders, the Scout Folk Ensemble's mission is to preserve vanishing Hungarian folk customs, such as (primarily) dance but also Easter-egg decorating, delivering maypoles, learning folk songs, and sewing their own folk costumes. Its anniversary performances held every five years are mainstays of Cleveland's Hungarian cultural scene. Performers number in the hundreds, and each performance attracts audiences of well over a thousand people, most of them Hungarians. In the 1970s and 1980s the group toured North America, giving performances in cities where other Hungarians lived, such as Toronto and New Brunswick. In 2001 40 members of the group went on an ethnographic folk culture tour, spending extended time in Kazár, a Hungarian village, living with villagers and learning the dying folk arts, and touring the Transylvanian part of Romania, also visiting Hungarian villages. In 2011 and in 2016 the group undertook similar tours, again to Kazár and also visiting Hungarian villages in Slovakia, Ukraine, and Serbia. Each tour solidified and strengthened the Hungarian identities of participants, as they were able to see Hungarian folk traditions live and in person, and upon their return they passed on many of the lessons learned to the younger scouts.

What sets the scouting movement in Cleveland apart from most other organizations is that not only do they maintain language skills and impart culture to successive generations, but that they are able to do so into the third and sometimes to the fourth generations in the absence of a geographical Hungarian neighborhood. The Hungarian scouts in Cleveland have "evolved to become an important cultural carrier," said local ethnomusicologist Walt Mahovlich, who is familiar with Cleveland's ethnic scene, and can compare its Hungarian population with its Romanian, Ukrainian, Polish, Slovak, Croatian, and Serbian communities. Mahovlich, a third generation Hungarian-American who founded and leads the band Harmonia, playing at balls and weddings throughout the Cleveland area, remarked that at Hungarian weddings he plays in Cleveland, at about three per year for the last two decades, "guests demand music from regions they are not from, such as *Kalotaszeg* in Transylvania, or *Csángó* numbers, which shows that what the scouts have been taught has now become an integral part of their life events and important to pass on." At every wedding he plays, the dances requested are "for fun, and not didactic [as it is in scouting]; the culture is reincorporated, but it has become a part of their tradition, and their identity is now a living tradition."[40]

The Hungarian Association

The Hungarian Association, known locally as the *Magyar Társaság*, is another cultural organization with a long and rich history. Although other organizations have more members, like the scouts, and others may raise significantly more funds, such as the Cleveland Hungarian Development Panel, and still others do much more outreach to American audiences, such as the Cleveland Hungarian Heritage Society, in terms of culture exclusively in the Hungarian language, propagating and supporting it through over half a century and still ongoing, the Hungarian Association rises above the others.

Its origins were in Innsbruck, Austria, where János Nádas formed a Hungarian Association that met weekly and organized discussions, debate nights, song nights, and bridge and chess tournaments for postwar refugees. After coming to Cleveland, he formed the Hungarian Association in 1952 to preserve Hungarian culture and presided over its operations for 40 years. Its activities consisted of Sunday afternoon gatherings, a lecture series, and political demonstrations drawing attention to the occupation of Hungary by Russian forces; language courses; international competitions in scientific, literary, and artistic fields; organization and teaching of college courses; and national conferences which later morphed into the Hungarian Congress. Upon Nádas' death in 1992, his brother, Gyula Nádas, took over leadership, steering the organization effectively until his death in 2007 at age 101. Dr. John Nádas, son of Gyula Nádas, is the current president with elections held every three years.

Now known mainly for its yearly congress and a ball held in late November for the last 57 years, the Hungarian Association also holds occasional literary or cultural events, but its current mainstay is the November congress. The congress is rather like an academic convention, with scholarly lectures, well-known keynote speakers, a literary and artistic evening, meetings of the Árpád Academy, an academic hall of fame, meetings of the Saint Ladislaus Society, invited guests from Hungary and its surrounding countries, and congress events culminating in a black-tie debutante ball on Saturday evening. This yearly event attracted thousands of attendees in its heyday and continues to be an ongoing Cleveland Hungarian event, with attendees numbering in the hundreds. Recent keynote speakers have included János Martonyi, Foreign Minister of Hungary, Major General Robert Ivány, a Cleveland native who was commandant at West Point, Géza Jeszenszky, Hungarian Ambassador to the United States at the time, and Father Csaba Böjte, founder of orphanages in Romania.

In its long and storied history, the Hungarian Association has also organized rallies supporting Hungarian minorities and causes, initiated college-level lecture series many times throughout the years, sponsored Hungarian studies at John Carroll University and at Western Reserve University, and edited and published various books about Hungarian topics. In addition, it sponsored and helped a variety of smaller civic organizations. The beginnings of the American Hungarian Educators Association can also be found under the auspices of the Hungarian Association,[41] as can the current journal *Hungarian Studies Review*, originally publishing as *The Canadian-American Review of Hungarian Studies*.

In 1965, under the auspices of the Hungarian Association, Dr. Ferenc Somogyi founded Cleveland's Árpád Academy of Hungarian Scientists, Writers and Artists Abroad, using the example of the Hungarian Academy. Dr. Somogyi held the title of Secretary General of this international organization which was an autonomous subsidiary organization of the Hungarian Association. Its purpose was to recognize significant scientific, literary, and artistic contributions to Hungarian culture. As such, the reach of the Árpád Academy was truly international, recognizing Hungarian scholars worldwide in the diaspora, outside of communist Hungary. Awarding gold, silver, and bronze Árpád medals for achievements, the Academy attracted many prospective members to submit papers and a large audience of supporters throughout its decades-long history, and it remains active even today. All of its activities served to further the simple, if unstated goal, of a theory of identity: the Hungarian Association, through its literary and social events, builds, sustains, and transforms identity, because it actually shapes Cleveland's Hungarians by offering cultural programs, and those who take part express their sense of Hungarian identity by communicating facets of it to others who share their views.

Arguably the most significant depositories of Hungarian literary and cultural life in Cleveland are the yearbooks of the Hungarian Association, the *Krónika – Chronicles of the Hungarian Congress*, published as proceedings and including pictures and lectures from each November Hungarian Congress. Forty-nine editions of *Krónika* were published in book form in Cleveland from 1962 to 2011, in the Hungarian language, with occasional articles in English, and on average each about 300 pages long. The first was edited by Béla Béldy, and thereafter until 1995 they were edited for 34 consecutive years by Ferenc Somogyi. From 1996 on they were edited by his son Lél Somogyi; the last one was published in book form in 2011, and summarized proceedings from 2009 and 2010. Thereafter, proceedings have been posted online on the Hungarian Association website.

A spot check of the *Krónika*'s contents every ten years reveals the cultural values of the Cleveland Hungarians, inasmuch as it shows the authors and lecturers who presented at its annual November conference. Who gets invited and who submits proposals illustrates the common values that at least the educated members of the community share. To provide a theoretical framework, one can apply Mihály Szegedy-Maszák's 1983 statement when speaking about Hungarian minority writers as he was comparing postmodern Hungarian literature with the Hungarian literature of Transylvania, Yugoslavia, and Czechoslovakia: "It is worth remembering that most writers who represent minorities seem to aim at preserving old rather than creating new values."[42] Cleveland Hungarians, much like the Hungarian minorities in the countries surrounding Hungary, also tended to preserve old values, values which they felt had been lost to a communist regime in Hungary. However, in this case, Szegedy-Maszák was wrong when he said that "works of art never reflect the belief systems of a society."[43] The Cleveland Hungarian Association's choice of lecturers and guests did in fact show the belief system of émigré communities.

The *Proceedings of the first Hungarian Congress* detail its origins in the spring of 1961. Several Hungarians gathered and were commiserating and questioning whether it was worth organizing community activities at all, when someone observed: "Don't you realize that we always only consider Cleveland when we want to do something? That with an enigmatic resignation we accept the Cleveland curtain of indifference and don't even try to break through the minefields of small local cliques to try to meet other Hungarians?"[44] This question led to the organization of the first Hungarian Congress on November 24–26 of 1961. The first yearbook published the Congress's lectures and proceedings along with commentary submitted via mail by Hungarians from all over the world. The topics deal with questions of émigré Hungarians' representation, Hungarian cultural roles in immigration, and the economic and social problems of Hungarians.

To give the reader a taste of the Hungarian Association's work, a summary of four of these yearbooks, each ten years apart (1971, 1981, 1991, 2001) may suffice. The proceedings of the tenth Congress, published in 1971, also contains lectures and worldwide correspondence dealing with such topics as "Ten years in a quarter century of emigration," "Thoughts about making and broadening contacts with the Old Country," "The emergence and maintenance of independent western Hungarian culture," "The worldwide responsibility of Hungarians." A separate plenary session for the younger generation was titled "The question of maintaining our Hungarianness and building our contacts." Official business meeting minutes and presented awards were also included.

The proceedings published in 1981 continued in the same vein. Lectures by 50 individuals had as their main topics the concept of the Hungarian family in a free country (*a magyar család a szabad földön*) and the Hungarian future in a free country (*a magyar jövő kilátásai a szabad földön*). The former contained lectures such as "Can one raise Hungarian children with non-Hungarian spouses?" and "Incorporating Hungarian young adults into Hungarian organizations," while the latter included "We want to join together as a strong nation," "The future of the Hungarian-American book," "Judging the Kádár regime," and "History versus propaganda." The yearbook also included parallel sessions of various organizations such as the Transylvanian World Federation's Cleveland Women's Society, the World Federation of Hungarian Engineers and Architects, with representation from 22 countries, the Society of Free Hungarian Journalists, the officers' conference of the Hungarian Scout Association, and the 53 member American Hungarian Stamp Collectors' Society, with 43 of those from the Cleveland area. Presented awards and business meeting minutes of the Árpád Association were also included.

The proceedings published in 1991 reflected a slight shift after the fall of communism in 1989. János Nádas, in the opening of the conference, was happy to report that Árpád Göncz, president of Hungary, and József Antall, prime minister, as well as Otto von Habsburg all had sent their greetings to the thirtieth Hungarian Congress, a feat unthinkable some years earlier. The scope of the conference, as in years past, remained the fate of Hungarians worldwide. For example, the session on politics included six lectures dealing with the relationship of the new democratically elected Hungarian government and its relationship to Hungarian-Americans. The other sessions dealt with economics, culture, youth, Hungarian minorities in the countries surrounding Hungary, pre-1945 Hungarian military matters, a literary and cultural evening, as well as the usual formal dinner and black-tie ball.

Ten years later, the proceedings contained themes and topics similar to the 39 previous conferences. The main session, titled "Questions of Hungarian Fate," offered lectures such as "Formation of current Hungarian identity in America today," "Whereto, new Hungarian?" "Pact of the Rose Hill 13," "Democratic party platform with extremist symptoms," "Future of Western Hungarians," "Youth in emigration," and "Propaganda Hungarian Style." As was true of its predecessors, this yearbook exceeded 300 pages, and its contents were almost exclusively in the Hungarian language.

The proceedings of the forty-ninth and fiftieth Hungarian Congress, held in November of 2009 and 2010, were published in hard copy in the last edition of *Krónika* in 2011. Its contents remained consistent with previous Congresses. The proceedings of each yearly conference contain the literary reviews, lectures, hopes, and aspirations of the literati of Cleveland and of Hungarians worldwide. The international nature of the conference presenters, very few of whom were employed by universities and enjoying their travel budgets, shows that the Hungarian Association specifically and Hungarians from Cleveland who attended in general considered themselves members of a Hungarian diaspora, a worldwide community of Hungarians, linked by a common heritage and common concerns.

Organizations and Businesses

Although the scouts have had the broadest impact on the Cleveland Hungarian community in the last 60 years, and the Hungarian Association contributed the most Hungarian-language events throughout the decades, other important organizations also manifest Hungarian identity, each with its own traditions and history. The oldest is the United Hungarian Societies [*Egyesült Magyar Egyletek*], originally formed in 1902 to establish the Kossuth statue, and later functioning as an umbrella organization for the Hungarian churches and many Cleveland Hungarian chartered groups. At one time the United Hungarian Societies encompassed over 100 member organizations, many of which are still active today. Year after year, decade after decade, the United Hungarian Societies organizes commemorations for March 15 and October 23. By communicating the shared values in commemoration of important dates in Hungarian history, this organization expresses and sustains Hungarian identity. This umbrella organization is also responsible for coordinating occasional larger events that bring together multiple Cleveland Hungarian organizations.

The two most important member organizations with the most ongoing events that attract Cleveland Hungarians from across the social spectrum are the Cleveland Hungarian Heritage Society and the Hungarian Cultural Center of Northeast Ohio. One of the most visible to downtown visitors, with its public museum and gift shop, the Cleveland Hungarian Heritage Society was formed in 1985. With humble beginnings in the basement of St. Elizabeth church on Buckeye Road, the Society established a museum chronicling Cleveland's Hungarian history. Its collection slowly grew, and in 1996 the museum moved to Richmond Mall, then, in 1999, to Euclid Square Mall, and in 2003 to its current 4,100-square-foot home downtown at the Galleria Mall. Its collection encompasses not only Cleveland's Hungarian history but also reflects overall Hungarian history, culture, and folk art as well. The museum has an ongoing monthly lecture series and rotates its exhibits, which encompass a variety of historical, artistic, and cultural themes.

Organizer of the yearly black-tie fundraiser called the Vintner Dinner, the Cleveland Hungarian Heritage Society has the greatest outreach to non-Hungarians, with its monthly cultural programming and physical presence downtown. With a membership of 167 households, its museum gift shop allows visitors and locals alike the opportunity to buy Hungarian books, handiwork, and fine art items, and its small but cozy research library has several thousand volumes, as well as archival materials. It also has off-site storage with over 450 videotapes of Cleveland Hungarian history from the Kossányi radio and TV station archives. In addition, its twice-yearly publication *The Review* offers members news about past and future happenings in the Society. The museum's permanent visible presence is a strong stalwart of Cleveland's Hungarian community and displays the community's vibrancy for all to see. As such, it showcases the inherited folkloric and historical heritage brought over from Hungary and the Carpathian basin, built and then sustained through the communication of identity.

The Hungarian Cultural Center of Northeastern Ohio is another organization with a long and rich past. Formed in 2001 with the merging of the St. Stephen Dramatic Club and the Geauga Magyar Club, the former had been in existence since 1904 and the latter since 1975. Now a prosperous social club with numerous regular functions, the organization has 251 active members under the leadership of Mary Jane Molnár, a Cleveland-born Hungarian. Its yearly functions include summer, spring, and fall events attracting hundreds of area Hungarians, held at the organization's picnic grounds in Hiram, which is about a forty-five minute drive from Cleveland.

The 40 acre property was acquired in 1984, and it features a soccer field, an industrial kitchen, several pavilions, and an ornately carved, three meter-wide by seven meter-tall *székely kapu* [traditional Transylvanian Hungarian carved wooden gate]. The club's monthly newsletter, *Hírek* [News], written and edited by the club president, Mary Jane Molnár, is an important compilation of every Hungarian event in the Cleveland area. The club reaches beyond its own events and provides information about the greater Cleveland Hungarian communities as well. Its activities draw from a cross-section of people from other organizations as well as its own members.

Other organizations that contribute to the vibrancy of Hungarian social life in Cleveland include the Hungarian Business and Tradesmen's Club, founded in 1923 and once boasting over 1,500 members. It now has about 650 members, about 30 percent of whom are of Hungarian ancestry. Its social hall and bar is open from noon to midnight seven days a week, with Hungarian food served for lunch three times per week to about 50 people per day. Although not as many of its members speak Hungarian as in its heyday, the club has attracted some recent Hungarian immigrants and has a long tradition in Cleveland's Hungarian neighborhood.

The Hungarian Cultural Gardens, also an old and venerable organization, was originally dedicated in 1934.[45] Although it languished during the 1980s, it has recently organized Gulyás Cookoffs, wine tastings, and golf outings as fundraisers. In 2010 one of Cleveland's American citizenship swearing-in ceremonies was held in the garden.

The Cleveland Hungarian Development Panel is a small but efficient organization, formed as a nonprofit in 1990[46] by a group of Cleveland Hungarians to establish business connections and help further US–Hungarian relationships in the area of education, health and human services. One of its first successful endeavors was the donation of medical equipment for hospitals in Hungary. Its yearly event is the Paprika Ball, a formal evening held in late February or early March at the downtown Ritz-Carlton Hotel. Cleveland dignitaries and benefactors regularly attend, and the Panel has raised and donated more than a million dollars in its almost thirty-year history.

The William Penn Association headquartered in Pittsburgh, Pennsylvania has an active Cleveland branch with 2,295 members, many of Hungarian descent. Originally formed in 1886 by 13 Hungarian coal miners in Pennsylvania as the Verhovay Aid Association, the fraternal society provides life insurance, death benefits, and fellowship to its members. Merging with the Hungarian Baptist Society in Cleveland and later changing its name to William Penn Association in 1972, the organization remains the largest and only Hungarian-American fraternal insurance association today. Branch 14, the Cleveland branch, organizes meetings six times per year, usually at the First Hungarian Reformed Church in Walton Hills with an average attendance of 20–25 members. The branch also takes part in a yearly fraternal picnic, organizes annual trips to Hungary and a Hungarian heritage camp every August that teaches the Hungarian language and culture to its participants.

The oldest Jewish benevolent society in Cleveland was the Hungarian Benevolent and Social Union, organized in 1881 by 24 Hungarians of the Jewish faith and chartered in 1883 to provide life insurance and fellowship to its members. It changed its name in 1919 to HBSU to reflect the fact that membership was not limited to those with Hungarian ancestry, and is now known as the Heights Benevolent and Social Union. In the 1980s it incorporated as a fraternal organization, with two lodges: one in Cleveland and one in Florida that is made up of former Cleveland residents.

A relatively recently-formed organization is the Hungarian Genealogical Society of Greater Cleveland. Founded in 1996 by Gustav Enyedy, a chemical engineer who traced his own family's roots to eighteenth century Hungary, the organization grew out of a lecture he gave at a meeting of the Magyar Club. The Magyar Club had been losing members, and in an attempt at generating interest, Enyedy asked if anyone else was interested in forming a group to study personal ancestry. After people reacted positively, the group began with 18 members, with Enyedy serving as president for the first six years. Enyedy also founded, wrote, and edited the group's newsletter, *Forrás* [Source], which was at one time published intermittently twice yearly. The group is open to anyone interested in genealogy from the old Austro-Hungarian Empire, and although an overwhelming majority of its members are Hungarian, it includes Slovaks, Germans, and Croatians as well. Mostly comprised of second and third generation Hungarians, not many of its members speak Hungarian, but all are interested in Hungarian events and history. The Society boasts about 45 members, with about 20–25 members showing up at its monthly meetings at various suburban public libraries.

Being Hungarian, maintaining traditions, and belonging to an organization can bind people together, inasmuch as they share a common heritage and many common interests. But what is the relationship between Cleveland Hungarians and the country they live in? No longer living in an insulated ethnic community but rather fully integrated into American society, Hungarians work day jobs but volunteer and take part in Cleveland's Hungarian scene in their spare time and on weekends.

According to Susan Papp, 311 Hungarian-owned or supported businesses thrived in the Buckeye neighborhood between 1925 and 1960.[47] By 1980, that number had dwindled to fewer than 50. Today that number is four: Security Key near East 126th Street on Buckeye, owned by Joe Jámbor; J P Quality Printing on Larchmere Boulevard, owned by John Pathko; Orban Flower Shop; and the Balaton restaurant on nearby Shaker Square. These are pretty much the only Hungarian businesses in or near the old Buckeye neighborhood. This does not mean that Hungarian businesses disappeared from Cleveland. Andor Vasady-Nagy compiled a list of Hungarian businesses in Cleveland in 1967, listing 7 delicatessens, 5 bakeries, 10 Hungarian restaurants, and 4 taverns.[48] In 1966 Imre Sári Gál counted 20 Hungarian doctors on Cleveland's West Side and 22 on its East Side, and 350 Hungarian engineers.[49] And if one examines the advertising section of the Cleveland Hungarian Scout Folk Ensemble's anniversary performance program booklets from 1978 to 2008 (anniversary performances held every five years), one finds 24 Hungarian businesses advertising in 1988, 46 in 1993, 34 in 2003, and 38 in 2008. Some of the fluctuation is due to more or less effort expended by the program booklet volunteers to attract business advertising, but the number of Hungarian businesses in Cleveland, with something of a turnover, has remained relatively stable over the years.[50]

Today there are more than a dozen Hungarian-speaking doctors and dentists practicing in the Cleveland area. At least eight lawyers speak Hungarian, as well as numerous accountants. Hungarian-speaking engineers are also far too numerous to detail specifically, and finance seems to be a newly embraced profession for numerous local Hungarians.

Hungarian bakeries are another well-represented business of which there are several. The oldest is Lydia's Hungarian Strudel Shop, on Stumph Road in Parma Heights. Founded in 1938, the business moved to its current location in 1993. The current owner, Lydia Rakosi, is the great-great granddaughter of the founder, Elizabeth Rakosi. Lucy's Sweet Surrender, in business since 1957, was founded by Lucy Ortelekán and taken over in 1994 by Michael Feigenbaum, a native Cleveland Hungarian. Transylvania Bakery is owned by Lajos Mezősi, who immigrated to Cleveland from Transylvania. It has no retail presence but can be seen at many Hungarian social functions throughout the year. Tommy's Pastries, founded by Péter Patay in 1989, is famous for its *pogácsa* [biscuits], and about 90 percent of his customers are Eastern European, with about half of those being Hungarian. Attila Farkas founded the Farkas Pastry Shoppe in 1966 with his father and served customers until 2016. It remains in business, but with a non-Hungarian owner.[51] Also notable are European's Best Restaurant and Bakery in Strongsville and Mertie's Hungarian Strudel Shop in Cleveland.

The only Hungarian butcher with a visible presence today is Dohár-Lovászy Meats, with a stand at the West Side Market. Owned by Miklós Szűcs and Angyal Dohár, the business was started by Emery Lovászy in the 1940s. In addition, many families still stuff their own sausage, often smoking it to dry as well.

Hungarian restaurants have come and gone in Cleveland. The Balaton on trendy Shaker Square is one of the oldest, established in 1964 by Terezia Nevery. The restaurant has authentic Hungarian decor, its waitresses speak Hungarian, and its Hungarian menu has an excellent reputation. Other well-known but now closed Hungarian restaurants include Szarka's Restaurant, Little Budapest, the Erzsébet Étterem, and the Debrecen Restaurant. Finally, though not a restaurant per se, Ida Rózsahegyi's catering business has for decades served weddings, funerals, church dinners, New Year's Eve dances, and private parties, as well as the Hungarian Business and Tradesmen's Club each week. Most Cleveland Hungarians are familiar with and praise her traditional cooking.[52]

In addition to the food service industry, Hungarians in Cleveland started a variety of other types of businesses through the years that do not cater to Hungarians alone. Their owners often can be seen at local Hungarian social events and the community takes pride in their success. One of the most successful Hungarian-owned businesses in recent times is Cellular Technology Limited (CTL). Founded by Professor Dr. Paul Lehmann, the global biotechnology firm specializes in immune monitoring and employs many Hungarians locally and abroad. In Cleveland, fully one third of the work force is Hungarian, over 20 individuals. Aurora School of Music in suburban Aurora, about a half hour from Cleveland, was founded in 2003 by Vera Holczer, who studied piano at the Budapest Bartók High School Conservatory. She started teaching from her living room, and the school grew immensely, building a state-of-the-art music facility in 2016 and now employing 39 staff members who teach nearly a thousand students in daily lessons. The Mayfield Academy of Self-Defense and Karate is a studio founded by black belt grandmaster Ferenc Kovács, a Hungarian Military Academy (Ludovika) graduate who saw combat in the Second World War, trained military cadets in numerous countries, then arrived in Cleveland in 1952. His martial arts school has been around for over 50 years, and Kovács also trained local police departments.

Several extremely successful Cleveland area businesses were started by Hungarians of the 1956 wave of immigration. These include Miklós Peller's structural engineering firm, which designed several landmarks in the Cleveland area, such as Blossom Music Center, the summer home of the Cleveland Orchestra. Other successful firms include Danny Vegh's Billiard and Recreation Supply, Mar-Bal, Inc (Jim Balogh), Graber Metal Works and later Ultrasteel Corporation (Steve Graber), Accurate Metal Machining (Lajos Loiczly), and Vantage Financial Group (George Szeretvai). Another successful refugee was Steve Menyhárt, who joined his aunt and uncle's plumbing business, founded in 1928 by Alex and Elsie Menyhart, and grew it after his arrival in 1957. His son, Péter Menyhárt, is now the third generation at Menyhart Plumbing and Heating Supply.

Local Hungarian jewelers include Young's Jewelry on Puritas Road in Cleveland (Aladár Solymosi, senior and junior), Jewelry Art in the suburb of Hudson (Györgyi Bőjtös and Barbara Johnson), Steve Papp Jewelry in the suburb of Solon, and Barany Jewelry in Brunswick. Successful Hungarian architects include László Bőjtös, who designed both of the Hungarian Reformed churches in greater Cleveland, and István Gáspár.

Businesses founded by later immigrants include Szente Landscaping, owned by Béla Szente, Ibi David Salon owned by Ibolya Dávid, and Concierge CPAs, owned by Borbála Bántó. Another accounting firm is George Csatáry's, who is also a Cleveland Hungarian. Floor sanders include Cleveland-born Jim Dienes and Attila Nagy, and contractors include Pálffy Construction, Tivadar Lukács, and Chris Falk, among others.

Not in Cleveland per se, but a since-sold Hungarian-owned senior and nursing home in the vicinity, the Lorántffy Care Center, was established by Tibor Dömötör, a 1956 refugee, reformed minister, and part-time poet in Akron. The center, which had an extensive Hungarian library, Hungarian-speaking staff members, and Hungarian cooking, has always had patients from the Cleveland area.

The above incomplete list merely gives a sampling to illustrate that the Hungarians in Cleveland actively take part in American life and contribute to Cleveland's economy while also contributing to Cleveland's Hungarian churches and organizations on a volunteer basis. By purchasing advertising in program booklets of social happenings, they also help defray the costs of cultural events. They and the countless Hungarian white-collar and blue-collar workers have integrated themselves into the American business climate.

Arts, Music, and Radio Programs

No study of Cleveland Hungarians' culture should neglect its ongoing weekly radio programs, its musicians, and its artists (the community's writers will be addressed in the following chapter). Hungarian radio programming is but a shadow of what it once was, but the Cleveland area still boasts several weekly radio programs catering to those of Hungarian descent.

One of the best known programs is broadcast on Cleveland's public radio station, WCPN, on Sundays from 7 to 8 pm. Known as the Kapossy Family Hungarian Hour, it was started by Dr. Andrew Szabó and hosted for over 20 years by his wife Kathy Kapossy. The program is now hosted by Kapossy's daughter and son-in-law, Andrea and Andrew Lázár. The program is bilingual, geared toward educating about Hungarian music and culture, plays a range of Hungarian music and brings interviews with Hungarian local and notable guests, and gives announcements of upcoming Hungarian events in and near Cleveland. The roots of the Kapossy Family Hungarian Hour go back to the late 1960s, when it broadcast from the commercial station WZAK.

There is also a 3-hour weekly radio program in Cleveland conducted entirely in the Hungarian language on John Carroll University's station WJCU. Called the Bocskai Radio program, its origins date to the early 1980s with a show playing Hungarian pop and folk music. Today the program offers air time to several area Hungarian churches in its first hour, then a mix of older and contemporary Hungarian music, with news and local announcements. Of the area Hungarian radio programs, it is the only one conducted entirely in the Hungarian language; the rest play Hungarian music but are either bilingual or conducted in English. The program's website, www.bocskairadio.org, offers background information, current news, and is currently the most all-encompassing compilation of Hungarian events and culture in the Cleveland area. The program is staffed entirely by volunteers, and a separate monthly program is compiled and announced by two Hungarian scouts.

A third station broadcasting from Cleveland proper is WCSB. It was started in 1984 and hosted for its first two decades by noted Cleveland Hungarian personality Kathy Kapossy, then briefly by her widowed husband John

Palasics, and is now hosted by Bob Kita, who grew up in the Buckeye neighborhood, broadcasting on Saturday middays from 11 to 12:30. This radio program plays mainly music and airs some local announcements but avoids any mention of current events or politics in Hungary; its listening audience was estimated by Bob Kita to be around 250 people on any given Saturday.

Other programs include WKTL's "Souveniers of Hungary," hosted by the Check family in Struthers, Ohio, near Youngstown, broadcasting Saturdays from noon until 1:30 pm. In the Akron area, WAPS 91.3 has a Hungarian program on Sunday mornings from 8 to 9 am. Hungarian television programs used to be broadcast by Miklós Kossányi's NBN network, which was carried by local cable television stations under the auspices of the SCO-LA network. Since the closing of NBN, viewers can still access one hour per day of programming on cable that is restreamed from Hungary, and includes a half hour of news. Other Hungarian television opportunities include DunaWorld TV, which can be accessed by purchasing a satellite dish and paying monthly fees, but most Cleveland Hungarians now watch streamed programs from online websites, and broadcast television is starting to lose much of its appeal.

Definitely worthy of in-depth research, though beyond this book's scope, is the impact of music in cementing social bonds among Cleveland's Hungarians. Mária Tóth-Kurucz conducted a short study of Hungarian folk singing among the older generation of Hungarian-Americans entitled *Daloló Öreg-amerikások* [Singing oldtimers], published in 1976, but no significant work has been done since, with the exception of the Hungarian Scout Folk Ensemble's collection of oral histories published in 2008, *Clevelandben még élnek magyarok? Visszaemlékezések gyűjteménye* [Do Hungarians still live in Cleveland? A collection of oral histories]. The scouts and scout folk ensemble in Cleveland do, however, sing an extensive repertoire of Hungarian folk songs, with many members knowing at least a hundred such songs and some knowing many hundreds.

A staple of Cleveland's earlier Hungarian music scene was the "Night in Budapest;" from 1957 until 1970 this was Cleveland's biggest society event. The gala was founded by noted Cleveland Hungarian politician Jack Russell, and it honored famous Hungarians and featured local Hungarian Gypsy musicians.[53] First held on Buckeye Road, it was moved to the downtown Sheraton Hotel, with average crowds topping a thousand people. The program booklet from 1968 had many photographs showing Buckeye Road youth dressed as Hungarian hussars, 200 ladies in the costume of the Carpathian countryside, and a ballroom jam packed with many hundreds in attendance.

Throughout the 1950s, 1960s, and 1970s, and somewhat persisting into the 1980s, Cleveland also boasted an extremely vibrant cafe music scene, especially in the Buckeye Road neighborhood. These included the Gypsy Cellar, Settler's Tavern, the Bit of Budapest, and others. The Tokaj Orchestra, Jóska Rab, Ernie Kiraly, and Alex Udvary were some of the more famous musicians. László Roósz had an immensely popular band in the 1950s and early 1960s that played all the Hungarian balls and many dance-parties. Frank Borisz founded his Popular Hungarian Continental Dance Orchestra in 1953 and performed for forty years in Cleveland and in surrounding states, recording 6 record albums. Gypsy musicians played an integral part in the Cleveland Hungarian music scene until the early 1980s, especially among the *öregamerikás* [old-timer] generation. Primarily from Gypsy families that moved from Košice in Slovakia to Braddock, Pennslyvania (near Pittsburgh), then settled in Cleveland to serve its Hungarian population, this group called themselves Romungro Gypsies. In the mid twentieth century, as many as 50 Hungarian establishments on Buckeye Road and in the Lorain Avenue neighborhood employed these musicians. This was in addition to the many weddings, dances, and parties that hired them. Hungarian violinists or pianists often had a group of Gypsies backing them up. Among the most famous Cleveland Gypsy band leaders of the 1950s through the 1980s were Frank Richko, Rudi Ziga, Rudi Balog, Bela Barat, Bela Berti, and Ernie King. Both John Udvary, who came to Cleveland in 1936, and his son Alex Udvary were fixtures on the Hungarian music scene, playing nightly at the taverns but also performing with the prestigious Cleveland Orchestra. Also collaborating with Gypsy musicians was the Hungarian band leader Joe Jeromos. Another famous Hungarian musician who grew up in Cleveland playing in the gypsy style was Emery Deutsch; he left for New York and later Miami, and composed the national hits "Play, Fiddle, Play" and "When a Gypsy Makes His Violin Cry." Like him, though, nearly all of the Hungarian Gypsy musicians had left Cleveland by the 1980s as the number of venues and the prospects for regular employment had drastically decreased.

But Hungarian music did not die out completely with this exodus. István Mózsi was a concert pianist who frequently played with gypsy musicians in lounges like the Gypsy Cellar and at Settler's Tavern on Buckeye Road in the late 1950s. In 1957 Mózsi was asked by István Molnár to organize a larger band for the Gendarme Ball (*Csendőr Bál*), and Kálmán Hegedeos joined him in the early 1960s to form the Hegedeos-Megay band, which played at various Cleveland Hungarian weddings and events. The group's name changed to the Hegedeos Orchestra, and though its members varied in number, it was a staple of Hungarian events. They played for most Cleveland Hungarian balls from 1962 until the early 2000s, also traveling to Detroit, Cincinnati, Pittsburgh, and Chicago. They played for over 300 Hungarian weddings, including about 30 second-generation and several third-generation Cleveland Hungarian weddings.[54] In the twenty-first century, Béla Czirják also played many events.

A mainstay of the Cleveland Hungarian music scene in the past two decades is the band Harmonia, which regularly plays the Vintner Dinner, the Paprika Ball, the scout ball, the Hungarian Association ball, as well as numerous weddings, smaller receptions, and private events. Its founder, Walter Mahovlich, is a third-generation Hungarian-American, and the band also provides top-notch Hungarian folk music for the anniversary performances of the Hungarian Scout Folk Ensemble, shows that attract over a thousand audience members.

A measure of the importance of music for community social events is the extent to which organizers will go to import Hungarian bands and musicians from other North American cities if local Hungarian musicians are not available. In the past these have included Gábor Vaski and his Night Moves Orchestra from Toronto, or Szinkron from Hamilton, Ontario. A current favorite is Öcsi (Kálmán) Magyar and his Continental Orchestra as well as Életfa Ensemble from New Brunswick, New Jersey, players of authentic Hungarian folk music.

A Cleveland choir that sang in Hungarian performed at many March 15 and October 23 commemorations from 1972 at least until 2007. Formed originally by members of the St. István Choir and members of St. Emeric church, the group took the name Mindszenty Choir in 1974 on the occasion of Cardinal Joseph Mindszenty's visit, with his permission. At its 25th anniversary it had 60 members, mostly from St. Emeric church.[55] Today the West Side Lutheran church has its *Kis Magyar Kórus* [Small Hungarian choir], with a dozen members directed by the Reverend Zoltán Tamásy. Finally, not well known in Hungarian circles outside of its Sunday church services but nevertheless providing quality Hungarian language choral performances is the church choir of the Hungarian Bethany Baptist church.

In addition to musicians and vocalists, many local Hungarians have also served Cleveland's arts community. George Kozmon is by far the most well-known and respected Hungarian artist in Cleveland's Hungarian community. Cleveland-born and bred, he received his BFA from the Cleveland Institute of Art, and his paintings can be found in many public and private collections in the USA and abroad. He also illustrated the covers of both of Ernő Kálnoky's local Hungarian books, the cover and inside illustrations for István Fekete Jr's novel *Itéletidő* [Judgement time/weather], and all of the book covers for author István Eszterhás from the 1980s until the last publication in 1998. Imre Bogárdy, an engineer by training who also occasionally pens verse, is an accomplished watercolor artist, and his works are often on display at Hungarian events in the Cleveland area. Margit Dózsa produced ceramics with Hungarian folk motifs for decades, firing clay in a kiln in her home. Zsolt Gregora was a woodcarver, painter, and printmaker who produced linoleum cuts with Hungarian themes and was primarily recognized as a photographer who built his own kaleidoscopic camera lens to create images based on nature. László Dús was best known as an abstract-expressionist printmaker, but it was his technical innovations that earned him international fame. John F. Puskas, born in Cleveland in 1917, was an enamel artist with an international reputation who taught at Cuyahoga County Community College, Case Western Reserve University, and served as artist-in-residence at Kent State University. Kálmán Kubinyi, also born and raised in Cleveland's Hungarian community, was an influential etcher and engraver. Rudolf Radnay and his wife Erzsébet Bauer were acclaimed painters who came to Cleveland after the Second World War. Andrew Karoly and Louis Szanto, originally from New York, painted over 30 murals for local Cleveland businesses, including many in Society Bank's office and branches. Dave Szekeres and Judy Takács are also accomplished local Hungarian artists.

Magdi and András Temesváry, who started the Hungarian Scout Folk Ensemble in 1973, are folk artisans in the area of folkwear, glass engraving, and woodcarving; they have since moved to California. Gyuri E. Hollósy can also be listed here, as he studied at the Cleveland Institute of Art and has numerous major sculptures in the Cleveland area. In addition, his works commemorating the 1956 Revolution grace Liberty Square in Boston, Massachusetts, and a street corner in the Hungarian neighborhood of New Brunswick, New Jersey. The sculptor Béla Bácsi, who currently lives and works in California, also lived in Cleveland for a while and still has relatives here, while Elemér Polony was an abstract and mosaic painter who taught in Cleveland and then moved to Los Angeles. Tamás Frecska, a sculptor and screen printer who used to live near Cleveland in Medina, is now retired to Florida. Younger artists who grew up in Cleveland's Hungarian community but have since moved away to pursue artistic endeavors include Krisztina Lázár, Zsóka Némethy, the twins András and Péter Tábor, and Gabriella Verbovszky. From March to June of 2012, the Cleveland Hungarian Heritage Museum held an exhibition curated by George Kozmon titled "4under30," a collection of art by four young artists, each of whom was born in Cleveland and grew up immersed in its Hungarian community, attending the Hungarian school and scouts, and dancing in the Hungarian Scout Folk Ensemble.[56]

A recent phenomenon for Cleveland's Hungarian culture is the Kőrösi Csoma Sándor [KCsP] program, named after a famous Hungarian explorer. Funded by the Hungarian government, the program started in 2013 by sending 50 young professionals from Hungary to diaspora communities worldwide. The program later expanded and in 2017 sent 114 young professionals worldwide, including 24 to North America. The goals of the program are to strengthen the Hungarian language skills and Hungarian identity of the diaspora communities and to spur personal contacts with Hungary. These community organizing fellowships, which include living and housing stipends, are awarded for six to nine months, and in Cleveland the Cleveland Hungarian Heritage Society has hosted and mentored five fellows and Bocskai Rádió one. Living and working among Cleveland Hungarians, the fellows take part in the many community activities of various churches and organizations, catalyzing Cleveland's Hungarian culture.[57]

This program notwithstanding, Cleveland Hungarians clearly comprise a community that continues to maintain its language and heritage in an American environment, producing ongoing intellectual and artistic cultural products, thereby forming and maintaining the identities of its members. Independent of US government support, the community stands on its own, imports and produces its own traditions, culture, and literature, and is generally self-sufficient in terms of language policies. Aniko Hatoss, when examining the Hungarian diaspora in Australia, found that communities that are active agents and advocates for the maintenance of their cultural and linguistic heritage rather than passive recipients of government support are more likely to thrive;[58] bottom-up movements have endured, and so it is with Cleveland's Hungarians.

Galvanizing Events and Politics

If meaning is something conveyed or significant, and culture is the totality of socially transmitted behavior patterns, then large-group galvanizing events are the most meaningful elements of culture in a community because they convey the values that crowds hold. In addition, they serve to unite individual members of a community through their common presence. Every now and then a major event serves to galvanize and unite Cleveland's Hungarian population. Various organizations and churches work together to prepare for a common cause, and attract masses of people. No matter how different people are, i.e., which organization they belong to, which wave of immigration they or their ancestors arrived in, where they live, what their religion or political persuasion is, what their age or level of language skill, no matter their socioeconomic status, they unite as Cleveland Hungarians for a common cause. Some of the most notable such events are outlined below.

In 1974 Cardinal Joseph Mindszenty visited Cleveland on a worldwide pastoral tour of Hungarian communities after 15 years living closed within the American legation and embassy in Budapest. On May 25, he arrived amidst much pomp and ceremony, including police motorcycle escorts, a press conference, the mayor providing his personal limousine for the entire visit, parades with mounted police, honor guards by the Hungarian scouts and the Knights of Columbus, performances by Cleveland's Singing Angels, representatives from other nationalities, a gala banquet at the Recreation Center, and flag blessings. While in Cleveland, he visited Hungarian-related sites, churches and businesses. Thousands turned out, with multiple venues filled to capacity with overflow crowds, many wearing Hungarian traditional formal attire, the *díszmagyar*, with all of Cleveland's Hungarian organizations and churches taking part. Mindszenty also visited Hungarian churches and crowds in nearby Lorain, Barberton, and Akron.

Another pivotal event was the return of St. Stephen's Crown by President Jimmy Carter to the government of Hungary in 1978. The vast majority of Cleveland's Hungarians were anticommunist, and mass protests and demonstrations were held to try to avert the return. Busloads of demonstrators from Cleveland went to Washington, D.C., and local congressional representative Mary Rose Oakar worked together with local Hungarian leaders to lobby President Carter. Thirty-five Cleveland Hungarian organizations signed onto a resolution organized by Cleveland's Hungarian Association, joining a total of 150 Hungarian churches, associations, and federations in the United States, Canada, and Australia requesting that Carter not return the Crown until Soviet troops were withdrawn from and free elections were held in Hungary. However, the decision had been made, and the crown was returned after over 30 years of safekeeping by the US government. The impact of the return led to a warming of relations between the two countries.[59]

Another event that drew thousands of Cleveland Hungarians was the visit on November 9, 1991 by the Reverend László Tőkés, the hero of the Temesvár (Timişoara) siege that sparked the 1989 Romanian revolution and the demise of the hated dictator Ceauşescu. The visit included a banquet and a speech at the First Hungarian Reformed Church, which was still at 10706 Buckeye Road, and the church hall was filled to capacity.[60]

Something that attempted to mobilize most Hungarians in Cleveland but unfortunately did not succeed was the dream of a Magyar Park. Kálmán

Hegedeös and István Gáspár, while searching for a commercial real estate investment, happened onto a property for sale in Walton Hills. The property consisted of over 17 acres with a party center adjacent to a golf course, a roadside ice cream stand, a playground, and a caretaker's residence. They made an offer to buy the property in 2000, but after realizing its potential as a possible Hungarian community center, transferred the buying rights to a nonprofit organization set up for the express purpose of establishing such a Magyar Park. Community leaders became involved, a website was developed, and a capital campaign began under the motto *ezer család, ezer dollár,* hoping that a thousand Cleveland families would each donate a thousand dollars, thus raising the purchase price of $675,000, with enough left over to renovate the facilities to house a Hungarian library, community center, and picnic grounds. The Cleveland Magyar Athletic Club donated financing for the marketing campaign. About $240,000 was raised from the Hungarian community in Cleveland, but the seller backed out, litigation ensued, and the whole attempt imploded in 2003, with many people losing prorated parts of their investments. Had the seller not backed out, the capital campaign might have been successful. The organizers of the endeavor, including George Csatáry and others, worked tirelessly for the good of the entire Hungarian community, but in the end their efforts were not to be realized.

An event that certainly did unite almost all of Cleveland's Hungarians was the 50th anniversary of the 1956 Revolution. An extended week of commemorations culminated in a daylong event attended by thousands of people at Cleveland State University's Wolstein Center. The event included dance performances, children's activities, film screenings, and a keynote address by Congressional Representative Tom Lantos, who was born in Hungary and survived the Holocaust and Soviet occupation before emigrating to California.

Having the greatest recent impact on Cleveland's Hungarian social life, as well as being a stirring demonstration of community cohesion, was the closing of Saint Emeric's church, home to the Hungarian School and the scouting movement. Around 2004 the Cleveland Roman Catholic Diocese embarked on an evaluation of its physical resources, real estate, and church populations. Predicated on the fact that the city's population had spread into the suburbs in the 1970s and 1980s, the diocese was faced with near-empty, financially strapped churches in the cities and inner-ring suburbs, and booming parishes in the outlying suburbs. The diocesan leadership felt that this disparity needed to be addressed, and in 2007 launched a clustering program, grouping neighboring churches into groups of three and at first having them come up with recommendations to better allocate their resources and later make recommendations about which buildings and parishes to keep and which to close in their cluster. Thus the three Hungarian parishes of Cleveland, St. Margaret, St. Elizabeth, and St. Emeric, were grouped together not because of proximity but because of ethnic identity, with a mandate to decide by the end of 2008 which two should close. At the time of its decreed closing in June 2010, St. Emeric parish listed 340 registered families, but it also had a list of ailing and nursing home parishioners, which two lists together totaled about 390 families. In the years before the closing, the parish and scouting communities showered the bishop with a letter-writing campaign and lobbied extensively, and ongoing demonstrations were held at the church as well as at the downtown cathedral and bishop's office complex. Attendance at Sunday Hungarian Masses also grew in the last year, increasing to about 140, depending on weather conditions, with Christmas and Easter attendance approaching 400. Several funerals of prominent Cleveland Hungarians in the years preceding the closing filled the church to about 600 people. All to no avail.

The parish community, under the leadership and tireless efforts of Miklós Peller, voted procurator by the parish members, first filed a petition to the bishop in accordance with Canon Law protocol, and then filed an appeal with the Vatican Congregation of the Clergy. About four to five families transferred to St. Elizabeth, but most of the community, about 80 members, got together regularly at a nearby Irish parish, St. Coleman, located near Lorain Avenue on West 65th Street, where the local American pastor celebrated a bimonthly Hungarian-language Mass, reading aloud in accented Hungarian and giving his sermons in English. The media in Hungary devoted significant attention to this process.

In 2010, just months before the closing of the church, the scouts signed a three-year lease with the Diocese and were allowed to continue to use the Scout Center and the church building, including its basement and classrooms, as long as they did not use it for liturgical purposes. In effect the scouts became the caretakers of the church building, safeguarding it for eventual community use after its reopening or selling by the Diocese. Finally, in March 2012, the Vatican overturned the parish closing, ruling that the bishop had erred on procedural and substantive grounds. St. Emeric parish reopened in November 2012 after a hiatus of two and a half years. The Diocese reinstated Reverend Sándor Siklódi as its pastor, and over 500 people attended the joyous reopening, celebrating for two full hours, almost all of the crowd praying and singing in Hungarian in unison. Cleveland Hungarians of all religious persuasions came and celebrated together, demonstrating the meaning and importance of Catholic liturgy in the Hungarian language and tradition. Cleveland's Hungarian community had united behind a common goal and had persevered.

Another ongoing event of a more secular nature is held by the *Regös* group. Every five years since 1978 the Hungarian Scout Folk Ensemble has celebrated anniversaries of its founding in 1973. These performances, held in 1978, 1983, 1988, 1993, 1998, 2003, 2008, 2013, and 2018 have always united Cleveland's Hungarian scouting community to put on a Hungarian folk dance show for the greater Cleveland Hungarian and broader public. The shows are extravagant cultural events, and the two-hour gala performances held at college or civic auditoriums usually attract over a thousand people in the audience, with over a hundred performers from all age groups onstage and backstage. The scouts spend over a year preparing for these performances, and always get excellent reviews among the Hungarian public. The performances serve to unite and excite Hungarians in Cleveland, because the show entails much more than just the scouts on stage; many non-scouts help with food preparation, program booklet advertising, set construction, folk costume embroidery and sewing, and the myriad of other tasks that a two-hour staged theater production entails. The show embodies the spiritual homeland concept, for it attracts an audience and performers from various geographic areas, some bussed in from far away, who share the value system of appreciation of Hungarian folk culture in Cleveland.

If common events bring the community together, then politics are the ways that groups of people in communities interact and transact and either highlight or overcome their differences. In the 1950s and 1960s, Cleveland Hungarian politics were mainly local. Jack Russell was Cleveland City

Council president, several influential judges were active on the Hungarian scene, and the Buckeye and Lorain Road neighborhoods were fairly tight geographic entities; thus local concerns were expressed and resolved at the ballot box. But as suburban flight took place in the 1970s and beyond, the Hungarian population of the neighborhoods moved farther out into the suburbs and lost their impact on the electoral process. City politics became less interesting and less relevant to Cleveland Hungarians because they were no longer a distinct voting block. They turned their attention to overarching Hungarian issues with a more international flavor, especially the DP generation that had fled communism and the 1956 generation that had firsthand experience of it.

Political involvement, then, became a question not so much of local events but rather of fighting communism, expressing solidarity with and trying to help Hungarians behind the Iron Curtain, and demonstrating along with émigré members of other Captive Nations against a common enemy. Thus the political affiliation of Hungarians in the Cleveland area reflected the political parties that they felt best addressed these goals. And while the main goal of defeating communism was not really won by these émigré groups, their consistent efforts enhanced their own group identity. As Judith Fai-Podlipnik says in her analysis of the political activism of Hungarian émigrés: "For the most part, the efforts of post-World War II Hungarian-American organizations proved fruitless, except for assisting some refugees. Yet they never ceased to try helping their homeland to free itself from the Soviet grasp."[61] Indeed, Aladár Szegedy-Maszák once compared émigré politics to "the growth of a dead person's beard and nails,"[62] but these political efforts had an unseen benefit for their group cohesion. Ieva Zake writes:

> The ethnic refugees persisted in their efforts to tell the West what they knew about Communism, but often ran into the danger of appearing as zealous fanatics or right-wing extremists. Often, they were led to excess. And frequently they were misinterpreted, or, at best, ignored. Yet they continued in their struggle using ethnic anti-communism as a way to assert themselves in their adopted country and to hold their communities together. Anti-communism was, and for some of these refugee groups, still is, not just a political ideology, but also a foundation of their group identity.[63]

In the United States, the political party most often associated with anti-communism was the Republican Party. And in a survey of political involvement of Cleveland's Hungarians conducted in 2017 for this book, the results tended to fairly consistently reflect a conservative politics and a tendency to identify with the Republican Party. The sociological and political surveys were advertised and available right next to each other in numerous local venues. In the 1950s and 1960s, the political tendency was more or less split into quarters: 29 percent usually or always voted Republican, 19 percent usually or always voted Democratic, 33 percent were not yet US citizens, and the rest skipped the question. The Republican numbers gradually increased while the Democratic numbers stayed fairly consistent in the 1970s and 1980s, probably as more and more DP and 1956 refugees became US citizens and started to vote in American elections. Half the respondents tended to vote mostly or always Republican in these decades, 17 percent voting mostly or always Democratic. In the 1990s, these numbers stayed consistent, and were similar for

Cleveland Hungarian voting tendencies

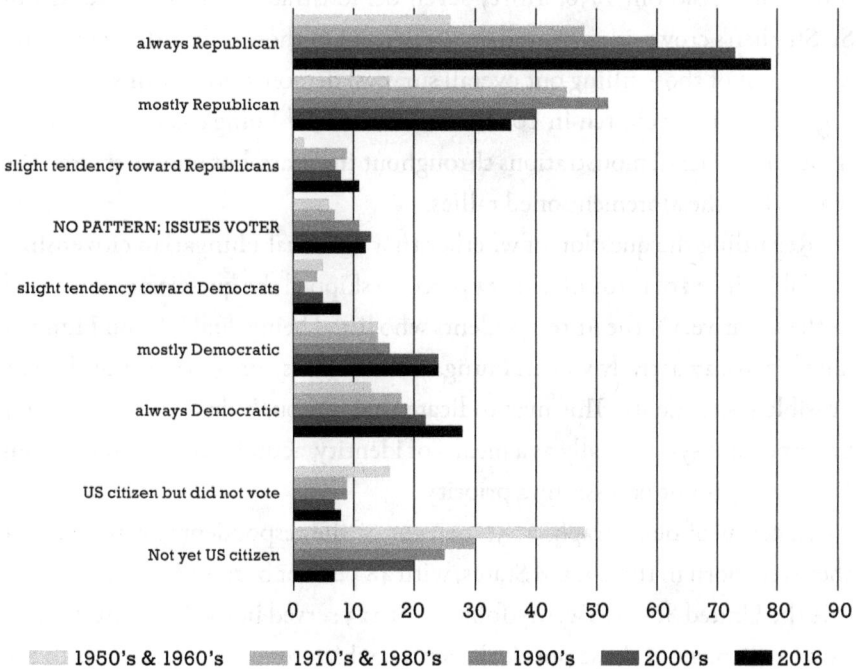

Legend: 1950's & 1960's | 1970's & 1980's | 1990's | 2000's | 2016

the early 2000s. The ratio of those in the political middle was also fairly consistent, staying 4 to 6 percent throughout the decades.

In the election of 2016, 54 percent marked their voting tendencies as mostly or always Republican, with 24 percent choosing mostly or always Democratic, maintaining the overall pattern of a little over half of Cleveland Hungarians voting Republican consistently through the decades. Also telling was the information that the respondents chose to share in the category marked "If you wish, list for whom you voted for President (Clinton, Trump, etc)." Of the respondents, 24 wrote Clinton's name, 22 wrote Trump's name, and 4 wrote things like "I could not vote for either presidential candidate."

The survey also reflected Cleveland Hungarians' participation in political demonstrations regarding Hungarian issues. Although 127 of 223 respondents skipped the question, reflecting an overall tendency not to get too involved in political issues, the legacy of 1956 is still important even 61 years later: 20 of the 96 respondents to the question about taking part in political demonstrations listed demonstrating in Hungary against Soviet oppression in 1956, and 29 of 96 listed demonstrating in Cleveland or the USA against Soviet oppression in 1956. Thirty-seven demonstrated against the return of St. Stephen's crown in 1977, and 61 (64 percent of those politically active, and 21 percent of those filling out overall surveys) demonstrated against the closing of St. Emeric church in 2009–2010. Cleveland Hungarians participated in other smaller demonstrations throughout the years, but none attracted the masses like the aforementioned rallies.

Regarding the question of whether they had dual Hungarian citizenship, available since 2011, 162 of 223 (73 percent) skipped the question or answered in the negative. Of the 61 respondents who listed being dual US and Hungarian citizens, 27 actively vote in Hungarian elections, just 9 percent of the 288 possible respondents. This may indicate that although dual citizenship may be important symbolically as a means of identity, actually voting on issues an ocean away is not necessarily a priority.

In terms of demographics, 52 percent of the respondents answered that they were born in the United States, with 48 percent born in Hungary or outside the United States. Twenty-four out of 223 served in the US military, a ratio of 11 percent of those politically active, which roughly corresponds to the author's previous research done identifying 336 Cleveland Hungarians who served in the US military since 1950.

The end of the Cold War saw the revitalization of official political contacts between the Hungarian government and émigré communities. Attesting to the strength of Cleveland's Hungarian community, an honorary consulate was established in 1993. László Bőjtös was named to the post, later he was promoted to honorary consul general and as such has functioned as a liason between political visitors from Hungary and Cleveland, as well as taking care of consular and citizenship matters.

CHAPTER FOUR
Language and Literature

In contrast to tradition and culture, language is perhaps the most individualized way of depicting what it means to be Hungarian in Cleveland, for it is the most fluid, albeit the most easily measurable facet of meaning. One can argue that Hungarian language use – why, when, how much – best shows what it means to be Hungarian in Cleveland. With the exception of spouses, very few non-Hungarians learn the Hungarian language; thus if one actively uses the Hungarian language in Cleveland, it is pretty safe to say that being Hungarian is a part of that person's identity, that it means something.

Newspaper and Book Publishing
Since the 1950s

For a Hungarian arriving or living in Cleveland in 1950, several locally published Hungarian newspapers would have been readily available. This would have included the daily *Szabadság* [Freedom], the oldest of Cleveland's Hungarian newspapers. Founded in 1891 by Tihamér Kohányi as a weekly, the paper peaked in the late 1920s, when it had 35,563 subscribers. Its vicious rival was the New York-based *Amerikai Magyar Népszava* [American Hungarian people's voice], founded by Géza Berkó in 1899. Both papers became dailies early on and remained so until the 1950s, when both were owned and edited by Zoltán Gombos. *Szabadság* eventually moved to New York and New Brunswick, NJ, merging with *Amerikai Magyar Népszava* to form *Amerikai*

Magyar Népszava / Szabadság, now being published online in New York and edited by László Bartus.

The weekly *A Jó Pásztor* [The good shepherd] was another readily available newspaper, published in Cleveland from 1934 to 1963. Religious newspapers would have also included the weekly *Katolikus Magyarok Vasárnapja* [Catholic Hungarians' sunday] and beginning publication in Cleveland in 1952, *Erős Vár: Amerikai Magyar Evangélikusok lapja* [Strong fortress: American Hungarian Lutheran newspaper]. The Catholic newspaper *Katolikus Magyarok Vasárnapja*, well known nationally, was long published in Cleveland and was billed as the oldest Hungarian Catholic newspaper in the United States and Canada. Established in 1894, the paper ceased publication shortly after its 100th anniversary. Its yearbooks are also interesting repositories of Cleveland Hungarian thought and culture; they contained poems, essays, data lists, history, religion, and literature, almost like an almanach.

Erős Vár: Amerikai Magyar Evangélikusok Lapja was also an official church newspaper. A 2008 edition shows that it was published in Lakewood, a suburb of Cleveland, and that the publication was in its seventh-eighth year. Indeed, the newspaper began appearing in Cleveland in 1952, was published elsewhere from 1957 to 1962, then since 1962 has been edited and published in the Cleveland area, and is now in its eighty-second year.

Many local Hungarian newspapers and periodicals have since folded or stopped publication; their back issues can be found in several local libraries. For example, the 1959 editions of *Szabadság* were all in Hungarian, and content included world news, opinion columns, two entire columns of Hungarian Cleveland classified advertisements, as well as separate advertisements by five different funeral homes. One of several newspapers later absorbed by *Szabadság* was the weekly *Amerikai Magyar Világ* [American Hungarian world], published in Cleveland from 1964 to 1978. Twenty pages, it was edited by Zoltán Gombos and sold in at least ten Buckeye Road neighborhood stores, mostly delicatessens and drugstores. A short-lived newspaper of an active youth group of the 1970s is *Patria*, published once in the spring of 1974. *Képes Magyar Világhíradó*, also known on its masthead as *Illustrated Hungarian World Review*, was a magazine published mostly monthly in Cleveland from 1963 to 1977. Lajos Füry and József Lendvay were its editors, and

Judith Petres Ewendt was its chief editor. Its photographer, József Lendvay, was known locally as "Photo Joe" and he documented most Cleveland Hungarian events with his camera, working tirelessly from the 1950s through the 1980s.

Az Újság [The newspaper] was an 8 page 16 by 20 inch paper written all in Hungarian, with no pictures. This locally published newspaper contained obituaries, church news, articles of events, and advertising from Hungarian businesses in Cleveland, including Hungarian books for sale, with a back page of crossword puzzles and jokes. Later it merged with the *Detroiti Magyar Újság* [Hungarian newspaper of Detroit] to form *Magyar Újság* [Hungarian newspaper], which was edited by Zoltán Kótai and published in Cleveland from 1976 to 1980. *Magyar Újság* boasted 66 years of publication with a Christian and Hungarian bent. This weekly paper had three pages of international news, all in Hungarian, a page and a half of advertising from local Hungarian businesses, a page of poetry, a page of church listings, a half page of obituaries, and a last page of crossword puzzles and jokes.

Printed by the Cleveland Hungarian printer Classic Printing, *Új Idő: Ismeretterjesztő és Irodalmi Folyóirat* [New times: a journal of literature and common knowledge] was a 20-page periodical appearing monthly from 1981 to about 1988. Edited and published by József and Ildikó Vigh, it contained poems, essays, photographs, crossword puzzles, and news about Cleveland Hungarians. Its advertisers were mostly Cleveland Hungarian businesses, but advertisements from Hungarian businesses in Canada, New York, and New Jersey also appeared on its pages.

Also published in Cleveland from 1962 until 2007 was the 8–12 page monthly *Szittyakürt* [Scythian bugle], billed as the official newspaper of the *Hungária Szabadságharcos Mozgalom* [Hungaria freedom fighter movement], a far-right leaning political movement. This newspaper contained historical and political articles, mostly anticommunist, along with news of some Cleveland Hungarian events. This newspaper was also printed by Classic Printing Corporation, a printer of choice for several Hungarian periodicals, newsletters, and newspapers published in Cleveland from 1967 to 2001.

Newspapers published in Cleveland tended to lean to the right side of the political spectrum, which is not surprising given the anticommunist leanings of most of the community. The exceptions were the left-leaning papers edited by Zoltán Gombos. The advertising in all of these newspapers, however, served to connect and tie the community together, and not only did the articles and pictures serve as a link among community members by reporting on their social events, but the poems and essays also served to enhance the language skills and broaden the thought processes of the readers, as well as to reinforce their existing views. Indeed, newspapers are the first draft of history, and fleeting and transitory as they may be, their archives can shed significant light on the values and conflicts of the communities they served. The yearbooks from churches and organizations also serve as important historical and literary records, for they contain pictures, reports, membership data, and often advertising. These yearbooks are frequently written in the Hungarian language and are often scattered among the various organizations and churches, and unfortunately there is no central depository for them.

Hungarian language books were and are readily available to the Cleveland area's readers, though they used to have many more outlets for distribution. Perhaps the oldest was the Kossuth Bookshop on Lorain Avenue, started by Klára Zsigmond and Endre Thurner in the early 1950s. It featured Hungarian embroidery and books, as well as newspapers, LP records, and gift items, and also lent Hungarian books for ten cents each. After Zsigmond's death in 1971, the store moved to the family residence on Lakota Avenue in Cleveland and continued selling Hungarian as well as German books. The house was a veritable maze of stacks and boxes of books and inventory. The business closed after Thurner's death in 1992.

Another similar business was the Nádas bookstore, operated out of Gyula Nádas' home on Grace Avenue in Lakewood. Begun originally in the early 1950s as an importer of typewriters with Hungarian keyboards, this quasi-bookstore sold books, newspapers, Zsolnay and Herendi porcelain, original oil paintings, typewriters, and other Hungarian items. Set up in the Nádas residence, this house also had mazelike aisles in the living room and halls, stacked floor to ceiling. A spreadsheet of inventory compiled in the early 1990s and used until around 2000 shows a total of 2,993 Hungarian books alone.[64] Its listings shed light on what one local bookseller anticipated his buyers would read, based on years of Cleveland Hungarian business experi-

Number of individual book titles by various Hungarian authors, circa 1990–2000 (list is NOT exhaustive)					
Sándor Csoóri	4	István Fekete	14	Lajos Füry	12
Áron Gábor	6	Géza Gárdonyi	8	Jenő Heltai	10
Ferenc Herczeg	8	Gyula Illyés	16	Mór Jókai	34
Frigyes Karinthy	9	Gyula Krudy	22	Imre Madach	7
Sándor Makai	7	Dezső Malonyai	8	Sándor Márai	15
Kálmán Mikszáth	21	József Mindszenty	8	György Moldova	9
Ferenc Molnár	13	Ferenc Móra	8	Zsigmond Móricz	17
Lajos Nagy	10	László Németh	11	József Nyírő	5
Viktor Padányi	4	László Passuth	26	Sándor Petőfi	10
Jenő Pohárnok	5	Jenő Rejtő	14	Miklós Surányi	19
Dezső Szabó	19	Magda Szabó	6	Zoltán Szitnyai	10
Áron Tamási	7	Jenő Tersánszky	8	Albert Wass	24

Titles Available in Nádas Bookstore

ence. It includes Hungarian translations with 17 titles by Claire Kenneth, 14 titles from Agatha Christie, 12 from Jules Verne, 9 from Charles Dickens, 8 by John Steinbeck, and 8 by H.G. Wells. The table shows a sampling of those Hungarian authors with four or more separate titles stocked in the Nádas bookstore. This list is not inclusive of all the Hungarian authors stocked, but does indicate which authors were popular. Not only does it contain a representative selection from the traditional canon of Hungarian literature likely to be familiar to persons living in Hungary, but also worth noting is the number of titles by émigré Hungarian authors not widely read in Cold War Hungary such as Lajos Füry, Áron Gábor, Sándor Márai, Cardinal József Mindszenty, József Nyírő, and Albert Wass. These authors wrote of themes important to émigré Hungarians, of Hungarian identity and nationalism, of displacement and of Soviet occupation, of villages left behind, rife with romanticized childhood memories, of being imprisoned under communism, as well as of pre-Second World War society.

An outlet on the East Side in which to buy Hungarian books and items was the *Magyar Áruház* [Hungarian store] in a storefront on Buckeye Avenue. Originally begun as a scout store [*Cserkészbolt*], it later stocked many items from Hungary and was owned by Dénes Dietrich, who was also scoutmaster of one of the Hungarian scout troops in Cleveland; he was also the initiator of the Scout Picnic, the Scout Ball, and the Teleki Scout Park.

Later, in the 1980s, the Classic Printing workshop became a center of Hungarian publishing. Although it did not have a retail storefront, a small number of Hungarians gathered there regularly to discuss sports and politics and to purchase newly printed books, and the printshop saw regular Hungarian traffic, as it was the printer of choice for Hungarian book and newspaper publishers of all political persuasions, both religious and secular. Through the years all of these outlets have closed, from the Kossuth bookshop to the *Magyar Áruház*. Their owners passed away and Cleveland's Hungarians do not read as many Hungarian books as in the latter part of the twentieth century. Out-of-town Hungarian book distributers have largely taken the place of these bookstores, and online ordering is possible from Pannonia Books in Toronto and Magyar Marketing in Indiana.

Important among the 8,000 books found in the Cleveland Hungarian Heritage Society's museum in the Galleria Mall are its émigré fiction and twentieth century history and politics sections. The émigré fiction section of this small library has 293 Hungarian books published outside Hungary, including multiple volumes from Albert Wass, József Nyírő, Lajos Füry, István Eszterhás, and Áron Gábor. The publishers range from Cleveland to Canada, Argentina to Australia, which shows a bond among émigré communities; their common fates tend to connect them, especially in the themes they write about. The émigré poetry section of this library contains 215 books, including numerous volumes from József Kovácsy, Tibor Tollas, Ferenc Mózsi, Irén Négyesy, and Péter Hargitai, among others.

While most brick and mortar outlets for Hungarian books are no more, book purchasing certainly has not died out completely. Many Cleveland Hungarians buy books when visiting Hungary, as anything is available there, unlike during the Cold War, when Hungarian government authorities prohibited certain authors from publishing in Hungary, and émigré authors tended to be strongly anti-communist. Today anyone can visit the Cleveland Hungarian Heritage Museum in the Galleria Mall on East 9th Street in downtown Cleveland, which boasts an impressive book corner in its gift-shop. Another outlet is the book donation program run by the scouts. As older Cleveland Hungarians die, they often leave behind personal libraries of hundreds of Hungarian books. By word of mouth, a tradition slowly evolved in which their descendants began donating these books to the scouts, who in turn took these to the annual scout festival Labor Day weekend, where they were in effect recycled by the public. Hardback books are sold for two dollars and paperbacks for one dollar, and the proceeds are used to send care packages to Hungarian language schools in Subcarpathia in Ukraine. A storage cleanup at St. Emeric in October of 2012 counted 150 boxes of books, each with approximately 20–40 volumes, yielding 3,000–6,000 Hungarian items. The average traffic at the scout picnic is a turnaround of about 400–700 Hungarian books sold yearly, which shows that Cleveland Hungarians do still read Hungarian books.

While the availability and quantity of imported books is illustrative, it is book publishing within a community that shows what topics are truly important to that community, i.e., which themes authors feel the need to share their thoughts about. Additionally, the number of books published reflects the literary output of any given community, and in Cleveland's case, that trend increased from the late 1950s to peak in the 1980s, and it has seen a decline since then. For example, the Cleveland Hungarian Heritage Museum's library contains no books published in Cleveland from the 1930s to the mid 1950s. At least 5 Hungarian books were published in Cleveland in the late 1950s, including 2 by the local author István Eszterhás, the editor of the newspaper *Katolikus Magyarok Vasárnapja* and whose son later became a Hollywood screenwriter. The 1960s saw at least 10 Hungarian books published in Cleveland, mostly literature and poetry, while the 1970s saw at least 14 Hungarian books. These were also mostly literature and poetry but included personal memoirs and some works of history. The 1980s continued the trend with at least 14 Hungarian works published in Cleveland, with literature, poetry, and more nonfiction, mostly with historical and political topics. The 1990s saw a drastic drop, with only 5 such books on the shelf. The trend continued with only a handful published in the twenty-first century.

The lack of a significant commercial market, tied with the obligation that many authors felt to make a personal financial sacrifice in order to disseminate their ideas, most notably anticommunism, led many authors to self-publish their works. Examples include György Csikós's memoir of his Siberian captivity, *Apró események a pokolból* [Tiny events from hell] (1984), as well as József H. Csia publishing his brother István's 152-page volume of poetry titled *Zarándok az Úr pitvarában* [Pilgrimage in the Lord's anteroom], written under the pseudonym *Szemtanú* [Witness]. István was a career military officer in Hungary, imprisoned for six years by the communist authorities, and his uncle Sándor, to whom the book of poetry is dedicated, was executed in 1945. Attila Simontsits coauthored a collection of military photographs from the Horthy era, *Harcunk 1920–1945* [Our fight], and compiled a chronological documentation spanning 1,141 pages, *The Last Battle for St. Stephen's Crown*, published in Cleveland in 1983. These self-published books deal mostly with the themes of the actual and later political fight against communism, a recurring struggle of the community.

Another topic was the education of the community's younger members. The émigré Hungarian Scouts Association, which changed its name after 1989 to Hungarian Scout Association in Exteris to reflect the reestablishment of previously banned scouting in Hungary, was the publisher of textbooks from two Cleveland Hungarian authors during the Cold War, including Zoltán Bócsay's history of Hungary titled *Vázlatos Magyar Történelem* [Outline of Hungarian history], published in 1984, and Ernő Kálnoky's 1979 geography textbook titled simply *Magyar Földrajz* [Hungarian geography], and his Hungarian folklore booklet *Magyar Néprajz* [Hungarian folklore] from 1977. The covers of both consist of original artwork by Cleveland Hungarian-American artist George Kozmon. All three of these books were written with the express purpose of teaching scout leader candidates the basic knowledge of Hungarian history and geography required for leadership advancement in the scouting movement, and they were used by hundreds of Cleveland Hungarians mostly of the second generation.

Also falling into this category were the children's books published by the Árpád publishing company: their series of children's Hungarian reading textbooks, *Séta betűországban* [A walk in letterland], *Szép magyar világ* [Beautiful Hungarian world], and *Kincsesláda* [Treasure chest], served for many decades as the textbook of choice for Cleveland's Hungarian school, as did the children's writing workbooks by Panni Nádas Ludányi called *Irka-firka* [Writer-scribbler].

Dealing with literary, historical, and modern political themes, several Cleveland Hungarian publishers churned out frequent books from various local and international Hungarian authors. The largest two were Kárpát Könyvkiadó and Árpád Könyvkiadó, each of which produced at least five or six Hungarian books each decade from the 1960s through the 1990s. Also publishing in the late 1950s and early 1960s was Magyar Könyvtár, producing fictional works of literature from Gyula Bedy, Erzsébet Ágnes Bodnár, and István Eszterhás.

Functioning as an independent publisher as well as the printer of choice for minor local publishers, the Classic Printing Corporation, owned by László Berta, was a mainstay of Cleveland Hungarian book, pamphlet, newsletter, newspaper, and flier printing for over 30 years. Located on Madison Avenue near West 95th Street in Cleveland, the printshop was a gathering place for Hungarian writers and social leaders throughout the 1970s, 80s, and 90s. No fewer than 34 Hungarian books printed by Classic Printing in its Cleveland shop reside on the shelves of the Hungarian Heritage Society library, but the actual number printed in the city is much higher, probably close to 700, as Classic Printing was founded in 1967 and operated until 2001. Erika Berta, László's widow, remembers her husband printing many Hungarian newspapers and printing many of the Hungarian books at half or quarter price or even for free, just to support Hungarian publishing in Cleveland. She remembers Hungarian books being published in the Classic Printing shop about every month and a half.

Thousands of miles from Hungary, making the effort required to write and publish a book in the Hungarian language shows a sense of belonging to the spiritual homeland, with ties to Hungary and to the Hungarian language. A book has no individual relevance; it is inherently a communal effort. Even if the author is long gone or dead, the book was meant for an audience and meant to be shared. What books are available to any community, but in this case to Cleveland's Hungarian community, show how communication has built and continues to build and sustain identity, for the communication of that Hungarian author was meant to express a certain value, a certain identity to its reader.

Not residing in any of the public libraries but worth mentioning are un-published family memoirs, which were accessed by the author because of his personal relationship with the authors or their descendants. Not disseminat-ed and thus not reaching a wide audience, these pamphlets and typed man-uscripts are nevertheless important historical documents, precisely because they are not intended for a wide audience. Memoirs of famous historical fig-ures carry the danger that the person is trying to justify his or her actions and thus may not always be entirely trustworthy, although they are valuable in their own regard. Memoirs written for family members, however, tend not to embellish the truth; although memory tends to fade in the twilight of life, many of these memoirs are written about extremely personal events. Much as every American remembers exactly where they were and what they were do-ing when they first heard the news about the assassination of John F. Kenne-dy or the attacks on the Twin Towers on September 11, 2001, so too are the events of fleeing Hungary during the Second World War and the events of 1956 seared into the memories of the participants, and many can recollect with amazing clarity even 60 or more years later.

These unpublished memoirs, written in Hungarian in Cleveland but most-ly limited to family distribution, include the 1956 memoirs of Miklós Peller, "Éjszakai Menekülésem a Vasfüggönyön át" [My nighttime flight across the Iron Curtain] and "Csengőfrász: a Szentkirályi család története," [Doorbell terror: the story of the Szentkiralyi family] written by Ödön Szentkirályi.[65] Written from a broader perspective and including pre-war Hungarian mem-ories and incisive observations of tumultuous historical events as well as ear-ly years as Displaced Persons in Cleveland, several other memoirs also stand out. These include: "A Fricke család emlékeiből" [Memories from the Fricke family], an approximately 140-page typed memoir written by Valér Fricke, a Hungarian representative in Parliament during the Second World War who later fled to DP camps and then to Cleveland and whose pre-war Bocs-kay formalwear is still worn by his greatgrandchildren at Cleveland Hun-garian balls. Another is "Bad Kreuznach, Romilly, Mailly le Camp," written by Gábor Papp, the founder of Cleveland's Hungarian School. Also falling into this category is "Nagymama naplója" [Grandmother's Diary], written by Hanna Strada about her aristocratic childhood and later life as a refugee, translated by her daughter Maria Strada Friedrich and published in a bilingual hardcover limited edition for family use. Now in the Cleveland Hungarian Heritage Society's library are the memoirs of John Uray, which also make for interesting reading.

These unpublished manuscripts, much as Hungarian books published in Cleveland during the time span of this study, exemplify a communication theory of identity. Cleveland family- and published authors thought of themselves as being distinctly Hungarian, although they lived in the United States. By writing in the Hungarian language, their communication built, sustained, and expressed their identity, using the social aspects of writing and publishing to give meaning to their own personal lives. Their writings helped maintain the Hungarian language in the Cleveland area and construct a narrative, as it were, of the values of the community.

Hungarian publishing in Cleveland since the 1980s, however, has waned; today the only periodicals regularly published in the Cleveland area in the Hungarian language are the newsletters of local Hungarian organizations and churches. These include regular church bulletins, which like other organization's newsletters, in and of themselves constitute historical records, for they all detail ongoing and special events. Most church bulletins are one to two pages, but the exception is *Ébresztő* [Awake], a 16 page full-color periodical of the Hungarian Bethany Baptist church, which has published monthly in Hungarian since 1999 with a circulation of 100-120. *Jó munkát* [Good work] is the yearly newsletter of the American Hungarian Friends of Scouting. Written in Hungarian, it is mailed yearly or biannually to over a thousand households mostly in the Cleveland area. The bilingual *Review*, the official newsletter of the Cleveland Hungarian Heritage Society, appears twice a year and chronicles the museum's social events and cultural activities. Although not written in Hungarian, the *Hírek*, sent out monthly by the Hungarian Cultural Center of Northeastern Ohio, is a treasure trove of information about Cleveland Hungarian events and is the most all-encompassing in its coverage of those events. All of these local initiatives use communication to promote and express identity.

Out of town Hungarian newspapers are also available, although they tend to be read by the older generation. If we revisit the 2011–2015 American Community Survey five-year estimates, in which about 82,819 people spoke Hungarian at home throughout the USA, with 6,399 of those living in Ohio, we find approximately 4,445 people who speak Hungarian in the home in the greater Cleveland area. Thus, almost two-thirds of Ohio's Hungarian population can be found in the greater Cleveland area. What are some current Hungarian newspapers that these Hungarians read, other than their local community newsletters? The weekly *Amerikai Magyar Népszava*, now published in New York but formerly was *Szabadság* of Cleveland, for example, has approximately 500 subscribers in Ohio, out of about 6,000–10,000 nationwide. In addition, the online edition garners an average of about 600 hits per month from Ohio. If we interpolate from these ratios (US, Ohio, Cleveland), we may surmise that 300–350 Hungarians in the Cleveland area subscribe to *Amerikai Magyar Népszava*, and that around 15 people per day access it online from the Cleveland area. Also worth mentioning are other online news sources straight from Hungary and its surrounding countries, but it is hard to ascertain exactly how many people from the Cleveland area access websites in Hungary. Since 1989, however, news sources from Hungary are freely available, although few of them target Hungarian-Americans exclusively.

The most popular website for local Cleveland Hungarian news today is unarguably www.bocskairadio.org. In fact, this website has taken over the role that major Cleveland Hungarian newspapers like *Szabadság* used to play in the 1950s. The website publishes on average about 15–20 new articles monthly and reposts an additional 60–80 news items, mostly from Hungary. Around 300 local photographs are posted monthly, as are about 10 short films per month. Its local email blast reaches 1,689 email addresses with weekly news updates. While it is hard to ascertain exactly how many listeners its radio program reaches on any given week, the yearly fundraising radiothon (which most public radio stations engage in, including WJCU) attracted around 150 individual donors each in 2016 and 2017, with 135 donors in 2014 and 2015.

But the volunteer local news organization's reach has grown beyond the Cleveland area. For example, readership online has increased from around 7,000 US readers and around 3,400 readers from Hungary in 2013 to at least

Website visits	Individual Users (unique IP addresses)	Individual pages visited	Percentage of visitors with IP addresses in USA	Percentage of visitors with IP addresses in Hungary	Percentage of visitors with other IP addresses*
2013	23 345	13 222	45 898	53%	26%	21%
2014	44 228	27 263	82 160	47%	34%	19%
2015	75 544	53 781	123 888	40%	34%	26%
2016	94 857	70 797	145 610	39%	33%	28%
2017	100 075	72 497	153 500	26%	46%	28%

Bocskai Rádió Website Traffic

* Other IP addresses mostly include Romania (6-14%), Canada (2-3%), Germany (around 2%), Slovakia (around 1%), Serbia (around 1%), and the United Kingdom (1-5%).

22,000 readers from the US and around 24,000 from Hungary in 2017. Six of its video reports about Cleveland Hungarians were broadcast by DunaTV in Hungary in 2017, and its video reports published on the Bocskai Rádió Facebook page attract between 3,000 and 10,000 views, with the most popular being its live broadcast of Fr. Csaba Bőjte's visit to Cleveland in November of 2017, which was viewed at least 34,000 times. A look at its current website traffic statistics reveals an increase in individual logins from about 13,000 in 2013 to over 70,000 in 2016 and 2017. Individual page views (articles clicked on or videos watched on the website) numbered around 150,000 yearly in 2016 and 2017.

Although some of these website visits must be discounted due to an indeterminate number of them being automated webcrawler software, Facebook follower numbers and video views reinforce the analysis that Bocskai Rádió has become the most significant news outlet publishing in the Hungarian language in Cleveland, mostly replacing the role of local print newspapers. However, one must be careful when drawing conclusions from website traffic data alone, because automated bots do webcrawls to visit sites but are not human visitors. In addition, those organizations posting pictures more frequently get higher website traffic, and more reliable information is the number of Facebook followers of an organization, as will be discussed in the conclusion.

Local and Visiting Authors

An exhaustive analysis of Cleveland Hungarian writers is beyond the scope of this work; nevertheless, some authors must be introduced briefly. The Cleveland Hungarian poet who most captured the essence of Hungarian-American life was György Kemény. He was born in 1875 in the Hungarian village of Garadna and arrived in Cleveland in 1891, immediately starting to write for *Szabadság*, and later founding his own journal titled *Dongó* [Wasp]. His epic and lyrical poems captured what Hungarian-American life was really like in Cleveland, Pittsburgh, New York, and other cities.[66] Other notable Hungarian authors in Cleveland include those who arrived in the first half of the twentieth century, among them László Pólya (1870–1950), József Reményi (1891–1956), and Árpád Tarnóczy (1884–1957).

The arrival of the DP and 1956 immigration wave created a new wave of Hungarian literature in Cleveland, one tied closely to prewar Hungary's Horthy era and to the 1956 Revolution. These newer arrivals included the poets Imre Sári Gál, György Gyékényesi, Tihamér Halmay, Lajos Illés, Márton Kerecsendi Kiss, József Kossányi, József Kovácsy, Mária Tóth-Kurucz, and Eszter Farnos Zilahi, among others, and the prose authors included Dóra T. Dombrády, István Eszterhás, Gyula Bedy, János Kerecseny, Fréda B. Kovács, Ágnes Huszár Várdy (who has since moved to Pittsburgh), Ágnes Bognár, and Judit Petres. The Hungarian Association's yearly November conference provided a forum for many of these and other Hungarian writers, and a forum for Cleveland's Hungarian audience to hear and interact with these and visiting émigré authors. While most Cleveland Hungarian writers evoked Hungarian national pride and demonized communism, the Jewish perspective seems to be missing from collections of Cleveland Hungarian writing. The notable exception is the poet Oszkár Bán, whose siblings died in the Holocaust. He wrote several collections of poems, including one published in Cleveland. Local unpublished poets include Imre Bogárdy, Jenő Szedenits, and the late Gusztáv Veres, who often took part in and recited their own poetry at commemorations of 1848 and 1956.

Four local writers who published in the Hungarian language are worth highlighting: a nonfiction writer, a poet and scientist, a poet and dramatist, and an editor and fiction writer. Their ties to the community over the span of years, including their participation in social events and work spent on behalf of the Hungarian community, as well as the quality of their published literature set them apart from the many others who published in Cleveland in the Hungarian language. They are Dr. Ferenc Somogyi, Dr. György Gyékényesi, Márton Kerecsendi Kiss, and István Eszterhás.

The most prolific Cleveland nonfiction writer was Ferenc Somogyi, who was born in 1906 in Nárai, a small village in Vas County in Hungary. His first published work was a collection of local folk customs, for which he won an award in 1925. He studied law, history, political science, and literature at the University of Pécs in Hungary, then began teaching at the university level in Hungary through the 1930s. He was elected to the Hungarian Parliament in 1939. The Second World War swept him to a DP camp near Feffernitz in Austria. From 1948 to 1956 he edited and published the émigré journal *Vagyunk* [We exist], first in Austria and after his immigration to Cleveland in 1950.

In Cleveland he continued his scholarly work and community service, starting a Hungarian culture lecture series at Western Reserve University, editing the Hungarian Association's *Krónika* for over three decades, which was a book-length summary of the Hungarian Association's conference published yearly, and assembling the organizations's thirty-year historical summary in 1983. He taught countless Cleveland Hungarians in his decades of public service, in its Hungarian school or at the university level as chair of Hungarian Studies at Western Reserve University. He was a founder of the Hungarian Association, cofounded and codirected the St. Stephen Free University in Cleveland, and served as the general secretary of the Árpád Academy of Hungarian Scientists, Writers, and Artists Abroad.

He published well over 500 scholarly articles, edited numerous compilations of Hungarian cultural and literary works, and penned 26 books. His four major works, however, are an overarching synthesis of Hungarian history titled *Küldetés: a magyarság története* [Mission: the history of Hungarians], which had two editions and three printings, the latest in 1978, a two-volume literary history spanning Hungarian literature to 1925, and a history of Hungarians in Cleveland, published in 1994. Objectivity and well-documented research characterize these four books, as they do all of his published materials. For his eightieth birthday, Steven Béla Várdy and Ágnes Huszár Várdy assembled a 616 page collection of 27 independent studies titled *Triumph in Adversity*, a fitting tribute to Somogyi's life work.

Küldetés, his history of Hungarians, arose from efforts to provide students of Cleveland's Hungarian school with a textbook. His goal was to provide a history of the Hungarian people that included not only the people of Hungary but also émigré communities, and according to its introduction, strove to delineate the mission, or rather, the calling of the Hungarian people, calling in a sense of destiny. His two-volume literary study, *Magyar nyelv és irodalom* [Hungarian language and literature] spanned Hungarian literature from its oral precursors to 1925, with clarification of basic concepts, easily readable prose, and numerous examples illustrating the epochs in the Hungarian literary canon. Somogyi wove his literary samples into the prose to give the reader a true sense of styles of literature produced in the various historical eras. Both volumes taken together offer an expansive overview of Hungarian literature, and make for fairly easy reading; Somogyi's prose style is light and down-to-earth, yet not at all lacking in detail or depth. He was unarguably Cleveland's best nonfiction writer in the latter half of the twentieth century.

The most prolific Cleveland Hungarian poet after 1950 was József Kovácsy. A DP refugee and a mechanical engineer by training, he published six volumes of poetry from 1987 to 1997, each over 500 pages long, the first two self-published and the rest by Árpád Publishing. His poetry, however, lacks the deep insights provided by Gyékényesi and Kerecsendi, and most of his poems deal with themes of revenge and hopelessness, betraying a bitter and negative tone, and his rhetoric is that of the Hungarist movement, a far-right extremist group.

Much less prolific but much more involved in Cleveland's Hungarian community was Dr. György Gyékényesi. Born in 1932 in Hungary, in the small village of Gyékényes bordering Croatia, his family fled when he was 12 years old, and after spending time in DP camps, he arrived in the United States in 1951. He served in the US Air Force from 1952 to 1956, then studied mechanical engineering, eventually earning a Ph.D. in 1972 at the University of Michigan. He worked at NASA, and also organized a Hungarian Theatre in Cleveland, with yearly drama productions. His first collection of poems, *Karikázó* [Circler], was published in 1972, and his second, *Karámország*

[Corral country], was published posthumously in 1974; both were published in Munich, Germany.

Gyékényesi's poems are pleasant in tone, sometimes echoing well-known folk verse, and they span the breadth of human life experiences, from early life to young love to to mature love to growing old. Other poems examine nature, science, or the art of literature, with allusions to historical and literary forbearers. For example, Gyékényesi takes the universality of death and applies it to the immigrant experience in America with his poem *"Mikrokozmosz"* [Microcosm]. The poem starts with the funeral of a seven-year-old child, but then shifts the mood with a familiar children's verse about candles burning. Although the candles are at the wake and in the cemetery, the mood is neither somber nor depressing; it is almost childlike and playful. *"Ég a gyertya ég / el ne aludjék / apád nézi anyád nézi / ravatalon ég."* The middle of the poem speaks of the military with Hungarian mythological imagery, but again with an almost playful tone, quoting a Hungarian childhood folk game, "Give us soldiers, King," in which children mimic medieval power structures, transferring rhymes into physical prowess. "Adj király katonát / nem adok / ha nem adsz hát / szakítok..." The middle stanza has a somber, almost macabre tone, detailing 5 million undead corpses, all due to the military, but echoing the death of a simple citizen, placing one death into a broader context of deaths, and also adding the aspect of time, with mention of Csaba, the mythological military leader who rides the Milky Way with the souls of anciently departed Hungarian soldiers. Finally, the ending two stanzas speak of immigrants coming to America, packed into the holds of ships, an unknown number arriving to New York, but ending with yellow earth covering everything, bringing the poem full circle to death and a burial, but with a one-word conclusion: "in America." This has connotations far beyond a simple immigrant's journey; it evokes the emotions of an entire life, from one country to the next, from childhood to active youth to the end of life, with a pun on the word *"hajó"* [ship] and *"ha jó"* [if it's good]: *"Amerikába jöttünk / tujisten hányan / hajó orrában / hajó farában / betakar a sárga föld / Amerikában."* This both suggests and ends with the opportunities available in America, a positive spin on a simple death, echoing Gyékényesi's own short lifetime, and his poetry endures beyond his early death.

Márton Kerecsendi Kiss was another poet and playwright—now accepted into the literary canon in Hungarian literary circles—who lived and wrote in Cleveland, in his case, from 1965 to 1990. He was born in 1917 in the Hungarian town of Kerecsend. He became a teacher and worked for years in the village of Biszke, teaching in Hungary's first Roma school (which he founded in 1938; its building in Bicske now bears his name). At the same time, he was a successful poet and writer, working alongside such literary greats such as his mentor Gyula Illyés, as well as Zsigmond Móricz, Áron Tamási, József Nyírő, István Fekete, and István Sinka.

His drama "A Harmincadik" [The thirtieth] stems from his experiences as a teacher in a company town: a law stated that companies had to establish a primary school for their employees once the number of children reached 30. The drama's plot is about everything the aluminum company does to avoid opening a school, including firing employees or transferring families each time the number of children approached 30.

After the war, Kerecsendi spent a brief stint in a refugee camp, then in Italy, and in 1947 he arrived in Argentina, where he founded and edited a Hungarian newspaper, *Magyar Út* [Hungarian road], along with István Vörösváry. In 1957 due to the deteriorating economic situation in Argentina, he emigrated first to Toronto, Canada, then in 1965 to Cleveland, where he worked in the basement of Cleveland's City Hall but continued writing and publishing in his spare time.

Although other Cleveland Hungarian poets may have written and published more poems than Kerecsendi, he was definitely a part of the everyday social and literary life of Cleveland. His writings received critical acclaim in émigré literary circles, even though he was dismissed as a mid-level nostalgic poet by some literary critics in Hungary, who by and large did not praise émigré writers due to the prevailing attitude among the communist authorities. Most of his literary output while living in Cleveland consisted of poetry whose themes capture the émigré experience.

"*Keserű Szívvel* [With a bitter heart]," for example, showcases the work that maintaining culture amidst materialism and assimilation entails. Despite the poem's title, the majority of it is positive, and the ending also is very positive, more of a message that it is indeed possible to overcome materialism and assimilation. The poem begins with a bare-bones outline of Kerecsendi's emigration three decades earlier, subtly alluding to Soviet brutality, betrayal by the Allied powers, and a difficult life in refugee camps, but nevertheless forgoing specifics, explicitly stating that there is no need to rehash the details, that his life was just directed by fate: *"Három évtizede élek honomtól távol, / mindenki tudja, kiknek jóvoltából. / Nem sorolom fel azt sem, miért jöttem. / Így adta a sors, amikor beborult fölöttem."* The second stanza continues with descriptive imagery of life in refugee camps, and in the third stanza Kerecsendi fondly remembers the people in the camps who helped him in the tough times, who later found human rights, food, and peace in their new countries. The fourth stanza continues with the years passing by and the former refugees finding respect, happiness, and contentment among the churches and community organizations. The fifth stanza details the positive aspects of their immigration; the émigrés respected each other, prospered, and remained Hungarian. Their work ethic and the fact that they were on the right path raised them, including Hungarian school, scouts, newspapers, churches, and civic organizations. Their lives prospered and the Hungarian community assembled: *"Becsülték egymást. Gyarapodtak. Magyarok maradtak: / felemelte őket a szorgalom s a tény, hogy jó úton haladnak. / Magyar iskola, cserkészet, újság, templom, sok-sok egylet... / Életük dúsan felvirágzott, a magyarság összesereglett."*

But then comes a shift in the sixth stanza, a little more than halfway through the poem. Something happened, perhaps the material success. The émigré in the new homeland, with a pause in the poem, somehow forgot his calling. The poet hesitates to describe exactly what happened, because it is scary and it hurts to talk about this topic. But then he calls on his own calling as a poet, saying that perhaps only the poet is capable of saying these words out loud, perhaps he has an honest responsibility to society. The next three stanzas detail the poet's criticisms. A set of parallel constructions express the poet's frustration: he spoke, they did not listen. He wrote, they did not read. He sang from the heart, they turned away. He woke a flame in their hearts, they stomped it out. He called them with ancient holy scripture and native words, and they went along instead with real estate salesmanship. Indeed, the language and structure evokes an almost biblical feeling of prophet vs. people.

Yet the poet does not resent his audience; instead, the last two stanzas speak of the rich hearts of the people, then evokes the thousand-year history of the Hungarian people, ending on a positive note, that despite the losses and storms of the Hungarian people, they did not give up. Although Kerecsendi wrote in Cleveland, an ocean away from Hungary, he is now accepted into the Hungarian literary canon as a solid reputable poet. He suffered from Alzheimers for ten years before his death in 1990.

Another prolific Cleveland writer was István Eszterhás, who wrote mostly fiction. He was born in 1907 in Kispest, Hungary. He studied law in Budapest and was an accomplished and prolific writer at a relatively young age, publishing six works in Hungary between 1935 and 1942. He spent time in DP camps before arriving in New York, then continued writing after arriving in Cleveland in 1950. With a few exceptions, most of his books were novels self-published in Cleveland, of which there were 14.[67]

Some of his novels take place in his native Hungary and describe idyllic village life with humor and pathos. Others describe life as a refugee, coming to America, and being Hungarian in the United States. Some of his works delve into the historical fiction realm of Revolutionary War America or Turkish rule in Hungary. His memoir *Száműzött a szabadság igájában* [Exiled in the yoke of freedom] tells of his decades of work editing the Cleveland Hungarian newspaper *Katolikus Magyarok Vasárnapja* and includes insightful ruminations on being a refugee vs. being an émigré.

Two of his novels can serve as case studies of what topics were important to Cleveland Hungarians in the 1980s. *A bíboros és a rendőr* [The cardinal and the cop] (1985) is dedicated to the memory of Cardinal Joseph Mindszenty. It is a fictional account of what Mindszenty might have been thinking before and during his decision to leave the American embassy in 1971 after 15 years of self-imposed house arrest and exile. The book's chapters show an uncanny insight into the historical details and political nuances of the time, whether of the Hungarian government or of the Catholic Church. Considering that Eszterhás never lived under communism, his work shows a mastery of the ideological language of the times, as well as a mastery of the psychology of a deeply spiritual man with full realization of his historical fate. In addition to showing a keen understanding of political and ideological nuance, his novel also displays an emotional nationalism, albeit one steeped in empathy for the Hungarian communists as people, doing the best they can in difficult situations. Eszterhás shows sympathy and an understanding of humanity, the mark of a true writer.

Another work full of empathy and several levels of meaning is *A hézag*, published in 1983, which could translate as the rift, or the gap, or the chasm. The subtitle is "satire – in the form of a novel,"[68] and the author's note on the inside cover specifically states the moral of the story: the overall point is to caution Hungarian-American readers about language use: they should not mix English with their language. But the novel is also directed at the iron bridles that Hungarian speakers face in Romania, Slovakia, Serbia, and Ukraine. This novel has stood the test of time, for its lessons can also be understood to apply to today's Hungary, in which English words are mixed often and freely with native Hungarian, often to the consternation of older emigrants in the United States who see such language use as an adulteration. But the novel is far more than just a linguistic warning. Eszterhás knows and understands not only the perspective of the average resident of the Buckeye Road neighborhood in the 1970s and 1980s, but he also sees the fine machinations of both Hungarian and American media, and the ideological and psychological motivations of Hungarian-Americans, as well as of political operatives in Hungary. Again, what makes Eszterhás stand out is that though he did not experience life under communism, he captured its essences and details perfectly.

The novel's basic plot line is that a communist operative in Hungary hatches a plan to fleece his American-Hungarian relative for the sake of socialism, and travels to Cleveland to put his plan into effect, with the full blessing of communist authorities. To do so, however, he must play the stupid tourist so as not to show his true identity, that of a true believer in communism. The humor of the novel lies not only in its multiple levels of meaning (e.g., the dramatic irony of the reader realizing the sheer stupidity of the truly clueless narrator acting as a clueless tourist who stumbles over the most basic of linguistic issues) but also in the difficulty of someone from Hungary understanding Hunglish, Hungarian with many English words mixed in.

Already in the first chapter the reader is introduced to Eszterhás' mastery of the ideological language of Kádár's times, when the narrator tells of his plan to steal his relative's money by enticing her to retire back to Hungary: "Yes, native land! Which is important to emphasize, because today the party really pushes the 'native land' expression instead of 'homeland,' especially in the direction of our compatriots living abroad, who we don't want to accept into our socialist homeland, but we do allow them to vacation in the native land. This is smart, they really figured this out, homeland nix for the Westerners, but every fascist, half-fascist, or fascist-seeming Hungarian can come to vacation in the native land, with hard currency of course, as vacationers."[69]

Later the narrator, after being warned at home not to read émigré newspapers, curiously takes one into his hands in Cleveland and immediately regrets it. It is full of lies, and he is amazed that they are allowed to print such falsehoods. Here Eszterhás reveals his mastery of language and of parallel layers of meaning. For the falsehoods that shock the narrator are actually the truth, conveniently ignored or labeled as lies by the propaganda of the Kádár regime. This comical, not-too-smart narrator unwittingly reveals insightful truths not only about Cold War politics but about propaganda as well. Yet his words are tempered with a sense of humanity, with understanding and empathy toward the narrator's condition and background.

In the end, the narrator returns to Hungary without his aunt's money. As he lands in Budapest, the same feeling engulfs him that all returning Hungarians experience. "Coming home from the West, whoever is Hungarian and steps off the plane onto native soil, at *Ferihegy* everyone's steps weaken, as if the dear native soil were to actually reel underfoot ... everyone feels this who goes West and returns via *Ferihegy* airport."[70] The narrator refers to a specific nostalgic feeling, but the reader cannot help but wonder if Eszterhás is not in fact referring to the expanded horizons of the traveler, that native Hungarians are not as confident after meeting émigrés, perhaps because they have been exposed to a different sort of Hungarian identity, one sustained and maintained in freedom and material prosperity.

Indeed, the ending of the novel is also quite telling. While trying to understand the rhetoric of the comrade sent from Moscow to indoctrinate the Interior Ministry employees, the narrator realizes that there is a rift, a gap, a chasm between Hungarians (the spacing of the final six lines of the novel is important, for it slows the reader down, emphasizing each and every word):

Original	Translation
MI A HÉZAG?	WHAT THE HELL?
	[with a pun on the word rift]
Ja. A hézag.	Yeah. The rift.
Sok a hézag köztünk.	Many rifts between/among us.
És egyre nől.	And constantly growing.
A sok hézag.	The many rifts.
Köztünk.	Between us.

But the final word of the novel not only means "between us," as in separating us, but it also carries another meaning, that of togetherness, with connotations of bridges between us, or across us. Thus the end is positive, emphasizing the togetherness and sense of common identity that unites Hungarians, whether they are communists and live in Budapest, or anti-communist and live in Cleveland. And that is the hallmark of true literature, which unites and highlights our common humanity. Eszterhás was indeed a master fiction writer. He was, however, investigated by the US Office of Special Investigations in 1990 for possible war crimes, and it was then that his 1936 book *Nemzetpolitika* [Nationality policy] came to light. He was almost deported, and charges of its anti-Semitism caused a rift between Eszterhás and his son Joe, the Hollywood screenwriter. According to his son, Eszterhás regretted having written the book.[71] His last book was published in 1998, a work of poetry, and he died in 2001.

In addition to the writers living in Cleveland, also telling is the type of visitor that Cleveland's Hungarians attracted to their cultural gatherings through the years. The Hungarian Association Congress, a scholarly conference still being held yearly in Cleveland, attracted better-known Hungarian émigré authors such as Albert Wass, and the novelist Áron Gábor was a regular visitor to the conference.[72] Perhaps because Gábor's own life contained many parallels and similar experiences to many in the DP and 1956 generations, e.g., imprisonment under the communist regime, forced labor under the Soviets, and emigration, and because he wrote about them so vividly, Cleveland Hungarians could easily relate to his writings. A 1968 original recording of his voice when he addressed the November conference shows his and the community's sentiments; he follows the writer Albert Wass.[73] In the introduction to Gábor's speech, János Nádas, the organizer of the conference, says that Gábor not only comes to "appall us, but to strengthen us in our perseverance, that we can all be advocates for Hungarian issues and for the millions locked behind the Iron Curtain."[74] This sentiment summarized the atmosphere of Cleveland's Hungarian literary circles during the Cold War: anti-communist and of strong Hungarian feeling.

These forums of Hungarian writers from all over the world convening in Cleveland considered themselves first and foremost Hungarian. Europe, Australia, South America, or the United States were their places of residence, but meeting other Hungarians reinforced their identities as being primarily Hungarian. Not knowing their newly adopted countries' languages, by day they worked mostly in factories. On the weekends, they could recreate the intellectual life they had been forced to leave behind in Hungary. Their communication built, sustained, and transformed their identities, and these conferences allowed participants and local audience members an opportunity to reinforce the Hungarian aspects of their lives.

Áron Gábor was born in 1911 in the Hungarian city Kaposvár. He earned a law degree at Pázmány University, then became a reporter for two liberal newspapers, *8 Órai Újság* [8 o'clock newspaper] and *Reggel* [Morning]. He was a war correspondent during the Second World War, writing a book about his experiences along the Don River on the Soviet Front, *Túl a Sztálin Vonalon* [Beyond the Stalin line], a book for which he was sentenced to death. As the general secretary of the Hungarian Red Cross after the war, he was arrested by Soviet authorities. The author's account of his 17 months imprisonment by Soviet authorities while still on Hungarian soil developed into his first novel, *Az embertől keletre* [East of man], which later became the first of a four-volume series, all of which were written as autobiographical fiction.

His sentence was unexplainedly commuted to five-years forced labor and life exile by the Moscow Special Committee, and he was shipped to Siberia. Gábor later wrote his second novel, *Szögletes szabadság* [Freedom framed], about his years in the gulag. Upon release from the gulag he went to the nearest police station, trying to get home. "Where is your passport?" they asked him. "Passport? I was brought here to Siberia in a cattle wagon—no passport," he replied. Even in the great Soviet empire everyone needs a passport to travel, they told him, denying him his way home. Thus he spent an additonal ten years as a legal resident of a Russian village in Siberia; his observations living amongst the Russian people he detailed in *Évszázados emberek* [Centenarians]. After 15 years of imprisonment and exile in Siberia, he was allowed to return home and attempted to reintegrate himself into the post-world-war communist Hungary of 1960. This Hungary of 1960 had experienced and already repressed the 1956 Revolution and was well on its way to goulash communism under János Kádár. Reintegration was difficult for Gábor, and after five years of trying to fit in, he emigrated to West Germany, smuggling his manuscript of *Az embertől keletre*, which was published in Munich two years later.

He continued writing the rest of the novels in the series while also publishing regularly in émigré periodicals and visiting Hungarian communities dispersed around the globe, including North and South America, travelling as far as Australia, and presenting at Cleveland's Hungarian Association conference numerous times. He died in 1982, but he is still mostly unknown in his native Hungary.

When Gábor addressed a Cleveland Hungarian audience in 1968, he alluded to the success of their Cleveland Hungarian social institutions, just as the writer Albert Wass had done several minutes earlier, and told them that they owed it [to Hungary] to maintain the facets of the thousand-year-old Hungarian history and culture that they had saved [as refugees], and not only to gather at Hungarian conferences but also to engage Americans politically, to take advantage of their rights as American citizens, to tell what they knew about communism, that there was a drama on the other side of the Atlantic.[75] This perspective, that émigré Hungarians had to speak up for those still behind the Iron Curtain, was an often-repeated theme among Cleveland Hungarians during the Cold War, and an oft-repeated theme in Áron Gábor's speeches. Thus one can see that Hungarian literary life and publishing flourished throughout the Cold War.

Language Use and Instruction

The members of Cleveland's Hungarian community who are active tend to have decent Hungarian language skills. Indeed, the author's sociological survey administered in 2017 to Cleveland's Hungarians yielded the following summarized results: the great majority (70–75 percent) characterized their language skills as "strong", and an additional 15–23 percent as "medium."

Understanding spoken Hungarian

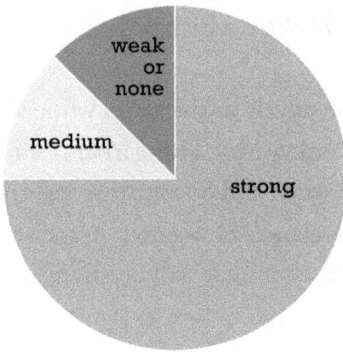

weak or none

medium

strong

Ability to speak Hungarian

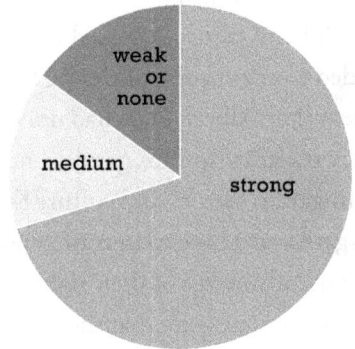

weak or none

medium

strong

Ability to read Hungarian

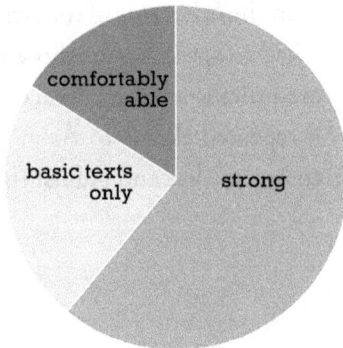

comfortably able

basic texts only

strong

But how did these Cleveland Hungarians learn and maintain their language skills? Beyond the family, the easiest way to ascertain the strength of an ethnic community is to examine opportunities for its language instruction, and the means by which it passes on the language to each successive generation, for language is an important part of culture and identity formation. Even before the founding of Cleveland's current Hungarian school, Hungarian language instruction was alive and well in Cleveland. Elementary schools with large concentrations of Hungarians began providing instruction in Hungarian at St. Elizabeth's Church in 1893, St. Emeric's in 1905, and St. Margaret in 1922. Another school was the Kossuth school, started in 1954, which taught Hungarian in the evenings at the East Side Hungarian Lutheran Church.[76] Over time and due to the forces of Americanization and assimilation, this language instruction gradually withered, being replaced by summer courses taught by the priests and ministers in the various churches in the early 1950s, and then by the Cleveland Hungarian school starting in 1958, along with later smaller startups. Their language and identity was a form of sustainable ethnicity, by virtue of constant maintenance and expression of Hungarian communication, whether on Sundays at church or on other days in secular organizations.

One direct precursor to Cleveland's Hungarian school was Hungarian instruction started by DP refugees in 1951, held at St. Margaret. Organized by Endre Román, it had about 50 students, and declined in the late 1950s. The Cleveland Hungarian School was then started in 1958, when Gábor Papp, as scoutmaster of a local Hungarian scout troop, saw that the language skills of his scouts were beginning to lapse.[77] He thus decided to begin ongoing weekly Hungarian instruction, and ended up directing the school for 30 years. Instruction was and is for two hours on Monday evenings, with volunteer parents being the teachers. Instruction begins at the kindergarten level with games, songs, and the alphabet, continuing at the elementary level with reading, writing, basic Hungarian history, geography, and literature, and culminating with high school-level exams. A poem recitation contest is an ongoing part of the curriculum, as are basic musical and religious concepts. Recently the school added beginning language instruction for adults, and there are now four classes exclusively for adults, in addition to the nine levels for heritage speakers. The school charges a nominal tuition of about $100 per year, which includes books and teaching materials, and covers rented classroom space. Enrollment for school year 2017/2018 was 57 students and 19 adults. Over the course of its 60 plus years, the school has had several homes, including renting classroom space from various public schools or residing in church basements. Recently it has been headquartered at St. Emeric church, also using the rooms of the adjacent Scout Center. The heritage language school is currently directed by Judy Szentkiralyi.[78]

Hungarian language instruction in Cleveland also included that of John Palasics, as well as of Fréda B. Kovács at Harvey Rice elementary school and of Ilona Vaskó and Ilona Sándor at St. Margaret church in the late 1970s, as well as two Hungarian schools on the city's East Side. One was the Reményik Sándor Magyar Iskola, which was formed as a result of a 1962 three-day Hungarian conference held at the lakeside Point Chautauqua. This school taught on average 50–60 Hungarian students until sickness and neighborhood disintegration led to its demise around 1967. The other school was the Gárdonyi Géza Magyar Iskola [Hungarian school named after a famous Hungarian writer], formed in 1969 by László Zala, the East Side Hungarian scoutmaster. White flight from the Buckeye neighborhood led to the slow demise of this school as well. Both schools were staffed by volunteers, mostly parents, and held class once a week. In the 1980s Bernadette Pavlish and Andrea Mészáros started an informal Hungarian school at a church on Ford Road, so they would not have to drive over to Cleveland's West Side to have their own children learn Hungarian. They worked with about 30 children, mostly aged six and seven years, for about six years.

A recent addition to Cleveland's volunteer Hungarian schools is that of the West Side Lutheran Church, formerly on West 98th Street. When her own son was two years old, in 2001, the Reverend Éva Tamásy started a small kindergarten so that he could spend time in a Hungarian environment with Hungarian friends. This small venture has since expanded and serves as a complementary venue to the original Hungarian School for those who wish for their children to receive additional Hungarian instruction on Thursday or Friday afternoons. About a dozen students attend as of 2017, with over half also attending the Hungarian School on Monday evenings at St. Emeric. Friday afternoons the first two classes are taught before scout meetings, allowing families to attend both this school and scout meetings on Friday evenings. Thursday evenings host the third, fourth, and seventh grades.

The most recent addition to Cleveland's volunteer Hungarian schools, thus bringing the total to three, is instruction held at the First Hungarian Reformed Church in Walton Hills. Led by the pastor's wife, Bea Krasznai, this school entails Sunday School for children during Hungarian-language church services, then a break for lunch or a snack, and then an hour of language instruction every Sunday. The students number about 20, split into three groups.

Transforming the identities of children, forming them from average monolingual Americans into bicultural and transnational Hungarian-Americans, is a perfect example of a communication theory of identity, as well as of the concept of a spiritual homeland: parents and volunteers try to impart a sense of belonging to the worldwide Hungarian diaspora in general and to Cleveland's local Hungarian community in particular.

Hungarian language instruction in Cleveland also includes the college level. In postsecondary education, József Reményi began teaching Hungarian literature in 1929 at Cleveland College, the adult education unit of Western Reserve University and Case School of Applied Science (today Case Western Reserve University). In the 1950s and 1960s, Dr. Ferenc Somogyi taught Hungarian art, literature, and culture under the auspices of the *Szent István Magyar Szabadegyetem* (a lecture series held at local Hungarian churches), *Magyar Önképzőkör* (a subdivision of the Hungarian Association), *Magyarságismereti Akadémia* (a two-year course also organized by the Hungarian Association), and he became the director of Hungarian Studies at Cleveland College. It was there that Hungarian language instruction was also offered by Ilona Vaskó.

Cleveland State University began offering Hungarian language courses in 1969 with Róbert Oszlányi. From 1974 to 1994 Theofil Lant taught Hungarian, and from the 1990s the program waned. The vacuum was filled by Lakeland Community College, where Imre Márkus, an engineer from Transylvania, taught as an adjunct faculty member from 1992 to 2012. Over 800 students took part in his courses over this 20 year period. In 2013, however, Cleveland State University's Hungarian program saw a resurgence, with the signing of an agreement between the University and the Fulbright Commission, which brought five Fulbright scholars from Hungary, one per academic year, from 2014 to 2018, each of whom taught beginning and intermediate Hungarian courses as well as courses about Hungarian culture. These Fulbright scholars were Rita Gárdosi, Dénes Mátyás, Péter Müller, Mónika Fodor, and Enikő Bús each of whom also took part in Cleveland's Hungarian community by giving lectures at the Hungarian Heritage Museum, teaching Monday evenings at the Hungarian School, and attending cultural events as well as teaching during the daytime at Cleveland State University.

New in terms of Hungarian language instruction in North America is Cleveland State University's newest online offering. Broken into two Hungarian language courses for beginners, the courses were developed in 2015 with the help of a Hungary Inititatives Foundation grant, and it attract students from all over North America. The courses are offered through the Continuing Education part of the university and are available to the general public. The courses offer lectures and assignments completely online, so that no attendance is necessary. The unique feature, however, is the use of 25 short instructional films shot at Hungarian locations throughout Cleveland, using native heritage speakers in everyday language situations. These range from domestic household activities (morning and evening greetings within the family, arguing over bathroom usage, cooking in the kitchen), to campus social pleasantries, to shopping at the local Hungarian butcher at the West Side Market, and shopping or phone ordering from each of Cleveland's four Hungarian bakeries. Calling a Catholic priest and Lutheran minister and inquiring about church service times and asking for a hospital visit for sick grandparents, ordering and eating at the Balaton, Cleveland's premier Hungarian restaurant, and conversation during a grandparent visit also fall within the topics covered by the films. Since its inception, course enrollment has fluctuated between 11 and 21 online users per semester.

Although the numbers of children and students enrolled in Hungarian language instruction in the Cleveland area have waxed and wanted throughout the decades, what remains consistent is that there are dedicated parents and teachers who continue to provide instruction, who consider it valuable to impart the language to others. Each successive generation has a majority of its members who assimilate and lose the language, and each new wave of immigration tries again and again to retard the forces of language assimilation. Specific factors impacting language maintenance will be explored in the next chapter.

CHAPTER FIVE
Language Use Case Studies[79]

What is the relationship of Hungarian-Americans living in larger communities like Cleveland to their language? If only 5–7 percent of those reporting Hungarian ancestry in the greater Cleveland area report speaking the language in the household, then what exactly are the factors that influence their language maintenance? How is it that some are able to pass on their language to succeeding generations, but 93–95 percent do not? How exactly are they able to do it, and what role does the community play in it all?

Background and Methodology

Miklós Kontra has done extensive work in bilingualism and in sociolinguistics, and Csilla Bartha examined the language patterns and use of symbols of identity in Detroit's Hungarian community, but the most recent work in sociolinguistics is by Katalin Pintz. In an extensive study of a Hungarian-American community very similar to Cleveland, Pintz looked at New Brunswick, New Jersey's Hungarian community and found several factors that impacted language and cultural maintenance. Among these were close-knit friendships among parents who valued education and their ethnicity, and taking an active part in the ethnic community. The families she studied tended to "speak Hungarian as much as they can among themselves and to their children. Many of them watch DVDs, television shows, and the news in Hungarian through cable TV or the internet. It is also an important factor for them to find a Hungarian spouse. Nevertheless, they cannot and do not want to exclude themselves from the American cultural sphere."[80] This type of characterization contrasts with the ethnic neighborhoods of forty or fifty years ago, both in New Brunswick and in Cleveland, in which entire city blocks had families of mainly one ethnicity. Today, ethnic Hungarian communities in any given American city tend to stick together not geographically, but rather culturally, gathering on a regular basis from throughout the suburbs, perhaps weekly or more frequently, to take part in a city's ethnic activities.

Pintz also found that although some of the respondents did not like being forced to speak Hungarian as children, they nevertheless all "value this kind of parental education, for they would also like to pass on their mother tongue to their children."[81] Parental involvement and consistency was definitely a factor in keeping the Hungarian language alive. But perhaps even more important than the parents, or rather, due to the involvement of the parents, the community itself as a social environment reinforced and became the determining factor of ethnicity.

New Brunswick's Hungarians, she found—whether attending Hungarian church services, folk dance rehearsals, scout meetings, a Montessori kindergarten, or the weekend Hungarian school—are known for the high level of Hungarian that is spoken there. The main reason for this is the fact that "the members of the community form a close-knit unit based on friendships and family ties. They organize cultural events several times a week, ranging from scouting to Hungarian language education and dance classes. The members of the community are active in several Hungarian activities simultaneously."[82] There are many similarities between New Brunswick's Hungarian community and Cleveland's Hungarian community. Both consist of fairly close-knit groups based on friendship and family ties, both organize cultural events regularly, both include scouting and dance groups and Hungarian language education, and the experiences related in Pintz's study are common to many people's experiences growing up Hungarian in Cleveland.

A case study approach can shed more light on assimilation regarding language use. If, as the comparison of Hungarian ancestry to the Hungarian language spoken in the household affirms, the odds are that most Hungarian-Americans will lose their language in one generation, what then are some factors that allow the tiny fraction to maintain their language? Many times they are able to maintain the language even in the second and third generations, in spite of overwhelming odds favoring their assimilation. What sets these people apart from the rest, and what lessons can be drawn from their insights?

Eighteen Hungarians living in the suburbs of Cleveland, Ohio, were chosen for case studies. Although the sample is small, the interviews were quite in-depth and yielded valuable insights about maintaining language into the second and third generations after immigration. Study participants were chosen for their similar Hungarian-American backgrounds to provide a typical experience of growing up Hungarian in Cleveland, yet their backgrounds and life circumstances provided a fairly broad spectrum of family immigration eras, including offsprings of the DP and 1956 generations and more recent immigration. Their Hungarian language proficiencies and primary language spoken at home also varied, as did their degrees of Hungarian ancestry: the parents of most were both Hungarian, but a few had only one Hungarian parent; several had Hungarian spouses and several had American spouses. Fifteen participants were born in the Cleveland area, with two brought to Cleveland as toddlers, so almost all spent their entire childhoods in the Cleveland area. One interviewee came to Cleveland as an adult, but her four children were all born in the Cleveland area and take part in its Hungarian community.

Six separate group discussions were held, with three participants each (one group had four and one had two participants due to scheduling conflicts) plus the researcher. Small-group discussions were chosen to allow a degree of intimacy that comes from being around other participants from similar backgrounds, and to allow study participants to hear each other's answers, agree or disagree with each other, and spawn new thoughts based on what they heard from each other. Listening to each other answer the same questions allowed study participants to reflect upon what was being said and decide whether that applied to them or not. The group discussions were recorded and transcribed word for word for later analysis, with the first round taking place in the greater Cleveland area during October 2010, and the second round in June and July 2017. As the writing and analysis of the data progressed, study participants were given rough drafts of the qualitative study results and given an opportunity to revise and add to comments given during their group discussions.

One of the six groups consisted of three siblings, and all three members of this group have their own children and the perspective of more than twenty years' distance from their own childhood, which allowed for more introspection both about their family upbringing and also a considered viewpoint about their own decisions on imparting language and culture to their children.

Two of the groups lived in the same suburban neighborhood; thus their American environmental factors were the same. They graduated from or at the time of the interview attended the same suburban public high school, located about a half-hour's drive from Cleveland's downtown in a middle-class area. Another group had three members all attending the same suburban high school in Lakewood, an inner-ring suburb of Cleveland. Teenagers still in the process of forming their own cultural identities were chosen for four of the six groups because of the possible insights they could contribute, being in the midst of their own transformations; the mixture of teenaged and adult participants offered both fresh, recent insights as well as considered, mature reflection in their revelations. The experiences of all eighteen study participants, although unique in their own way, are fairly typical of Hungarian-Americans who are an active part of Cleveland's Hungarian communities. In selecting research subjects in this manner, one realizes that "observing life from separate yet overlapping angles makes the researcher more hesitant to leap to conclusions and encourages more nuanced analysis."[83]

The purpose of the study was to gain a deeper understanding of the factors impacting second-language maintenance and cultural identity formation in an ethnic community, specifically those factors influencing individuals growing up Hungarian in Cleveland. Before the interviewing started, the participants or their legal guardians signed a statement of informant consent to give them a chance to understand the research study goals and to clarify and safeguard their legal rights. The participants took part willingly, and it was easy to establish rapport with them. The rapport and the participants' openness were reinforced by earlier relationships; some of them grew up with the author, others have been known since their childhood, and some were former students. The recorded group discussions ranged from 40 to 90 minutes, and the primary language was English, although Hungarian vocabulary was also used sporadically by the participants, depending on the concepts discussed. One of the 18 participants chose to remain anonymous and was given a pseudonym (marked with an asterisk*) for the purposes of the publication of the study's results.

The youngest participant in the first group was Gabe (Gábor) Kovács, a sixteen-year-old eleventh-grader at the time of his interview. His father was born in Hungary and emigrated to the United States when he was 12 or 13 and thus spent his formative years in Cleveland. Gabe's father works in the electrical and computer field and has owned several businesses. His mother was born in a suburb of Cleveland and has never been to Hungary. She works in the healthcare industry as a physical therapist. Both parents were actively involved in Cleveland's Hungarian scouting movement. As a young child, Gabe's parents enrolled him, along with his younger siblings, in the scout troop on Friday evenings and in the Hungarian school on Monday evenings. The family attends a local Hungarian church on holidays like Christmas and Easter, and on major events such as baptisms and confirmations, but on average Sundays attends the suburban American parish church near their house. Gabe also was a member of the Hungarian Scout Folk Ensemble, the scout dance group which meets on Tuesday evenings. Gabe's language skills have remained pretty consistent throughout his childhood, understanding and speaking fluently with his reading and writing skills somewhat weaker but nevertheless competent.

Matt (Máté) Kobus attended the same neighborhood Catholic school as Gabe, and at the time of the interview was in grade eleven at the same suburban public high school as Gabe. Matt's mother was born in the Cleveland area; her father came to the United States after 1956 and her mother arrived in 1964. She also attended Hungarian school and was involved in Hungarian scouting as she grew up in Cleveland. Matt's biological father is American, a nurse anesthesiologist, and he was not too keen on Matt's mother speaking Hungarian to him as a young child, so she did not force the issue.

Later, Matt's parents divorced and his mother remarried. Matt's stepfather, an engineer who is not Hungarian, tolerates Matt's language use to some extent. Matt's language use improved dramatically as he grew older; at first he only understood and could produce a few words. Then around the third grade his school friend Gabe kept telling him about how cool Hungarian scouting was, but to join one needed a better command of the Hungarian language, so he improved to be able to join the scouting movement. According to his mother, she never forced him to use Hungarian; his improvement was of his own accord. Lately he visited Hungary with his grandmother, and now he switches to Hungarian when he speaks to his grandmother on the phone. Matt was also a member of the Hungarian Scout Folk Ensemble, the scout dance group of Cleveland.

Megan Ramsey, the third participant in the group discussion, is Gabe's first cousin; his father and her mother are siblings. Megan was studying to be a dental hygienist at a local community college and graduated from Gabe and Matt's high school in 2008. Her father, a carpet and tile installer, was an American of Scotch-Irish and French-Lebanese descent and spoke no Hungarian in the household. Her mother was born in Hungary but finished her university studies after emigrating to Cleveland. She is an engineer and lived for a long time with Megan and her own mother, Megan's Hungarian grandmother. Megan did not attend Hungarian school but did attend Hungarian scouting as she grew up and was also a member of the scout dance group during high school. She has been to Hungary twice: once when she was four years old and once when she was 12. Megan's Hungarian language use remained fairly constant as she grew up, understanding and speaking fluently, and reading and writing at a slightly weaker level, but still competent.

The second group also consisted of three members who attended the same suburban high school. Jennifer Hegyi was the youngest member, in the twelfth grade at the time of the interview. She never attended Hungarian school and was only involved in the scouting movement for one year, but she did have a private Hungarian language tutor for about a year when she was 12 or 13. She visited Hungary with her family various times as she grew up. Her parents were both born in Hungary and emigrated to Cleveland as adults in 1995; her father is in the roofing business and her mother is a nanny, and both speak Hungarian in the household. Jennifer understands and speaks Hungarian, but in Hungarian conversations with the author she had a tendency to respond only in English. Her reading and writing skills are weak, according to her own account, and she could not pronounce the name of the Hungarian town that she was born in.

Samantha Dévai* attended the same high school as Jennifer, graduating in 2007. She earned a biology degree in college and was in her first year of medical school at the time of the interview. She was involved in the Hungarian scouting movement from age five until the end of high school at age 18. She was also a member of the scout dance group during her high school years; she only attended Hungarian school for one year, however, in the eighth grade at age 13. Her parents both grew up in Hungary and emigrated to the United States in 1982 but still speak Hungarian in the household. Her mother works in child daycare and her father in maintenance. She has been to Hungary three or four times for ten days each time, and took part in a month-long tour of Hungary organized by the scouts when she was a teenager. Samantha's Hungarian proficiency remained somewhat constant during her childhood, remaining fluent in speaking, reading, and writing, but she has noticed a regression since she moved away for her college studies.

Samantha's cousin is Vivian Varjas; their mothers are sisters. Vivian's parents were also born and raised in Hungary and emigrated to the United States in the early 1970s. Her mother is a bookkeeper and her father works in maintenance. She graduated in 2002 from the suburban high school of her cousin, attending college and earning a special education degree. She now works as a special education teacher. Vivian never attended Hungarian school and started Hungarian scouting around the third grade, continuing until the end of high school. She also was a member of the scout dance group all through high school. Her Hungarian proficiency has remained stable, with solid fluency in understanding, speaking, reading, and writing.

The third group, consisting of three siblings, held the longest group discussion, probably because of their advanced age and maturity as compared to the other study participants, and because of their inherent familiarity and rapport with each other, having grown up in the same household. Their parents emigrated to the United States after 1956, their mother at age 13 with her parents, and their father after spending three and a half years in Austria before arriving in Cleveland. Their father worked mostly in a factory. The family attended a Hungarian Catholic church on major holidays and family events, but usually attended the local Catholic church because of the children attending parochial schools. Grandparents on the father's side would occasionally come to visit from Hungary for several months at a time. All three siblings took part in numerous Hungarian community activities as they were growing up in the Cleveland area.

Ann (Anci) Graber, the oldest of the siblings, grew up in the suburb of Westlake and attended Magnificat High School, a suburban Catholic school for girls. She started her involvement in the scouting movement as a young child and joined the scout dance group during high school. Upon growing up, she also assumed responsibility as costume caretaker for the dance group, and was also the treasurer for the Hungarian girl scout troop. She married Steve Graber, also the child of 1956 immigrants. He had an upbringing similar to hers, attending Hungarian school, Hungarian churches, and taking major leadership roles in scouting and the dance group. Steve's brothers and sister, although they were also born in the United States, speak, read and write fluent Hungarian; his sister's children also do, and they are involved in Cleveland's Hungarian community. Steve's brother, Richard Graber, founded Cleveland's Hungarian dance troupe Csárdás. Steve and Ann have three children, all of whom also speak Hungarian and also attended Hungarian school, scouting, and were members of the scout dance group. Their oldest daughter at the time of the interview was 22 years old and a college student, their second daughter was 21 years old and also in college, and their son was 16 years old and in high school. Ann works as a computer teacher at a local Catholic elementary school. Ann's Hungarian proficiency is excellent with the exception of her spelling; she attributes this to never having attended Hungarian school.

Karl (Karcsi) Patay attended St. Ignatius High School and owns his own construction and landscaping business. He was involved in Hungarian scouting from a young age, attended Hungarian school and was a member of the scout dance group. His Hungarian language skills, although fluent, were somewhat weak in reading and writing. In recent years his oral language skills have increased significantly due to his working daily with recent Hungarian immigrants. His wife Denise, an American with no Hungarian background, attempted to learn Hungarian early in their marriage, but today almost no Hungarian is spoken in the household. Their children are both boys, aged 13 and 9 at the time of the interview, and apart from some rudimentary words, neither speaks Hungarian. Karl is very proud of his Hungarian heritage and visits Hungary every 3–5 years.

Susan (Zsuzs) Linder is the youngest of the siblings. Also attending Magnificat High School, Susan was involved in scouting from an early age, attended Hungarian school only later, and also joined the scout dance group during high school. For three years she was the scoutmaster of the Hungarian girl scout troop, an influential position of responsibility in Cleveland's Hungarian community. Her husband at the time of the interview, Dave Linder, is an American with no Hungarian background. At home Dave speaks English to the children and Susan speaks Hungarian, with the common language being English. Their three children, twin boys aged 12 and a daughter aged 9 at the time of the interview, understood and spoke, read, and wrote Hungarian, and they attended the Hungarian school and scouts. Susan's Hungarian proficiency is excellent with near-native fluency.

The next group consisted of only two participants, both parents to multiple second and third generation children who still maintain the Hungarian language. Krisztina Tábor was born in 1958 in Cleveland; her parents arrived to Cleveland in 1951 as DP refugees, and her father, Sándor Szabadkai, had a local Hungarian radio program. As a child she was active in the scouts, *Regös* group, and Hungarian school, and as an adult she took leadership roles as director or camp director in all three. She attended college and currently works as a branch manager in a local bank. Her husband, Andreas, is Hungarian and German, and they have five children, all of whose first language was Hungarian. Three of her children have American spouses, but both of her young grandchildren speak Hungarian and are involved in Cleveland's Hungarian community. Krisztina's Hungarian proficiency is excellent with near-native fluency.

Livia Karetka was the only one of the study participants who did not grow up in Cleveland; she was born in Budapest in 1977 and arrived to Cleveland as an adult to work as a nanny and to study. She has a degree in music from a

Study Participants

Participant	Where grew up	Where parents grew up	Parental Hungarian knowledge	Hungarian language skills	Attended scouts
Chmielewski, Emese	Cleveland	Mom Hungary, dad Cleveland	Mom fluent, dad not	Fluent	Yes
Chmielewski, Erika	Cleveland	Mom Hungary, dad Cleveland	Mom fluent, dad not	Fluent	Yes
Dévai, Samantha*	Cleveland	Both parents Hungary	Both fluent	Fluent	Yes
Duna, Andrew	Cleveland	Both parents Cleveland	Both fluent	Fluent	Yes
Dunay, Sofia	Cleveland	Mom Hungary, dad Cleveland	Both fluent	Fluent	Yes
Graber, Ann	Cleveland	Both parents Cleveland	Both fluent	Fluent	Yes
Hegyi, Jennifer	Cleveland	Both parents Hungary	Both fluent	Weak	No
Karetka, Livia	Budapest	Both parents Hungary	Both fluent	Fluent	No
Kobus, Matt	Cleveland	Mom Cleveland, dad elsewhere	Mom fluent, dad not	Fluent	Yes
Kovács, Gabe	Cleveland	Mom Cleveland, dad Hungary/ Cleveland	Both fluent	Fluent	yes
Linder, Susan	Cleveland	Both parents Hungary	Both fluent	Fluent	Yes
Pál, Greg	Cleveland	Dad Hungary, mom USA, stepmom Hungary	Dad fluent, mom not, stepmom yes	Fluent	Yes
Patay, Karl	Cleveland	Both parents Hungary	Both fluent	Fluent	Yes
Ramsey, Megan	Cleveland	Mom Hungary, dad USA	Mom fluent, dad not	Fluent	Yes
Sundem, Sándor	Cleveland	Mom Cleveland, dad elsewhere	Mom fluent, dad not	Fluent	Yes
Tábor, Kiki	Cleveland	Both parents Cleveland	Both fluent	Fluent	Yes
Tábor, Krisztina	Cleveland	Both parents Hungary	Both fluent	Fluent	Yes
Varjas, Vivian	Cleveland	Both parents Hungary	Both fluent	Fluent	Yes

* Pseudonym

Hungarian university and took some courses in Cleveland in accounting and economics. She works as a banquet manager. Her husband came to Cleveland in 1989 from Petri, a small town in the Hungarian region of Transylvania, in Romania, at age 11 with his brother, two years older, and their parents. Her children are 14, 12, 10, and 8 years old, and all speak Hungarian fluently; they speak both Hungarian and English at home.

The fifth group all currently attend or recently graduated from Lakewood High School. Sándor Sundem just graduated; his grandparents on his mother's side were born in Austria and arrived in Cleveland in the early 1950s as members of the DP generation. His mother grew up in Chicago's Hungarian community; later, as a US military spouse, she taught him and his four siblings Hungarian at their various duty stations. Sándor arrived in Cleveland in 2011 at age 10 and immediately became immersed in scouts and Hungarian school and later *Regös*, but he had previously attended Hungarian language school camps directed by his mother. Their family attends a Hungarian church and his American dad had fully supported his children's Hungarian language instruction. Sándor's Hungarian fluency is self-described at about 50–60 percent of his English fluency; he can express himself but sometimes finds it difficult, and he reads more slowly in Hungarian than in English. He attends DePaul University.

Andrew Duna was born in Lakewood, and both of his parents also grew up in Cleveland's Hungarian community; his grandparents were 1956 refugees on his mother's side, and DP refugees on his father's side. He is in his senior year of high school; his Hungarian is at about 65–70 percent, he says, and has noticed that his vocabulary and fluency has decreased, but he can read Hungarian pretty well.

Andrew's first cousin is Sofia Dunay; their fathers are brothers. Sofia, the youngest interviewee at 15 years of age, was born in Budapest but arrived in Lakewood at age 3. She is a junior in high school and is also involved with the scouts and the *Regös* group. Her mother was born in Hungary and her father in Cleveland, and both sides of the family speak fluent Hungarian. Her Hungarian fluency is at about 80 percent, and her reading and writing is about 75 percent, and she mentioned sometimes missing the connecting words that make one fluent.

The last group discussion had a diversity of members the other groups lacked. It included Gergely (Greg) Pál, sisters Emese and Erika Chmielewski, and Krisztina Tábor, niece of the elder Krisztina Tábor, hereafter referred to as Kiki. Gergely Pál is 17 years old, born in Cleveland, and a senior at St. Ignatius High School. His father arrived in the United States from Hungary to intern as a veterinary student, and he met an American receptionist whom he married. His father moved to the Cleveland area in 1993. After his first wife passed away, he remarried, and Gergely's stepmother is from Hungary, so Hungarian is spoken exclusively in the home. Gergely considers his language competency in Hungarian to be about 80 percent, because most of the language spoken at home involves household terms, so he is more fluent in English. Gergely is involved in scouting, was a member of the Csárdás dance group and attended the Hungarian school, and is a member of the Hungarian Scout Folk Ensemble.

Emese is 21 years old, born in Cleveland, and just finished a degree from Capital University in Columbus, OH, in French with minors in Biology and Chemistry. Erika is 19 years old, also born in Cleveland, and is halfway through an undergraduate degree in urban design at Cleveland State University. Their father is an American of Polish heritage who spent a summer abroad in Hungary and met their mother in Budapest in 1989. Their mother came to the U.S.A. in 1992 and they were married in 1993. Both sisters attended Cleveland's Hungarian schools and various Hungarian churches, were involved in scouting from a young age, and participated in two dance groups, Csárdás and the Scout Folk Ensemble. In Hungarian school, their father was a student, their mother taught, and the sisters were students, so it was a family event. In 2007, when she was 12 years old, Emese went abroad to live with her aunt in Budapest, attending school from August to November. Erika also spent several months in Budapest attending school at a later time, but she lived in a dormitory. Although Emese spent the last four years away from Cleveland's Hungarian community going to college in Columbus, she writes to her grandmother once a week and speaks daily to her mother on the telephone, so she considers herself equally fluent in Hungarian, English, and French. Erika's playlist on her phone is almost exclusively Hungarian, but her self-described fluency is at 60 percent, because she doesn't know all the textbook terms. She spends about 85 percent of her time with Hungarian friends, who speak very mixed Hungarian and English when together.

Krisztina Tábor, or Kiki, as she is known among her friends, is 31 years old and was born in Cleveland. She is self-employed as a nanny and takes college courses. Her grandparents fled the communists at the end of the Second World War; her mother's parents spent time in Austria as refugees, and her father's grandmother, whose husband died in the war, was German, as was Kiki's grandmother. Her paternal grandfather was shot and wounded at a train station in Hungary during the war, got onto a Red Cross hospital train, and ended up in Germany at the end of the war. He came to the U.S.A. and met his German wife in Cleveland. Both of Kiki's parents grew up in Cleveland's Hungarian community, meeting through the Hungarian scouts and folk dance. Kiki grew up in the same environment, with scouts and folk dancing, and she is currently responsible for all of the folk costumes for the Scout Folk Ensemble. She spent several years attending school in Hungary through its Balassi Institute, and today reads and writes Hungarian at least three times a week, and speaks the language on a daily basis.

The eighteen study participants in their three group discussions yielded over 38,000 words of data. According to the traditions of qualitative ethnographic research, their answers were coded into similar categories. Rubin and Rubin define coding as a "process of grouping interviewee's responses into categories that bring together the similar ideas, concepts, or themes one has discovered."[84]

Three major themes emerged from their responses. The first theme was the impact of parenting on language maintenance, both the role of their own parents as well as their own subsequent actions as parents. The second theme, repeated quite often and quite emphatically and emotionally, was the influence of their friends and peers through organized events in the Hungarian community, mostly through the scouting movement. The third major theme was the value of speaking a second language and the respondents' ties to their Hungarian culture as a sense of identity. Additional secondary topics that emerged from the discussions were reasons that people did not maintain their ethnic language, and also the role of American spouses in supporting or discouraging language maintenance.

The Importance of Parenting

The interviewees strongly identified their parents as one of the most important factors impacting their language competence, even though some parents were of different generations, i.e., some of their parents were born in the United States, others had immigrated after 1956, and others much more recently. Parents had different reasons for speaking Hungarian to their children, but most of the interviewees, both at the beginning and end of the interviews, came back to their own parents and family as being the single biggest factor impacting their language use. The elder Krisztina Tábor voiced a typical household phenomenon of the 1960s and 1970s: "Growing up, it was all Hungarian; we never spoke English at home. In some ways it was forbidden, but I never would have thought of it. If my friends came over, my scout friends, we would speak English in secret, so our parents would not yell at us." Speaking of a generation later, Andrew Duna also alluded to what language was and wasn't allowed in his household: "When I was growing up, it was strictly Hungarian; that was the only language allowed in the house." Sándor Sundem had a slightly more flexible household, saying, "My dad was not Hungarian, so when he was home we were allowed to speak English to him, but when he was gone for work my mom would speak Hungarian to us so we could enrich our language skills." Sofi Dunay's parents also had a practical outlook after moving from Hungary: "Right after we moved my dad spoke English to us so we could learn the language, but after having been here for several years Hungarian comes harder, so we try to speak that mostly; at home it's 50-50."

One of the reasons given for parents speaking Hungarian in the family was the issue of broken English, i.e., that parents had immigrated to the United States and did not want their children speaking English incorrectly. "I remember my mom saying that she didn't want me to hear her broken English, so we spoke Hungarian at home," stated Jennifer Hegyi at the beginning of the interview. She returned to the same thought at the end of the interview as well, "My mom still speaks broken English so I still speak Hungarian to her." Vivian Varjas echoed this sentiment when she said, "[My] parents being more comfortable probably with Hungarian, especially when I was little was probably the main determining factor in me speaking Hungarian." Megan Ramsey's mother was a little more utilitarian in her sentiments, as Megan related, "My mom always wanted to teach her daughter Hungarian, because it's always good to know a second language. That's what she always told me, just for being in the business world or going traveling anywhere." Livia Karetka also mentioned that her husband's household spoke only Hungarian growing up, and that her parents-in-law still speak with a heavy accent.

Susan Linder, speaking of her parents, the Patays, reinforced the idea that parental involvement was paramount, but not from a broken English perspective. Rather, she was comparing her generation to a previous cohort, speaking of the overwhelming majority of Hungarian-Americans who assimilate: "I'd say our parents first and foremost because there are plenty of people maybe ten years earlier who didn't speak Hungarian to their kids because then they were really trying to fit into the melting pot more than that concept. So the fact that [my parents] spoke Hungarian to us and that brought us to *cserkészet* [scouts] and everything they did was... I would say that has to be number one as parents." Her sister and brother concurred. Karl mentioned at the beginning of the interview that "growing up, that's all we were allowed to speak at home." Not only was their father's English worse, said Susan, but all three siblings emphasized that no punishment or threats were ever used about their use of language. Indeed, all three agreed the reason they spoke Hungarian was respect. Karl mentioned that "I think [my father] was just very proud of where he came from and it was important for them, for us to speak Hungarian at home. It wasn't a very strict something like 'That's all you're going to speak at home,' but it was just expected of us." It was respect towards their father, they agreed. The elder Krisztina Tábor had the same approach when raising her own children: "We tried to foster an atmosphere where we encouraged Hungarian but tried not to make it a point of contention." Later, as her children married non-Hungarian-speaking spouses, the family dynamic changed: "Now there's a mix. When we're with the grandchildren, now the challenge is a constant trying to encourage without making it punitive; it's an ongoing thing."

Tábor's niece, Kiki, related her family's speech patterns and upbringing as follows:

Growing up we spoke mostly Hungarian, but as we got older and had English friends and were involved in school, depending on the subject they [her parents] kind of decided what language we were speaking; homework was more English, but if we were speaking of scouts, then we spoke Hungarian. The last year of high school my parents got divorced, my father remarried, so with him and with his new wife and her kids we speak English. Depending on who's at home and what topic, we mix a lot. My brother's wife is learning Hungarian. It's the same with my grandparents—depending on who's there determines what language we're speaking. We attended both Hungarian catholic and Hungarian protestant churches, so we had multiples of everything, also Hungarian school, Hungarian scouts, Hungarian dance troupe, and in addition to that I spent three years in Hungary via the Hungarian scout scholarship program [to the Balassi Institute]. In my opinion that completely changed my level of appreciation for the culture, knowledge of country and language skills, and reinspired me to take part and to give back to the Hungarian community coming back from an adult standpoint, whereas as a child it was something you were forced to do, even if you were grounded from friends, the Hungarian activities stayed.

Andrew Duna reiterated: "Ultimately, in the end, the main factor is your parents, because of how they enforce it, and how much they speak it with you, and how much you hear it from them." Sándor Sundem agreed that parents are one of the leading factors, but he stipulated that "there are other factors, like how often do you go to Hungary, or how often do you do activities that involve Hungarian speaking." Sofi Dunay summed up her thoughts in this way: "I think it's all about how much is spoken at home, and that's up to the parents. There's a certain level of work the child must put into it, but it's more about whether the parents enforce it or not." Gergely Pál alluded to the emotional perspective when he said, "My dad really worked hard to instill a very strong sense of patriotism towards Hungary by visiting it almost every single year." But he also added an economic aspect of child-rearing: "My dad used to give me money to read books in Hungarian." Indeed, the idea of parental responsibility was emphasized by most of the respondents.

Another important area of parental responsibility is the role played by non-Hungarian spouses. Karl related the support shown by his wife, Denise, who does not speak Hungarian: "She had all intentions of trying to learn Hungarian. She learned the colors, the numbers, and that, but you know what, life takes over." Difficulties in speaking Hungarian to his children he ascribed to his long working hours and some other private personal issues, never to his American spouse, but he did touch upon the difficulties experienced by an American spouse who marries into a Hungarian family. "She's pretty easygoing, but she has her things that bother her, too. And, you know, after the honeymoon was over, you know, she voiced to me that it did trouble her when we went to my parents' house and she didn't understand what people were saying. And it wasn't until Susan got married and Dave came along that she started feeling more comfortable." Susan confirmed, "Dave said he felt kind of like an outsider," and then Karl continued, "Yeah, you feel like an outsider and it's like, the last thing they want to do after they've been through that is to go home and to speak it at home, you know, for me, anyway, the times I was there."

Navigating the tightrope of emotions regarding language use and being attentive to wives or husbands in terms of multiple languages is a problem often voiced by Hungarian-Americans with American spouses. In a particularly nuanced insight, Ann put herself in her sister-in-law's shoes and turned her own familiarity with and preference for Hungarian to Denise's situation with English: "For me, to speak to an infant in English would've been foreign. There's no way you could expect [Denise's] nieces to speak to her little baby in Hungarian, a foreign language for her. I mean, you have to say those words of endearment in your own language and for us, it was Hungarian. I couldn't imagine speaking to ... even to a baby now, I speak Hungarian, because that's what comes natural to a baby." Susan agreed, stating, "So then you're speaking a language that the spouse does not understand. So in the situation, Dave was not just understanding, but was agreeable to not understand his children's first words. And that bothered him. I remember being in the car with him once, and we were going and the boys were babbling about something, and it was insignificant, it was nothing, and he said, 'What are they saying?' And I said, 'It's really, it's nothing, it's just...' But to him it was everything because he didn't understand it. And that bothered him. Not to the point where he would say 'Don't ever do this.'" Matt Kobus related a similar sentiment: "Well, my stepdad kind of gets angry if my mom is always speaking Hungarian to me, and he feels kind of like he's left out of it. And sometimes my mom's friends will tell my stepdad 'You should learn Hungarian' and that really pisses him off." Susan distilled these sentiments into the crux: "that's always a difficult part, leaving your spouse out of a conversation."

All of the American spouses mentioned in the interviews were seen by the respondents as being supportive of Hungarian in the home, but Susan did point to several frustrations of a mixed-language household experienced by her husband Dave:

> So if I'm having a heated discussion with the kids, and we're disagreeing on something, then they're ... if Dave's home, he'll be like, 'What are you telling them, because I don't understand.' He gets frustrated with that situation, where he wants to back me up in what I've just told them, whether that's to get ready for church and then I left to go get ready myself, he's like, 'What did you tell them? Because I can't reinforce what you just told them because I didn't understand that.' These breakdowns still occur, and then you have to kind of take a time-out and say, 'I just asked them to get ready for church. They know what they have to do and if you can reinforce that, that'd be great.

In fact, Dave's sister-in-law, Ann, relates how supportive he is linguistically. "Dave would say things like, 'Hozd here the piros labda.' Whatever he could say in Hungarian, he would really make an effort."

It is not easy being the American spouse of a Hungarian-American parent speaking Hungarian to their children, and these situations reflect the difficulties experienced in everyday situations. Sándor Sundem, 16 years old but displaying the wisdom of a much older person, noticed that "if you get a job that forces you to relocate somewhere else that can affect your language because you might not have the community around; I feel also if you marry someone that isn't a Hungarian and they don't fully support it then you might try to lessen your Hungarian side in order to make them happy or in order just to be with them without having issues." But Krisztina Tábor provided the most practical advice: "Spousal attitude can make a big difference in the final result. It's important for couples to discuss this topic in advance, so the child feels it's important to both parents."

As life goes on, the parental cycle continues into the next generation, where Hungarian language use may actually be reinforced by having children. Ann Graber realized that her own ethnicity was strengthened when she grew up and had her family: "Meaning my own kids. As soon as I started having my own children, my ethnicity was strengthened, I mean the language, because I wanted my kids to have the same thing." She spoke of her struggles to keep her son in the scouting program:

> There came that point in his life, I want to say between age nine and twelve, where he was like, "I don't want ..." It was a fight to go every Friday, an absolute fight, and it was, "You're going until you go to ŐV[85] and then it's up to you." Then along came Magyar iskola for ŐV and he did that ... He still had good friends. He went through the ŐV course for two years, went to ŐV tábor, and afterwards he hugged me and he said, "Thank you for making me do it. This was awesome, I'm so glad I'm a part of it." And he really, really enjoys it. There's that point where you've got to reach...

Not only is consistent parenting important, she stresses, but her insights also show that the transmission of culture succeeds when parents create the conditions for friends to influence their peers in a positive way towards Hungarian language and culture. Her brother, referring to his own childhood, agrees, saying, "As much as I fought it back then, especially in the younger years, is how much I appreciate it now." The elder Krisztina Tábor explained it this way: "The main advantage to scouts is that as a child, you realize it's not just you who has to do this, but you have friends, their parents send them and they do the same thing, so it's not, you don't feel like you have to learn and it's a burden, but because it's enjoyable. Not every minute of it, because you do have to exert some effort, but being among friends makes it more fun and that's what gets you through those years when otherwise they would say, 'I don't want to do this anymore.' I think that's a big plus."

Sticking with it is a struggle, but discipline and consistency have their rewards, as when Andrew Duna said: "Sometimes it would be annoying because on Friday nights it would get in the way of sporting events; I remember when I was younger sometimes I would miss practice to go to scouts, or with Hungarian school I had an every other week deal with my parents, so there was that behind it. It was kind of annoying being reminded to speak Hungarian, but obviously I appreciate it now." When prompted to explain what caused that realization, he replied, "Just the friends and the realization that I can now go to a different country and speak the language and think in different ways." His cousin Sofi Dunay realized that when "surrounded by the English language when my parents would remind us to speak Hungarian we would be annoyed, but I think overall we know that they want the best for us and we want to be able to continue speaking it as well as we can." Erika Chmielewski echoed this sentiment, but gave a more focused explanation of how her priorities shifted as she grew up: "Scouting being on Fridays, sometimes it was hard, you'd have to miss Friday night skate, which was a big thing when you're in middle school and with sports a lot of times it was hard to juggle, and to know where your priorities were, and as I got older my priorities straightened out more." The reason she gave for her shifting priorities was that she found what she really liked about Hungarian culture, which was "the more dancing and singing of it." So she found events where she could hear Hungarian bands play, or go to a concert or a dance.

Parental pride can also play a part, as can be seen in the story Emese Chmielewski related:

We grew up speaking mostly English. My mother would speak to us in Hungarian and when my father came home from work, we would switch to English. So the story goes my mom found a *babazsúr*, which is a Hungarian playgroup, and one day a woman came to the house and I was two years old at the time and couldn't speak Hungarian, I could understand it very well because my mother made sure that we would know it because my mom's entire family was in Hungary. I couldn't speak but I could understand and this woman looked at my mom and said, "I don't understand why your daughter can't speak" and my mom was like, well, she doesn't want to. This woman looked at my mom and said, "that's not your child's fault, that's yours." My mother was enraged at this point, thought that this woman was accusing her. But after she left the house, my mother was rethinking these words, and realized that the woman was one hundred percent truthful in what she had said, so at that point my mother really strived to find Hungarian community and made sure that we would be able to speak Hungarian because no matter how much we spoke English in the household because my father is one hundred percent American, she always made sure, with my father's help, that we would be raised in a bilingual household.

Parental outlook, then, whether stemming from not wanting to use faulty English or from pride, but applied with discipline and consistency, is the factor that very strongly influences Hungarian language use.

Peers and Community

Although most interviewees credited their parents, Matt Kobus felt strongly that in the matter of learning the Hungarian language peers were the most important, even more important than parents. Indeed, in terms of the amount of time during the interviews spent talking about parents or about peers, every interviewee devoted at least three to four times as many sentences to reminiscing about their friendships and peers, as opposed to parents, as they were growing up. Peer impact on Hungarian language use seems, from their own words, to be the stronger overarching theme that emerges from their transcribed thoughts. Andrew Duna, while saying that "home life is the most critical part," conceded that "whether you participate in the Hungarian community or not is also important," which showed an awareness of the social influence on language maintenance.

Samantha Dévai spoke of her American friends' attitude toward her own language use: "I think especially when we started taking language classes in high school, and [her friends] realized that it was, like, such a hard thing to get just the basic concepts down, I think that's when they're like, 'Oh my gosh, they have a whole other language already.'" Jennifer Hegyi concurred, adding, "They always say, 'Oh, I wish I knew a whole other language.'" Vivian Varjas reinforced the attitude described among American school friends, surmising, "I think they just are maybe envious, or they think it's really neat that we know an entire different language, an entire different culture aside from just being raised with the American ideals and the American language. I think that they can't even wrap their head around that we can communicate in another language and that we've known it since we were, you know, practically born."

But not all peer support is positive. In trying to ascertain what factors impacted their Hungarian language use growing up, the conversations among the respondents revealed some concerns and negative factors that illuminate why over 90 percent of Hungarian-Americans do not in fact speak Hungarian in their households. Chief among these was the pressure to assimilate faced by children. Kiki Tábor related how as a young child she so longed to fit in with her American peers that she changed her name: "When I was in second grade, my teacher asked all of us our names, and after hearing two Christinas and two Kathryns, I decided I was going to be called Katy, too, and so the teacher very kindly called me Katy." This name change later caused some confusion with Kiki's mother, because "at the parent-teacher conference where the teacher waxed politely about Katy this and Katy that, my mom corrected her, saying, no, my daughter's name is Krisztina." But Kiki wanted to fit in at such a young age, and only later would her Hungarian identity become much more important to her.

Emese Chmielewski also had an experience about the name Katy, but her experience was decidedly different, partially because she was much older, and partially because it showed a much different attitude on the part of her American peers: "Hungarianness was really a part of my core. I was bullied a lot because of my name; my name is Hungarian rather than English, but what is interesting is that my American father named me, not my Hungarian mother." One time a college acquaintance randomly called her Katy and Emese explained what happened: "I'm like, who in the world is Katy, and finally I looked at her, and I asked, hey, which one of us is Katy, and she said, oh, that's you. And I said, I'm sorry, did I not introduce myself? My name is Emese. Oh, no, no, no, you did but I can't pronounce it. Anyway you're in America so please call yourself Katy rather than Emese." American peers, then, are not always supportive in maintaining ethnic identity.

Both Samantha Dévai and the Patay siblings mentioned cousins who were not living in cities with large Hungarian communities and where there was no Hungarian scouting. Says Susan Linder, "Well, the fact that [our parents] happened to land in Cleveland, you know? Because if they would've landed in, I don't know, Kansas, you wouldn't have the same culture surrounding you that would support that." Samantha Dévai recounts a parallel situation: "And then my other cousin that's still here in the States, um, in another part of Ohio, he didn't participate in scouts very much, so I think his Hungarian language ability declined much more rapidly than ours." To this cousin's credit, Vivian says, "He did recently just go to Hungary, and now he's come back and pretty much that's all he speaks, so I think it made quite the difference for him, so he might be inching his way up to where we're at," much like the fact that Karl Patay, because he works with Hungarian laborers in his construction business, speaks better Hungarian, knowing more slang and having better pronunciation, than he ever did as a teenager.

When asked what the single most important factor was impacting Hungarian language use, Matt Kobus succinctly explained his theory of motivation: "I would probably say your peers, because in some ways those are the people you look up to most or are with the most and if you see that they're doing a certain thing, then a lot of times you want to do the same thing." Karl Patay reiterated this theme independently, saying, "You did the same things together, you know when you have the same interests and you get along with people, it's just natural to want to be with them." Sofi Dunay, after fumbling for the right words, came to the conclusion that "our American friends at school, they don't really understand a lot of what we do and even if we tried to explain, I don't think they'd be able to, so I think that just brings us all closer together in what we do that we understand each other, which I think is a big part of all our identities."

But having friends who speak Hungarian, whether in the scouts or in other organized Hungarian community activities, does seem to make a difference. Said Krisztina Tábor, "The ones who remained have a stronger connection, while the ones who've moved, their proficiency is lower." Jennifer

Hegyi, one of two respondents who did not spend many years growing up with the scouts, admits that she does not really know that many Hungarians that are her age, except for a few that don't live in Ohio. In addition, the reason she no longer has a private Hungarian tutor is that she "got really busy in school so I couldn't do any of it." Livia Karetka also mentioned a Hungarian friend with an American spouse who had no relatives nearby; maintaining Hungarian was very hard so the friend stopped and gave up, but another kept it up because of the scouts. Her other friend has two children, one who is a scout and one who is not; and the reason the one does speak Hungarian is the scout friends.

Megan Ramsey also spoke of an American school culture that was not really supportive of or understanding of bilingualism. She characterized some of her peers in school as being very sheltered or narrow-minded. "They don't really know much about culture and history and the old world. Like, they don't really care that much, I kind of feel." One in particular was surprised that Megan would go abroad. Megan describes the incident: "I just told my friend the other day at school that I'm going to Europe, and she's like, 'What?! Where are you going? You're going there alone?' I'm like, 'Yeah.' 'It's so dangerous, don't go.' I'm like, 'No, it's going to be fine ... I'm going to go to a school there, a study abroad program, everything's going to be fine. There's going to be professors, classes ... it's going to be all right.' And she's like, 'Oh, you're a daredevil.'"

Livia Karetka noticed, "What we do stands out from other typical American families, with our traditions," and also that [scouting's friendships] "gives them more reasons to keep it up because they know that there are other kids who can also speak Hungarian, and as they get older, they realize it can be a cool factor and American friends who study Spanish or Mandarin Chinese or French in school realize they'll never be as fluent as we are in Hungarian." Ann Graber remembers being chastised at her daughter's preschool: "I got in a lot of trouble from Deanna's preschool teacher, how could I do this to the child [speak to her only in Hungarian]? And I looked at her and I go, 'Don't worry, she'll learn English.' You know, I was not intimidated at all, because we had been through it, you know. And she knew her numbers, she knew her letters, she was fine."

This feeling of being somewhat different than the average American is not unique to Cleveland's Hungarian community; it goes beyond the community to cross into the realm of identity among other ethnic groups in the United States. "My best friend in high school was German and she was just as involved in the German, in, uh, *Deutsche Zentrale* [German central] as I was in *cserkészet* [scouts] and MHBK [Hungarian veterans organization]." This common trait points to a shared experience with other ethnic communities, albeit one not shared with the average American high school friends alluded to by the other respondents. Kiki Tábor had a similar experience when asked about her friends: "I would say at this point about eighty percent of my friends are Hungarian, with the twenty percent that aren't, who are American are ethnic in some way of their own: Ukrainian, German, Polish. They get it, they're involved in their culture and community in at least some aspect, if not as heavily as I am involved in the Hungarian community, they understand all the craziness and the cult aspect that some have described our scout life to be, and I find that I'm OK with that." Indeed, this description of a cult aspect puts into words the strong bonds felt among members of the community, bonds that set them apart from the rest of average American society. Kiki summed up the aspect of friendship by telling what connected her to her peers: "Despite the fact that we had different levels of schooling and different types of sports interests, the Hungarian culture gave us this unifying experience and this special thing that tied us together and transcended the other cliques and groups that would separate American friendships."

This view is reinforced by the example of the bond between Matt Kobus and Gabe Kovács, who relate the effect of their close friendship on their own language use. Says Matt, "Gabe's like one of my best friends. He's always been there for me, like I see when he speaks fluent Hungarian, so I look up to him for that." The effect on Hungarian language use is mutual, continues Gabe: "I think that the top five people [who impacted language development] would be my grandma, ... my dad, and my two other grandparents, because it just comes easier for them; and probably, um, probably Matt, actually, because, since when he joined *cserkészet* [scouts], he didn't know that much Hungarian, so I sort of pushed myself to speak it more with him so he would learn it."

Peer friendships, therefore, can have a negative or positive role in impacting ethnic language maintenance.

Most of the respondents really stressed these closer bonds that had developed between them and their Hungarian versus their American friends. Gabe Kovács explained it this way: "My best friends are probably the Hungarian ones, because I've been with them longer ... my entire life ... because our parents know each other, and we would go hang out with each other when we were like, three, and I never really had that with that many people that are American." When pressed to explain the reasons for a majority of her close friends being Hungarian, Megan Ramsey echoed Gabe's sentiment: "I feel like the Hungarian community respected me more because I spoke Hungarian and I was raised that way and they were raised the same way I was, pretty much." In another instance, she alluded to the role of the Hungarian community in Cleveland: "I always really enjoy going to the Hungarian balls that we had, and I think I gained a lot of friendship by going to that, and definitely the camps, all the Hungarian camps. I definitely gained a lot of friendship there, too, and I never really had that at my high school, like going out on camping trips, doing huge projects together to gain closer friends, or traveling."

Karl Patay, agreeing with his siblings Ann and Susan, also highlighted the difference between parents and peers on language use: "It wasn't the Hungarian that brought us together; it was our parents bringing us here, meeting friends and the times we had together, the bonds formed, the memories, and it was your life. I mean, school, your American friends were completely secondary. Everything you did was with Hungarian friends." This commonality was stressed again by Megan Ramsey: "When you meet someone and you want to be able to have things in common with. I felt like I didn't really have a lot of things in common with other students at high school. Maybe I never really gave it a chance, but because I was really really good friends with all the Hungarians." Ann Graber at another point in the interview stressed that "it wasn't our nationality sometimes, but the friends we had." To which both of her siblings immediately replied, "It was a way of life."

When asked to elaborate, Susan Linder explained: "The people that I hung out with in *cserkészet* [scouts] were the people I went to school with and

I had all the social events with them, too. And then through *cserkészet* we had *locsolás* [Easter folk tradition] and *tea* [dances] and *bál* [debutante balls] and all that stuff, so the social events were tied in." Susan's best friends, who were Hungarian, also attended her high school. Karl Patay, whose best friends did not attend the same high school he did, nevertheless agreed: "With me it was a way of life. I mean, we hung around, all our friends were Hungarian, typically. We socialized with them. It was just everything we did had something to do with *cserkészet*, *regös*, or ..."

Scouting and a Way of Life

The respondents also expressed the significant impact that being involved in Hungarian scouting from an early age had on their language use. Megan Ramsey, for example, said, "I started *cserkészet* [scouts] when I was four years old, and that's what really helped me keep up with the culture, the heritage, learning about it, speaking Hungarian." In her interview she mentioned attaining ranks in the scouting activities and how that motivated her to maintain her language; indeed, the Hungarian scouting movement demands basic levels of language proficiency and basic knowledge of Hungarian history, geography, and literature to attain each successive rank, and this motivates teenagers to learn, because they want to be with their friends to reach the next level. Ann Graber explained it thus: "And you'll thrive, you'll push yourself, you know, 'If so-and-so is going to *segédtiszti* [a rank in scouting] next year, I gotta do Magyar *iskola* [Hungarian school], I gotta get the *segédtiszti* material down. I want to go with him.' So it's achieving different ranks and increasing your verbiage, your knowledge, your literature, your history, everything, so that you can do it so you can keep up with your friends."

Friendship as formed in scouts formed a deeper commitment and did even more for their language maintenance than attending Hungarian School, the Patays all agreed. Karl explained the commitment: "It was a way of life. I mean, every Friday and Saturday at seven, and you look forward to it. And I think you hit the nail on the head [referring to his sister's earlier observation]. You did everything else so that you can go to *tábor* [camp]. And you studied because you wanted to have ... all your friends were going and you wanted to be there. And it was a great time, so then you did whatever you had to, and learning whatever it was, and read the book regarding the different camps, so you could be there with your friends. And it was a great life." Ann explained further: "Even Magyar *iskola*. I'll be honest, I hated going, but it was a social thing, too. Your friends were there."

The effect of scouting on language use commitment and its role in deepening friendships was perhaps most clearly explained by a sports analogy given by Ann:

> To go to camp brought us so much closer together because it's ... it's like playing the game of soccer: you cannot win a soccer game if you play on your own. You have to play as a team. And going to camp, you could not survive a week-long camp if you did not work together. And somehow that camaraderie that's driving ... I mean, yeah, there were tears, you know things sucked or whatever, and you leave the camp and get home and you'd say, "Man, that was the best time ever!" And you could hardly wait to see the friends again. That's something that a lot of people don't have, something like a scouting or an ethnicity like that, they don't ever really get to experience that, I don't think, because day in, day out you don't do that with schools.

Sándor Sundem expressed the same sentiment when he said that "those are the friendships to me that are going to last the longest, because you have those connections with [your Hungarian friends]." Indeed, the deep commitment to friends and community caused both Ann and Susan to consciously choose to stay in Cleveland and not go away to college. Susan vividly remembers getting into the Ohio State University for physical therapy school, and deliberately choosing to stay in Cleveland because of her friends and because of scouting. There was no way anyone could talk her out of it, remembered her older sister Ann. Her parents did not encourage Susan to stay in Cleveland: "It didn't need encouragement, because that's what we wanted," said Ann.

Samantha Dévai, Vivian Varjas, and all three Patay siblings spent numerous years not only in the scouting movement but also in the Hungarian folk dance group organized by the scouts, with membership restricted to those Hungarian-American teenagers who work with younger scouts on a regular basis and also are able to read, write, and speak fluent Hungarian. All but two of the interviewees were current or former members of the Hungarian Scout Folk Ensemble, known locally as the *Regös Csoport*. Now, as 20 years ago, the autumn harvest festival season runs throughout the fall, sometimes with overlapping performances at Hungarian churches in the Cleveland area. Ann Graber characterized typical involvement in the dance group: "We did a *szereplés* [performance] every weekend, if not two or three ... We would literally go to two, three on a weekend. And that's what we did September through May and that was our weekend activity. We loved it. It was what pulled us in ... we didn't go away to college because we wanted to continue to be a part of what we were in." Although the *Regös* dance group does not usually have multiple performances each weekend, only in the fall, Ann's memory shows the use of a narrative construction typical of Hungarian-American discourse, as shown by Mónika Fodor's work,[86] drawing on very real facts. The overall scouting movement in Cleveland does have a packed schedule, often with several parallel events on weekends year-round, and this packed schedule led to intense emotional ties and deep friendships.

The friendships are based on shared difficult circumstances, for it is far from easy to maintain the Hungarian or any ethnic language in the United States, as shown by the vast majority of the Hungarian population who assimilate. Susan ascribes the friendship commitments to a deep understanding: "You understand each other. You understand where everyone's coming from." Her sister Ann characterizes these friendships as "amazing. We've got such a base, such a core already that we could not see somebody for ten years, and you see them and you pick up where you left off, because you built so much on it." Susan relates a recent incident connecting with an old friend at the jamboree, a scout camp held every five years: "You still have that common connection. Remember Róni [Veronika Zidron]? She was up at *Jubi* [a scout jamboree] and I haven't seen her since *Körút* [a European tour organized by Hungarian scouts] and I ran up to her, I went up to her at Mass and I saw her and gave her a hug and then after *zászlólevonás* [camp's closing ceremony], you know, we connected, but I hadn't seen her in so long that, again, you just reconnect so quickly because of that commonality." Just as Urban and Orbe described, these deep understandings based on friendship honed through intense communication has transformed their identities, forming a common Hungarian bond among them. Andrew Duna characterized the community's values thus: "Scouting teaches you how to interact with people." And interaction forms social bonds. Taken to the Nth degree, intense interaction, such as is found in a tight-knit community, especially among scouting activities in the wilderness, forms lasting bonds. Gergely Pál, when asked about his friends, replied: "Percentage-wise, I have more American friends, but the friendships with the Hungarian friends are incredibly strong and uncomparable." When pressed to charactize the uncomparability, he explained: "The relationship is so much stronger when you're cutting down a tree, or building a tent, or going on a hike—these events help strengthen the relationship more than with Americans."

Karl Patay, who has not been involved in Hungarian scouting for the last 20 years, nevertheless felt such an emotional bond that during our interview, held at a Friday evening scout meeting in Cleveland, he expressed an almost visceral reaction upon seeing Hungarian scouts of a newer generation:

> I've been so far away from it for so long, it's—when I first came in, I went into that other building and I saw them all line up and I haven't seen it in twenty years, and it—it was surreal. And it was so neat, I almost wished I was a part of it again, because it was such a part of my life back then, that it gave me the shivers to see and hear all that, yet. And I had no idea that there were still so many kids involved. I had no idea... it's so emotional to me. I mean, it was such a main part of my life ... it's something I feel like I can step right back into tomorrow and I would just ...The memories that it brings back, every camp that we went to and the times we had, the camaraderie ... you can't take that out of me. As much as I've been away from it for twenty years, for 24 years it was everything to me ... I mean, it was a tremendous memory for me, just walking in there and just, it brought tears to my eyes just thinking, 'Wow, it's still here.' So walking in here and seeing all this and, you know ... I'm reciting everything they're saying, because I know it. And it's neat to see that.

Ann alludes to similar lasting emotional bonds when she talks about her daughter's friendship with Samantha Dévai, though they both attend different colleges: "Deanna will not speak to Samantha for six months and then the next thing we know, Samantha's on the phone, 'I saw something on Facebook, are you okay?' Yeah, and then they'll talk for an hour. *'Anyuka* [mom], I miss her. She's my best friend.' And that's the way it is." The same is true for her son: "Pisti grew up with all the boys, too, so he had Joey, Gabi, Keve, Bende [referring to some of her son's friends]. He's really close with these kids, and that's make it or break it." Ann goes on to conclude that "it's the language that pushes them together and the nationality, because they have that in common, thank goodness, but it's a lot of socialization."

Much as Katalin Pintz found in New Brunswick, NJ, the Cleveland Hungarian community is also close-knit because of their shared experiences and commitment. Ann recounts, "Even nowadays, our adult friends, we hang out with only Hungarian people. As adults. Married couples. Only Hungarian people. The American friends that I met as a kid starting going to school, 'What are you doing New Year's? Want to get together?' 'Oh, we're with our Hungarian friends.' 'What are you doing this time?' 'Getting together with our Hungarian friends...'" Susan agrees, stating that the families she hangs out with stem from her scouting best friends, including a friend who grew up in New Brunswick in the parallel close-knit Hungarian community and later moved to the Cleveland area.

But friendship alone is not enough; discipline was another recurring theme in the interviews. And discipline brings rewards, both in terms of parents and scout leaders, but even from grandparents. Ann Graber recalled: *"Nagypapa* [grandfather] would make us read in Hungarian, and we would go hide and say, 'Zsuzsi will go first' (laughs). Mostly I would go hide. I hated reading with them." Yet later in life, she transmits these same values to her own children.

Sometimes the discipline of the scout leaders brought forth pride and accomplishment, as evidenced by a situation Karl Patay related:

We were *róverek* [older scouts], so I was the, um, *örsvezető* [patrol leader] for Kanyó Zoli, Csorba Béla, Sanyi, and I don't know who else was in there, but I mean, Miki, and you know we went on a two-day *portya* [hike] and Levente tried to push us and he gave us something like twenty-five miles or something the first day and we were pissed. And I'm thinking, 'How the heck is he going to think that we're going to finish this in one day?' We start early in the morning, two o'clock, and Levente came by at eleven thirty with the van and at that point, we were determined. He was going to pick us up and finally take us to our destination where we were supposed to spend the night next to this creek. And we had compasses and you know how it was. We said no and we wouldn't take the ride. You know what, you're going to test us, so we refused it and we just kept walking.

Demanding a high standard evokes a proud reaction and camaraderie from the teenaged boys, and this is what tied them together. Karl continued, "but you know what? I'll never forget it, because it was [not] wussy." Andrew Duna, when asked why passing on to kids is important, concurred: "I learned to tough it out with the scouts, the values that it taught me as well as the friendships you make through it."

The Patay siblings also mention others who for various reasons left or drifted away from Cleveland's Hungarian community, that these people especially as parents often return years later and re-engage with the community. Karl surmises,

And you can probably go through *cserkészet* and see who is in there now and kind of drifting, and then when they became parents, maybe somehow for whatever reason, um, you know, maybe married someone Hungarian or something, it kind of drew them back in. They left for a time. I think Balássy Pali was gone for a while, and after he had kids, and now he's a major part of it, probably for the last ten to fifteen years. ... I think once they come back, I think they're lifers ... I think you kind of realize that maybe what you've been missing and then you don't want to lose it again.

The examples he mentions are all people who experienced Hungarian scouting as children, and later had their own children enrolled in the program. Kiki Tábor explained what she saw as a correlation between language level and lack of involvement in the community: "They don't use the language as often as we do, and don't have a strong reason to use it. If you don't use it, you lose it." But those who are involved in the community, do indeed have a reason to use the language, and thus through practice and use, their language skills get better.

Not only does the Hungarian scouting program organize activities that promote a deep and lasting bond of friendship it also has an effect on language use by what it demands from its leaders, many of whom are teenagers working with younger scouts. Matt Kobus relates how scouting impacts his own language use, saying, "Whenever I'm at scouts or activities I try and speak it because there's little kids there and I want them to speak better and I want to be a role model for them, I guess." By Matt's own account, his Hungarian language skills are at about half of where his native English skills are, but what being involved in scouting does for him is to cause him to be cognizant of others' and the community's language usage, which in turn leads to a conscious choice to use Hungarian, even if it is harder to speak for second and third generation Hungarian-Americans.[87]

In another thought-provoking example, being involved in scouting led to career success, as Susan Linder recalled. "I remember it was June, when I was interviewing for this job and they tried to set up an interview when I was going to *kiscserkész tábor* [cub scout camp]. I said, 'Sorry, I'm going to be cooking for forty-five kids, you know, at scout camp and going whitewater rafting the day after with my family, so let's do it the next week.' And they emailed me back, 'You're taking 45 kids to scout camp? And whitewater rafting? You're hired!'"

Visiting Hungary, Linguistic Insights, and Value

Most of the respondents also emphasized how much of an impact visiting Hungary had, not only on their language use but also on their sense of identity. Gabe Kovács linked his Cleveland Hungarian experiences, especially in the scouting program, when he said, "After I went to Hungary, I think I really realized that it's not just some sort of activity on every Friday night, it's actually who I am, I guess." Samantha Dévai agreed in an independent interview, explaining that for her, visiting Hungary "made it more real, because living here it just seems so isolated, it's just a small community in Cleveland, so being there and that actually being the predominant language made it seem like, ok, there's a lot of people that speak this and they're from there and it's not just us in the scouting community of greater Cleveland." Vivian Varjas's pride was brought out by her visit to Hungary: "Just seeing where the family came from, seeing the traditions, kind of, live and in action." She also explained that visiting Hungary positively impacted her language skills: "After returning, I mean, noticeably, it became even more, you know, spoken more at home, much more fluid and I was able to incorporate new words into the language base, so it definitely helped, even just being there for a few weeks. It showed huge gains in the language when I speak it, that's for sure." Sofi Dunay felt the same way: "Whenever we go to Hungary, I can feel myself getting better in vocabulary and word flow, and then after our return it fades." But then she tied visiting Hungary to her sense of identity: "It helps me remember how everything we do here connects to back home, like, I don't know, sometimes you forget that all this scouting and dancing, and everything is like, it's nice to see where it all started." Indeed, Andrew Duna tempered those thoughts with "being involved in Cleveland is stronger than visiting Hungary in strengthening identity, [but] visiting is an affirmation." Krisztina Tábor also noticed a definite difference in her own children: "Our children went later, in high school, and for them, their identity got a big boost. Because of connecting it not only to family, but culturally and language-wise, it really cemented a lot." Sándor Sundem felt that his visit provided him with meaning: "Since we live in Cleveland, that's what shapes us, the scouting, the Hungarian school, the camps, but going to Hungary helped us realize that it was all a part of us, that it was meaningful to do what we were doing here."

The timing of when to take children to Hungary matters as well, as voiced by Krisztina Tábor: "If families have the opportunity to go as a family, that's a remarkably good thing that helps cement things and carry them through the years as they become older, at ages seven to twelve: those are the years that a child becomes more involved in school, and it's hard for parents to remain strong when their kids are whining about it, but if they have an opportunity to go and see that there's an actual world there [in Hungary], that this is not just something your parents are making you do, I think that can be very important." Livia Karetka agreed: "Taking them at age fifteen is probably too late, and if you take them at a younger age and expose them to it, it will be familiar, not brand new and weird and awkward, not knowing the language."

The language spoken at home and among friends can vary from day to day, minute to minute, even within a sentence. The Patay siblings also brought to the surface some linguistic insights regarding their own Hungarian language usage. Speaking of the pragmatics of whether a conversation is mixed with English or Hungarian, Karl relates that "with Mom it's mixed, depending on how she answers the phone or how she starts the conversation. She'll start in English, too," as opposed to his father, who always started the conversations in Hungarian. This phenomenon of guiding or directing the language of conversation is well-known among Hungarian-American parents whose children's easier language is English. Continues Karl, "So, if she started in Hungarian, you know, '*Hogy vagy?*' [how are you?] then, you know, I'd be speaking Hungarian to her ... And it flows ... For example, coming here today, when Feri was here. When you start a conversation in Hungarian, most of it's spoken in Hungarian ... how something is started, I guess, who starts the conversation." His sister Ann concurs: "You don't want to lose it. The less you practice it, the harder it is to go back. Pisti [her husband] and I will speak in Hungarian amongst each other more than I do with my own kids."

But the reason English often becomes the predominant language in the household is that it is simply easier communication. Ann Graber explains: "Because you're at work all day, you come home, you do homework and everything. We'll discuss an activity and you want a response from your kids. Their first language, unfortunately, even though they spoke Hungarian as a first language, is English. If you want to get something out of them, you have to just say it in English. It's more important to have that communication going... it's easier for them, communications-wise." Karl Patay had the same language shift brought on by his long working hours. He remembers, "I was working ten to twelve hours a day, sometimes going, at one point, two jobs, and I was never home. You know, when I'd come home at nine o'clock or eight o'clock at night ... the last thing I'm going to try to do for the half hour or twenty minutes I see the kids is to try to teach them Hungarian. I wanted to just communicate with them. I wanted to see them, I wanted to hold them, I wanted to hug them, see how their day went, the goods and the bads, and that's a big difference between why my kids don't speak Hungarian and her kids do."

This ease is a natural phenomenon experienced by many children of immigrants living in the United States, which Karl characterized as "once we got into high school age, we would speak English amongst ourselves." Ann relates of how the shift from Hungarian to English came about as she saw it in her own children:

> They spoke solely Hungarian in the house up until *kis* Pisti [Stevie] started first grade. Kindergarten was still part-time; it was two full days and a half day. And the girls only spoke Hungarian together. There's six and four years between Pisti and the two girls, and as Pisti started coming home, he was ... all of a sudden he was cool, that he could speak English. The kids spoke Hungarian as their first language. Pisti didn't start preschool till he was four and a half, and when Deanna started when she was three and a half, she spoke Hungarian only and I would have to translate for her. So she understood English, but she didn't speak ... As Pisti started going to school, so first grade, second grade, the language all of the sudden switched between the three kids. That was, it was very noticeable. All of the sudden, the three kids, who spoke Hungarian at home to each other, started speaking English, cause now Pisti understood English.

This natural switching is what the scouting movement and the other community activities seem to mitigate, inasmuch as the natural tendency of the children is to choose English, the easier language in which to communicate amongst themselves. Parents enrolling their children in organized Hungarian activities such as scouting give their children, especially the teenagers, a structured outlet that channels the conversations to Hungarian by way of working with younger children. This allows the language to be maintained despite assimilation pressures, often late into the second and third generations, as one can see from the respondents and their children. Karl recalls his shift in high school where "I started getting more American friends, and in turn, talking with them and doing more things with them, I lost the Hungarian a lot."

But this assimilation can be reversed. Megan Ramsey switched her Facebook page to Hungarian, alluding to the differences between the Hungarian spoken in Cleveland and the Hungarian spoken in Hungary:

Somebody told me the other day, when he went to *Magyarország* [Hungary] when he was about eighteen years old, he told me that the way that he speaks Hungarian over there in *Magyarország* is really old-fashioned and he didn't understand the language between the friends and peers and the younger crowd, because it was really fast and it kind of, everything went with the flow and there was a lot of slang involved that we're not really taught over here, because our parents all came in the fifties, sixties and seventies, during that era. So I think that the way we were raised is a little bit more old-fashioned, I think, and the way, the reason why I changed my Facebook to Hungarian and that sometimes I do text in Hungarian, too, is because I kind of want to learn a little bit how real Hungarians, like the modern-day Hungarians speak, because one day I would like to go there and not feel like a fool, you know? And be able to communicate on like the same level as other Hungarians.

Krisztina Tábor agreed: "One of the difficulties here in Cleveland is we have less people that come here from Hungary, and when those people come here, they bring more of the true current Hungarian language, and it's very different from the Hungarian we learned that our parents brought over forty or fifty years ago." Réka Pigniczky, in her documentary film *Inkubátor*, examined the Hungarian-American communities of California, New Brunswick, Cleveland, and Philadelphia, and numerous interviewees in the film expressed this same disconnect between being Hungarian in the United States and being Hungarian in Hungary. In her narration, Réka speaks of an almost artificial incubator that her parent's generation set up for their children, emphasizing only the positive parts of Hungarian culture.

The Patay siblings reminisced about visiting Hungary in the 1980s, going to a dance in Füred, and feeling the same dismay the narrator in *Inkubátor* felt. Karl Patay tells of his sister Ann's entrance to the dance: "She's there, in her *hímzett díszmagyar* [handmade traditional dress], that she worked on for a long time, right, and many tears (laughs) and, but it shocked—I remember, this was my first impression—it shocked me to see the Americanized version of the Hungarian girls there. Nobody had anything on like that. They had westernized, just ball dresses on ... Like here we are, the Americans, with all the Hungarians, and they had nothing on that was Hungarian." Ann continues: "We knew more of the folk customs than they did. We feel bad when we discuss, you know, this and this and this, uh, *locsolás* and, uh ... they're like, 'Huh?'" Susan Linder mentioned a mutual friend, Klári, who said the same thing. Ann Graber surmises that "we're more Hungarian than they are," which her sister Susan clarifies: "Or at least that we try to preserve the culture much better than they do, but they don't have to otherwise, they live there." Preserving the culture because of a perceived need to, as opposed to in Hungary, where there less of a need to, is a theme heard not only in Hungarian-American circles, but also often among Hungarians in Romania, Slovakia, the Ukraine, or in Serbia as well.

Ann recounts that here in the United States, we grasp for anything that's Hungarian, probably because "we wanted to preserve it so much." Her sister Susan explains that she is "for preserving it, because we see that each generation is going to get weaker. It's just, I think, inevitably it will, so you try to ingrain anything that you can and grasp on to anything that you can. Even as I just look around in the house, and see the *Hollóházi* [porcelain] or the *Herendi* [porcelain] and stuff like that, and see that the kids appreciate that, so you hope that that's one little thing that they will take with them, you know, when they get to their own house. So it's—or your *hímzett terítő* [embroidery]... stuff like that that it's a part of us." Much as the people interviewed in *Inkubátor* expressed a disconnected view of Hungary, i.e., an almost distilled version of Hungarian culture, based on historical reality but altered by the geographical and chronological distance of emigration, so also did the subjects of this study express the importance of holding on to facets of Hungarian culture, indeed clutching steadfastly to them, because of the overwhelming odds favoring assimilation.

But the value of speaking Hungarian is not limited to its importance in maintaining identity; there are practical considerations that transfer to American life as well. All of the respondents emphasized the value of speaking a second language, in this case Hungarian. Gabe Kovács had the simplest, most common-sense insight, appropriately followed by a laugh, when he said, "We all speak it, so why not speak it?" The parents of Jennifer Hegyi felt that Hungarian was so important that they had a private Hungarian tutor for their daughter when she was 12 or 13 years old. Vivian Varjas, reflecting on the Hungarian language use in her childhood, stated that "it was something that made me stand out against the peers and I was always very proud of it." Matt Kobus linked the pride of being Hungarian to peer influence when talking about the gradual shift as he got older: "The scouts and making friends there [caused the change]. Knowing people there and realizing that other people take pride in being Hungarian, so I should, too, I guess." Livia Karetka echoed this sentiment: when her family went to Hungary for her sister's wedding, "we were able to communicate in Hungarian and they got along just fine, so it was really good. They were proud of it, not that they weren't before, but here [in Cleveland] they don't really see the benefits, but afterwards they did."

Even the American spouses mentioned in the interviews saw the value of speaking a second language. Susan Linder related how the subject of Hungarian language use with eventual children came up with her future husband Dave: "When we were dating, it came up, and it was a non-factor. It was the more the better ... Dave always said that it's a gift you can give to your children ... it's so easy to give it, why would you not? Why would you deny them that language?" Megan Ramsey also related how her father, who had originally been opposed to his daughter learning another language, changed his mind: "He actually changed his mind when I was like four years old because he has a niece, my cousin Bailey who ... was living in Belgium at the time ... and she was learning French. So then my dad realized that, you know, 'Maria should teach Megan some Hungarian.' Because of his niece. I guess he realized, because he was a new father ... he realized that it's best to know another language, because he wasn't raised that way. He was raised [monolingual] like typical United States citizen."

Andrew Duna and Sofi Dunay also touched on the value of knowing Hungarian when studying a third language in high school. Sofi mentioned that she realized while taking German and Spanish that she can make connections better due to her Hungarian skills, and Andrew pointed out how his Hungarian helps his English reading comprehension skills, and being able to roll his r's helps him with Spanish.

When asked whether they plan on speaking Hungarian to their own children, the respondents all answered in the affirmative. Sofi Dunay had the quickest answer, without a moment's hesitation: "Yes. Something that's been a big part of my life, I want my kids to be able to speak Hungarian; it's important to me and I want it to be important to them." Matt Kobus replied, "I think it would be a shame if the whole Hungarian thing ends with me in the family." Megan Ramsey, reflecting on her own childhood, said, "Most definitely, because I think it's just such a great thing to know, just knowing another language in general. So yeah, I would definitely put them through Magyar *iskola* and I hope they would like it a lot better than I did," laughing as she finished. Andrew Duna took his answer a step further, tying his language knowledge to his identity: "That's pretty much entirely who I am and ... what my parents also wanted was that I would be Hungarian and to relate fully to the community and participate in it." For Andrew, it seemed "strange to speak to a child in English, even a baby, that's how we've always been taught." He was able to project into the future and see the question in light of fairness: "And then it would be strange that my ... as much as knowing Hungarian has been a part of my life, that it wouldn't be a part of theirs, and to deny them the opportunities that knowing a second language, and knowing Hungarian, as well as being part of the community, that denying them opportunities to experience that fully would be terrible."

Emese Chmielewski answered with a short, matter-of-fact "yes". Her sister Erika Chmielewski alluded to community ties when she said, "My friends and I already have a plan that we're all going to have kids at the same time and they're going to be in a Hungarian band together, they're going to be Hungarian dancers, and they're going to be awesome at it, and they will be, of course, learning Hungarian so they can sing their songs." Gergely Pál, on the other hand, emphasized the idea of personal identity when asked if he would speak Hungarian to his own children: "Yes, for sure. My dad brought me up with a strong sense of how important it is to be Hungarian and without that important part of my identity, I don't know where I'd be, so I want to make sure my children, and their children's children will be Hungarian and can pass it on as long as they can." Gabe Kovács alluded to academic research, all the more noteworthy since he was 16 years old at the time of his interview: "I heard something, some sort of study once, that if you learn, if you're bilingual at a young age, that it's easier to learn, or something like that ... So I think it would be a benefit to them, and like it's just a cool quality to have." Indeed, decades of research in bilingualism has found that speaking two languages does, in fact, help when studying a third or fourth language.

Emese Chmielewski alluded to a cross-generational effort when she said that "one of the ways to maintain the Hungarian community in Cleveland is for each of us to make that sacrifice like our parents did before us, to really make sure that at home they follow a strong routine that we are going to teach our kids Hungarian, and we are going to sit down with them and show them the Hungarian alphabet, and if we don't know something we'll call up one of our Hungarian friends." Reinforcement and support from the community, then, are also a factor. Emese continued: "When you look at maintaining the Hungarian language, it's your sacrifices and it's the sacrifices of the community as a whole. Community means you're not alone; there's always someone to call—having that network and having someone you know who might be able to show your kids something more than you could give them—it's very important."

American or Hungarian?

Perhaps the most telling question was the last question of the interview, in which each respondent was asked whether they considered themselves American or Hungarian, and why. Their answers were easily divided into age groups: those below and those over age 25. The younger respondents mostly said they were American, although proud of their Hungarian heritage. Because almost all of them and some of their parents were born in the United

States, that is not surprising. Matt Kobus and Megan Ramsey were unequivocal in their answers. Matt: "I think I feel more American, like without a question. Like, you know, I feel proud to be Hungarian, there's just like a stronger pull towards the American patriotism." Megan continued in the same vein: "Um, I would have to say that I am more of an American, just because, just like Máté said, he's more patriotic towards America, and I'm more patriotic toward America. I was raised as a Hungarian, I guess, but only with food and the culture and the folk dancing and, you know, having Hungarian friends, so I do consider myself more Hungarian than any other type of nationality I have in the blood, but if I have to, uh, if anybody asks me, I'm an American. No matter what. Because this is my home, this is where I was born." Gabe Kovács alluded to his parents' role in forming his identity: "I consider myself, I don't know, half and half? That's what the answer usually is when I get asked that question. Because I am an American citizen. I was born here, raised here, but really I was sort of raised like a Hungarian, I guess, because my parents tried to do that and I think they succeeded." Andrew Duna alluded to his grandparents: "I consider myself American because I'm an American citizen. I've grown up in this country; my parents always taught me to respect it and all the values and opportunities it provides and that my grandparents came to seek refuge here. But the American part of me is a lot stronger."

Vivian, Samantha, and Jennifer were also unequivocal in their answers. Vivian Varjas: "Although I'm very proud of my Hungarian heritage, I still probably consider myself American, just for the sheer fact that I was born here and I did my schooling here and will most likely finish ... be living here the rest of my life, so I would probably say I'm American." Her cousin Samantha Dévai agreed, "I feel sort of the same way." Jennifer Hegyi, who was born in Hungary but came to the United States as a toddler, continued: "I think that I'm a little of both, but if I had to pick one, I feel like I'm more American, just because of how I was raised here and it's not the same as if I was in Hungary." Sándor Sundem connected both past and future when he replied, "I was born and raised here, I've fully gone through the process of being an American child. I am Hungarian heritage-wise but I am not a Hungarian citizen, I do not live there, and if I get a dual citizenship down the road I might move there eventually, but I would still define myself as being an American."

Other interviewees were not so sure. Gergely Pál said, "It's more the situation I'm in. It's a key part of my identity, and I don't think I can say that I'm just Hungarian, though. I was born here, my mom was American, my grandparents from her side are American, I go to an American school. The American side is not something I can distinguish from the Hungarian side; it's all mixed. I can't say one or the other—it depends on the situation." For Erika Chmielewski, it also depends on the situation. She implied that identity needs active nurture and participation, especially in the folk culture realm, where "if you go to Hungary and ask a random person on the street about 'can you do a *Mezőségi* [a Transylvanian folk dance] with me right now,' they'd be like, 'I have no idea what you're talking about.' And so I think when I'm in America I'm always talking about Hungary, thinking about the folk aspect of it, and I couldn't live in Hungary without explaining to everyone that I'm American." Her sister Emese used an extended metaphor to illustrate her combined identity:

I was once asked if my life was a movie, what would be the title and opening scene? I immediately said the title would be SUSPENDED, with the opening scene being a girl on monkey bars with her mother yelling in Hungarian, "*Emese, gyere le onnan!* [get down from there]" and the father yelling in English, and I think that's kind of how my life was, just no matter how many times I was taken to Hungarian school, to scouts, I always had an American father at home who embraced the Hungarian life, and no matter how many times I was at softball or soccer practice, I always had a Hungarian mom at home who was embracing the American culture and so I'm really trying to say that I'm neither and both at once.

The three Patay siblings, being older, offered different views on the same question. Susan also could not separate the two parts of her identity: "I can't say if I'm American-Hungarian or Hungarian-American. But it's both. And ... because I have such a reverence for the country that gave me and my parents freedom and that they really ingrained in us that, yes, our culture is one hundred percent paired in real life and it's what we are, but the fact that this country gave us the freedom to, you know, have your own religion, and ...

maintain your culture and do what you want that way. You can't... I can't separate the two. I can't say one or the other. You're not assimilated but you can keep the two separate, appreciating both, really. It's not one or the other." And both Livia Karetka and Krisztina Tábor agreed that they felt both American and Hungarian. Livia was proud to be both, and Krisztina felt the identity of both, adding that "to what degree varies from person to person." Sofi Dunay also could not answer the question: "I don't know. All of my family is either there or is from there, I have dual citizenship, I moved here when I was three, so I guess some of both."

Karl Patay got emotional as he explained that whenever he visits Hungary, he calls it *"Megyek haza"* [going home], just like his parents did, even though he was not born in Hungary, it is not a home to him, yet such a strong tie still remains. He feels the emotional bond that his parents had with their native country, yet consciously disassociates himself from negative aspects of Hungarian culture, offering an urban vs. rural dichotomy, while at the same time acknowledging that his identity has changed through the years.

> If you asked me when, up until I was twenty, twenty-four, I would say I was more Hungarian. At forty-four, I'm more American because of the disassociation with that life, not intentionally, but because again, of life. And not only that, but I've been back enough times to see that there's a lot of what I see in Hungary today that I don't want to be associated with. It's, you know, not the villages, but the big cities have become very westernized. You walk into Budapest today and, I'll never forget, three years ago when I was there, I thought I was walking through the Bronx. Graffitti everywhere. I don't want to be associated at all with the Hungary, with the big cities of today. What I want to be associated with is the life that my parents lived there and the life that's still being lived in the villages where they're still keeping rabbits and chickens and pigs in their backyards.

Ann Graber, on the other hand, explained that her Hungarian identity is a particular type of Hungarian-American identity, localizing it to her experience growing up as a scout in Cleveland. "I will say ... Hungarian-American, but the Hungarian-American ... I mean, I'm here, this Hungarian, OK? The *cserkész* Hungarian, the *regös* Hungarian, the *magyar iskola* Hungarian, the Cleveland Hungarian, the in exteris, or whatever is outside of Hungary. That's Hungarian-American." Her ties to her Hungarian roots have become stronger through time, as she acknowledges the effort that maintaining a Hungarian identity for herself and for her children entails. She continues, "The older I become, the more it's still very important to me, even more so. I do get tired of what I'm doing, I have to admit, because I've been involved for so long, I do get tired of it but that necessity is so strong. And now it's like you see it in your kids and that's why it's still so strong." Much like Attila Z. Papp formulated his unique community culture built upon inherited values, and just as Bőjtös defined a spiritual homeland, Graber's Hungarian identity was built and sustained through communication within the community.

Perhaps the most nuanced response was given by Kiki Tábor: "I have certain views, beliefs, and advantages that make me undeniably American, yet I would more strongly identify myself if not exclusively as Hungarian but definitely as European—European mindset, European preferences, having both the Hungarian culture and a German grandmother, it gave me a view of things. But at the same time, having lived in Hungary, I couldn't say that I'm one hundred percent Hungarian, I don't have that same nose-to-the-grindstone, downtrodden, post-communist mindset a lot of people have there— I definitely find the optimism to be more American. It's definitely a healthy blend of both."

Mónika Fodor found that "qualitative interviews about culture inquire about shared understandings, taken-for-granted roles of behavior, standards of value and mutual expectations." Furthermore, she writes that "a fundamental goal is to find out what people have learned through experience and how they are able to pass it on to the next generation."[88] What are the main factors, then, that impact Hungarian language and culture maintenance among these eighteen Cleveland Hungarians, and by extension among Cleveland's Hungarian community in general in light of their responses? Gergely Pál integrated the concepts of practice, emotion, and community in his view: "The key to maintaining language is practice, so reading, writing, speaking; but the way to really ingrain and help push that in children or anyone trying to learn or further their language, it's important to connect it to an emotion. The basis is the parents, and secondary is the community—you find something in the community that you love and it takes effort and sacrifice—and from then on it's great." The emotional aspect of learning a language can be reinforced by the community, but it is the parents who plant that seed, and who nurture and maintain the plant through regular contact with the community.

Parents who spoke Hungarian in the household, who took their children to Hungarian community events such as the Hungarian school, scouting, and the folk dance group, made a significant cultural impact on their children, as evidenced by their children's recollections even twenty years later. The Hungarian scouting movement and folk dance group, by placing strict demands on its participants, effected a deep camaraderie and strong bonds of friendship among the children and especially the teenagers, who are prone to listen to their peers instead of their parents. When peer friendships in American high schools are stronger than among Hungarian friends, language use suffers. When peer friendships among the local Hungarian teens is strong, their Hungarian language use improves. Thus having a child actively involved in Cleveland's Hungarian community events leads to a higher fluency and a stronger sense of cultural identity, as does visiting Hungary.

But it is important to emphasize that these factors that allow language maintenance even into the second and third generations are preserved by only a small percentage of Cleveland Hungarians. The vast majority, for one reason or another, succumb to the inevitable forces of assimilation. To represent the majority viewpoint, an extended follow-up interview was conducted after the initial 18 interviews with someone who was born and grew up Hungarian in Cleveland, but whose wife and son do not speak Hungarian and are only marginally involved in Cleveland's Hungarian community. Nick Falk grew up speaking only Hungarian in the household, attending on a weekly basis scouts, Hungarian school, and the CMAC for fencing and boxing; he can speak, read, and write Hungarian fluently. Among his friends, language proficiency varies from 50 percent to 100 percent. Many of his friends have married Hungarians and continue to speak the language in the home and be involved with scouting, Hungarian church, and the Hungarian school.

Falk sees a gaping hole in Cleveland's Hungarian community in that the non-speaking members are neglected and sometimes feel like outcasts. His own son, for example, really wants to be a part of the community and has made friends, and for years has volunteered in the basement kitchen for the Scout Picnic and at various scout camps, but his language skills preclude his being a part of that inner circle of those who speak the language fluently. His son's identity, however, is very much Hungarian; both of his cars carry the Hungarian crest near the license plate, and the first thing he did when going away to college was to hang a giant Hungarian flag in his dormitory room. Nick loved the outdoors aspect of scouting when he was involved in it as a child and a teenager, but like many of his age group, he drifted away from the community after age 18.

Ironically, efforts expended to strengthen Hungarian identity were one of the reasons it became less important to him. "I and my friends loved the rope bridges and hiking in Chagrin [a nearby park], but then scouting started to become less outdoorsy and became almost uniformed Hungarian school," he recalled. "I didn't want to go *szavalni* [recite poetry at commemorations], because I was doing it already on Mondays at Hungarian school." His younger sister's generation, on the other hand, really enjoyed the Hungarian folk culture aspect of the *Regös* group, and her cohort remained quite active in the community. Now, however, Nick's sense of Hungarian identity has changed. "As time progressed, my son came along, and I wanted to teach him, so I had a kind of a rebirth of Hungarian-centric feeling." When asked whether he considers himself American or Hungarian, Nick replied in his written commentary that it was a difficult question. "I consider myself to be an American of Hungarian heritage since I was born here. However, I am extremely proud of my Hungarian heritage and am seriously considering obtaining dual citizenship." When asked in person, however, he vacillated: "Now, as I grow older, I am Hungarian."

Twenty years ago he would never have considered retiring to Hungary, but now he is seriously thinking about it, because of family, culture, language, and the environment. "It's hard to explain the feeling I have when walking along *Andrássy út* [a street in Budapest] or in Kecskemét and seeing the apartment my dad lived in ... it's weird, not being born there, but I feel this draw to go there." He said, while later describing sensory details about visiting the Cold War Hungarian border from Austria in 1975: "I noticed the guard tower, saw the reflection in the guard's binoculars, looked across the border, and I thought, this is real." His connection to Hungary, then and now, is an extension of his Hungarian upbringing in Cleveland, and even 40 years later has a strong emotional component. This emotional component is what he would like to see in outreach to the non-Hungarian-speaking members of the community, a scouting experience not tied to language, but one that can incorporate language as a part of the experience.

The situation offers a Catch-22, however, because the stronger the expectations and ties to language or to the community are, the stronger group solidarity becomes. A line is drawn and those who do not speak the language are relegated to being outside the group. But if expectations and ties are loosened, whether in language or in any other realm, the group becomes more inclusive. Membership numbers are increased but solidarity and group identification tend to decrease. The scout leaders feel that the strength of the community is specifically because of the high expectations placed upon its members; lower language expectations, they feel, would dilute the strength of the community. But Falk is not alone in comparing Cleveland's Hungarian community to other ethnicities: "At the Feast of the Assumption, everyone is Italian, whether they speak the language or not," and that is the inclusiveness that he sometimes finds lacking in Cleveland's Hungarian community. However, he cannot but admire the community, whose parents and leaders expend energy to keep maintaining the language. A close-knit community that shares values is able to impart cultural identity to its members, even far removed from Hungary.

Indeed, the factors influencing language maintenance, mirror, albeit 52 years later, the concluding remarks of Joshua Fishman in his 1966 study. Fishman stated that the major hope for the future of the Hungarian language in the U.S.A. would be "undoubtedly the youngest generation of Hungarian Americans. However, it is unlikely that its current interest in Hungarian, gratifying though it may be, will result in marked and sustained proficiency unless there is strong general encouragement to bring this about."[89] His conclusion was that only governmental and intellectual circles could provide this encouragement, yet these 18 examples of Cleveland-area Hungarian-Americans have shown that consistent parenting, coupled with a strong ethnic community of school and scouts, may also provide an environment for many decades on end.

When only 5–7 percent of Hungarians in the Cleveland area report speaking Hungarian regularly in the household, odds are that 93–95 percent of those with Hungarian ancestry will eventually assimilate. These 18 case studies, as examples of Cleveland Hungarians who maintain their language and culture, show how to beat those odds. Even late into the second and third generations, it is still very possible to maintain an ethnic language and culture and pass it on to the next generation. It all depends on strong parenting and the peer friendships put into place and enabled by a tight-knit community.

Conclusion

So what it means to be Hungarian in Cleveland boils down to maintaining the language, culture, and traditions. Transforming over the decades from geographical neighborhoods to commuting social groups, Cleveland Hungarian identity remains multi-faceted and diverse, with the common factor being commitment and effort. Sustaining a Hungarian identity requires perseverance and frequent contact with others who share similar facets of ethnic identity. But what of the future? How will the legacies of earlier members of the community alter the lives of Cleveland Hungarians yet to come?

Legacies of Each Wave of Immigration

Of the six larger waves of Hungarian immigration to the Cleveland area, an in-depth look at the first and the last remains outside of the scope of this study. The first wave, that of the 1848 Kossuth era, is long gone, and its descendants have all assimilated into Amerian society long ago. At the other end of the timeline, it is too soon to tell the effects of the most recent wave of immigrants, the young professionals of the 1990s and early twenty-first century. Of the middle four waves, however, the descendants of each form an integral part of today's Hungarian community life in Cleveland. What effect have the immigrants or their descendants had upon the Cleveland of today?

The old-timers [*óamerikások* or *öregamerikások*] left behind a lasting physical impact. Although their neighborhoods have mostly dissipated into the suburbs, the churches they built are lasting mementos, many still in use today.

Their working-class efforts left today's Cleveland community with physical reminders of their history. No other generation has built as much. The following generations, however, left more of a spiritual, intellectual, or ideological legacy.

The influence of the 1956 refugees, in terms of their anticommunism and overall sense of Hungarian community, cannot be understated. Going through a searing emotional experience in which the country united in freedom for two weeks against a Soviet intervention, then fleeing their homeland and continuing its traditions in the United States, especially during the Cold War when commemorations of 1956 were banned in Hungary, gave the refugees a sense of mission and duty that rejuvenated Cleveland's Hungarians as well.

But it was the members of the DP generation who had the largest and most lasting impact on today's Hungarian institutional life of Cleveland. István Szappanos described a twofold legacy left by the DP generation.[90] First, it left an intellectual legacy by promoting and preserving a sense of Hungarian identity with literature and writings, continually recalling and recreating the lost life in the homeland. Second, it left a legacy of working with Hungarian youth of the second and third generations through teaching and working with younger scouts. This impact was added to by members of the 1956 wave of immigrants as well, most of whom also fled their homeland due to political persecution. Although some historians such as Miklós Szántó[91] have focused on the differences between the DP and 1956 waves of immigration, Gyula Borbándi, himself an émigré, writes of a merging of waves in his study of Hungarian émigrés. He found that the arrival of the 1956 generation caused the DP generation to reevaluate their own roles, tasks, and goals. The entire Western émigré community felt that the 1956 Revolution was a common, uniting factor, and the two waves of immigration cooperated on numerous levels.[92] Such was the case in Cleveland as well. To quantitatively measure the impact of the DP generation on Cleveland's Hungarian institutions, an analysis was conducted on the leadership of the largest secular organizations, looking specifically at their elected executive committees or boards of directors as of 2017.

For example, the Cleveland Hungarian Heritage Society, which operates the museum in the downtown Galleria Mall, has a 33-member board of directors, including its 4 officers; fourteen are members of the DP generation and three are their descendants, including all of the 4 officers. Also, of 16 people listed on its honorary board of directors, 5 are members of the DP generation.[93]

For the Hungarian Association, its 2017 board and planning committee had 14 elected members, with 9 of them being of the DP generation or its descendants.[94] The Hungarian Cultural Center of Northeast Ohio, however, does not fit this pattern; all 16 members of its executive board were either born in the Cleveland area or arrived in other waves of immigration. Along the same lines, the executive committee of the Cleveland Hungarian Development Panel also had only one of 12 members from the DP generation.

One can definitely see the impact of the DP generation when looking at the leadership of the Hungarian scouting movement in Cleveland. The 4 Hungarian scout troops of Cleveland fall under the jurisdiction of a district commissioner. Of 9 district commissioners serving since 1955, 7 were of the DP generation or its descendants.[95] Most of the work of Hungarian scouting in Cleveland is done by its scoutmasters, those who are responsible for the day-to-day operations of the troops, including organizing camps and outings, parental communication, and leadership coordination; the position is rather like being a CEO, for it involves management of a troop with multiple layers of leadership, activities every week, and at least 30 members. In 2017, for example, the boy scout troop had over 40 active members, the girl scout troop over 60, and in the 1970s and 1980s each of the troops had over 100 active members, all meeting weekly. For Hungarian boy scout troop #22, 8 of its 13 scoutmasters since 1951 have been of the DP generation or descendants thereof, while for Hungarian girl scout troop #33, of 17 scoutmasters since 1957, 6 were of the DP generation. For Hungarian girl scout troop #34, 8 of 12 scoutmasters since 1952 were of the DP generation or its descendants, while for Hungarian scout troop #14, all but 4 of its 21 scoutmasters from 1951 to 2017 have been of the DP generation or its descendants. And the precursor to today's 4 Cleveland Hungarian scout troops was troop #12, existing from March to September of 1951, founded by DP refugee Ferenc Beodray.[96]

A separate organization linked to the scouting movement is the American Hungarian Friends of Scouting, which is the sponsoring organization of the Cleveland Hungarian scout troops. It guarantees the financial stability of the scout troops and functions as their social liason. Of its 15 elected and appointed board members, all but 2 are members or descendants of the DP generation.

Thus we can see that as of 2017, most of Cleveland's major Hungarian organizations had over half of their current executive boards who were members or descendants of the DP generation. For the scouting movement, that ratio was even higher, with 39 of 63 scoutmasters, or 62 percent being members or descendants of the DP generation, and 7 of 9, or 77 percent of its district commissioners. It is safe to say that the DP generation has shaped, formed, and left a noticeable and lasting impact on Cleveland's Hungarian community life. As Joseph Széplaki wrote, "Every immigrant lives in a divided world partly by choice and largely of necessity. He divides his attention between the social, political, and cultural phenomena of two countries. He is ineluctably bound to his native land even as he tries to prove loyal, receptive, and responsive to his adopted country. Thus he is very sensitive to the customs, institutions, and events in both countries."[97] By working with Cleveland's Hungarian youth through the scouting movement and by serving on the boards of directors of other institutions, the members of the DP generation laid a foundation for the Cleveland Hungarian community, creating a spiritual homeland built upon inherited values that enabled and sustained the vibrancy of its current state. Additionally, because the DP generation's organizational life was strongly committed to the use of the Hungarian language, which tends to slow assimilation, this commitment allowed Cleveland's Hungarian community to be able to welcome newer Hungarian immigrants who found a home in a community that spoke and embraced their language.

Although the DP generation seems to have shaped Cleveland's Hungarian community the most in recent years, an additional unusual cultural dynamic in Cleveland is that most of Cleveland's Hungarian organizations and churches have members of all immigrant generations on their boards, which demonstrates an underlying commitment to inclusivity, as well as a realization that it takes several layers of Hungarians to preserve the community. One of the secrets to any vibrant community is the consideration of various perspectives, and including third and fourth generation Cleveland Hungarians, as well as DPs, 56-ers, and recent immigrants in discussions and community work enables a broad mix of viewpoints, fresh ideas, and creativity.

Outlook for the Future

In the field of cultural studies one can be struck by the repetitive nature of history. Joshua Fishman's observation about the 1956 generation in comparison to earlier waves of immigration generalized it as being preoccupied with the process of adjustment: "Their current interests are frequently materialistic or self-centered with cultural or group attachments being much weaker in comparison ... Consequently, the 1956 Hungarian refugees are still largely 'untouched' by other Hungarian-Americans."[98] Ironically, Fishman's assertion is now frequently applied by 1956 refugees, thoroughly integrated since their arrival into Hungarian-American communities such as Cleveland's, to characterize more recent Hungarian immigrants of the twenty-first century. This strikes even closer to the heart when one reads Steven Béla Várdy's characterization of the turn of the century immigrants from the Dualist Period (Austria-Hungary between 1867 and 1918):

> ... most of [them] were basically traditional, religious, and nationalist individuals. Moreover, their nationalism and attachment to their homeland became even more pronounced after emigration. True, this nationalism was rather unsophisticated and emotional, nurtured by the overromanticized traditions of the Hungarian Revolution of 1848 ... Its most visible manifestations included an almost irrational anti-Habsburgism and a sincere but somewhat shallow national exhibitionism (e.g., the wearing of national costumes, the flourishing of national colors, the indulgence in emotional and flowery oratory, the tendency to blame others for the misfortunes of the Magyars, the making of exorbitant claims for Magyar achievements). Yet it was still this nationalism—however showy, naïve, and superficial—that was the primary ideological nourishment and guiding force of most Hungarian-Americans. This force retained much of its vitality ...[99]

Could not something similar also be said about the members of the DP generation? They, too, were basically traditional, religious, and nationalist individuals, whose attachment to their homeland became even more pro-

nounced after they were forced from their native land by the war and by Soviet occupation. Is it any wonder that they exhibited not an almost irratio-
nal anti-Habsburgism, but rather an almost rabid anticommunism? And
yet, their nationalism, and the term is not used here pejoratively, but in the
nemzeti (i.e., patriotic) sense of the word one can argue, was neither showy,
naïve, nor superficial, but rather, was deep-seated, based on personal experience, and genuine, and it also served as a guiding force for the establish-
ment of viable Hungarian institutions in Cleveland, institutions which contribute vitality even today. And as Dirk Hoerder stated, just like the Central
Europeans in Cleveland in the nineteenth century, who were "active agents
of change in their own lives who devised strategies of risk diversification ...
[and] lived transcultural lives, able to move in two different national, or more
often, regional cultures,"[100] so too do Cleveland's Hungarians move in two
different national cultures: the American one they live in, and the Hungarian one they create for themselves in their ethnic community.

And could not something similar be said about today's newest immigrants
from Hungary and its surrounding countries? Those who join Cleveland's
Hungarian community, seeing the inevitable progress of assimilation at work
in the second and third generations, could also be said to have a deep-seated, personal, and genuine national exhibitionism, one which differs slightly in its manifestations from earlier generations of immigrants but nonethe-
less expresses a sense of identity, of Hungarian culture and norms far removed
from the mother country. Indeed, knowing the effort that maintaining traditions, culture, and language so far from Hungary entails, this sense of identity is not surprising.

But what might the future bring? Gergely Hajdú-Németh, who was born
and raised in New Brunswick, New Jersey's Hungarian community, asked
this same question in his lecture at Lake Hope, during the August 2011 Itt-
Ott conference organized by the Hungarian Communion of Friends [Magyar
Baráti Közösség]. Active in the scouts and the *Csürdöngölő* folk dance group,
and a past president of the American Hungarian Foundation in New Brunswick, he provided a very insightful template for the future based on what he
saw as the strengths of each Hungarian-American organization. Every organization needs a unique interest, a practical marketing draw such as leadership

for the scouts, human rights for the Hungarian Human Rights Foundation, or Hungarian dance for a folk dance group. Good organizations have members, leaders, and a succession plan that involves younger members. He emphasized the successful use of technology such as email and social networking sites to connect Hungarians with similar interests. He also differentiated between older, or first generation personal experience with Hungary and today's successive younger generations' family experience with being Hungarian. Finally, he stressed the importance of a solid financial base, of utilizing existing infrastructure, and of cooperation among Hungarian organizations.

Another useful perspective for the future can be found in Attila Z. Papp's summary of his findings in his 2008 sociological study. He writes that "most organizational functions are really geared to responding to the challenge of assimilation" and that the assimilation process may be "slowed and delayed by committed intervention in the community setting." The intensity of commitment on the part of organizational leaders and members, he states, is "particularly noticeable if we consider that the individual has to respond not only to assimilation challenges but also fulfill ordinary private duties involving career and family. Upholding and preserving ethnic identity therefore cannot be separated from other segments of social identity."[101] Cleveland's Hungarian organizations offer a community that provides a social means of preserving and propagating Hungarian identity, through the simple method of living among other Hungarians. He also shares an insight about Hungarian-American organizational life that is very much applicable to Cleveland's situation. In summarizing the "transplanted vs. uprooted" cultural argument, he finds that "the organizations' response to the pressures of assimilation relies on a particularly American mixture of self-reliance, rootlessness, and preservation of existing cultural patterns. Self-reliance means that individuals recognize their own problems and those of their community; they act to manage these problems; and in all this the American example of volunteer community cooperation is of great assistance. The community creates its own self-sustaining organizations, based on volunteerism, mutual trust, and solidarity." As the previous chapters have shown, Cleveland's Hungarian communities are quite self-reliant, work together to solve common problems, and preserve existing cultural patterns, most notably in their folk traditions and language maintenance. To remain viable, they must continue to do the same, maintaining their language, culture, and traditions.

Krisztina Oláh specifically analyzed the communication strategies of Cleveland's Hungarian community in her Masters thesis.[102] She recommended a multipronged approach that capitalizes on the strengths of Cleveland's Hungarian communities and addresses its shortcomings. She compared Cleveland's Hungarians with other Hungarian communities in North America such as Boston and Detroit, then used a SWOT analysis, which is a strategic planning method for business projects. It entails analyzing the strengths, weakness, opportunities, and threats (SWOT) of any particular problem. Applying SWOT analysis to the communication practices of Cleveland's Hungarian community, she found that the strength lay in the long history of Hungarian community life in Cleveland, a well-established social order. The weaknesses were the lack of a physical community center, the overall older age of the leaders of the organizations, and the lack of a weekly or monthly paper or newsletter on all Hungarian events. She found the threats to the community to be generational differences, the assimilation process, and the weak communication practices of the organizations. She felt that opportunity for the community resided in a "communications facelift," possibly a community center, and establishing a community newspaper or magazine. Her communications strategy devised specifically for Cleveland's Hungarian community includes as her main points: "Creating a common community website, editing a monthly magazine or newsletter, empowering social media activities, making current communication channels (radio, events, organization newsletters) more effective, issuing an integrated database on Hungarians, creating a consistent image of the Hungarian community, regularly sending press releases to American and Hungarian papers, and choosing a designated spokesperson." Some of her recommendations have already been adopted: www.hungariancleveland.org is a website that showcases a calendar with every submitted Hungarian event organized in the Cleveland area, and www.bocskairadio.org is a Hungarian-language equivalent, offering not only a calendar but also local news and advertising.

Keeping these factors in mind, one can compare Cleveland's churches and organizations with Hajdú-Németh's and Papp's templates as described above and conclude that although use of electronic media still seems to be lacking, the other factors do seem to point to a stability and a base that will ensure successive generations a strong sense of Hungarian community in Cleveland. Incorporating more of Oláh's suggestions, furthermore, would really strengthen and bring these communities closer together. Cleveland has a long, rich history of Hungarian activities, and its future vibrancy depends on the work and dedication of parents, priests, and organizational leaders. Although assimilation into American culture is an unavoidable and unstoppable process, it is nevertheless possible to maintain the language, culture, and traditions into the second and third generations. However, it takes perseverance, leadership, getting along with others, and good old-fashioned hard work.

And Cleveland continues to flourish, proudly maintaining its Hungarian language and traditions. The scouts, the dance groups, the Hungarian school, and the churches all continue their work on a weekly basis, day-in and day-out, and the Hungarian school's enrollment actually increased in the last several years. The Hungarian Cultural Center of Northeast Ohio continues to attract hundreds to its picnics and events, and the Cleveland Hungarian Development Panel still raises significant funds for Hungarian causes. The Hungarian Association continues to organize its November conference, with famous keynote speakers and lecturers, and Cleveland's Hungarian radio programs continue to broadcast every week. Perhaps most visible in downtown Cleveland, the Cleveland Hungarian Heritage Society museum and library continues to offer monthly lectures and quality outreach to Cleveland's American community.

And not only continuing work characterizes Cleveland's Hungarian community but new things are also happening. For the last eight years, Lóránd Csibi has organized an informal family campout on the Hiram picnic grounds of the Hungarian Cultural Center of Northeast Ohio. This summer event, which attracts mostly new Hungarian immigrants to Cleveland, mainly from Transylvania, has slowly grown, having over 150 participants in 2017, with Hungarian food and music and fellowship for a long weekend in August. The casual weekend also involves volunteer maintenance work on the club grounds, showing a community-oriented outlook. And in 2017, Fr. Mezei organized an August twentieth festival commemorating St. Stephen, a holiday that everyone in Hungary regularly celebrates but nobody in Cleveland has for over 50 years. The street festival included live outdoor music with Harmonia and the Hungarian electrofolk band *Holdviola*, was held on the grounds of and adjacent to St. Emeric church, and attracted over a thousand participants, drawing from all over the Cleveland Hungarian social spectrum.

And Cleveland Hungarians also connect online, with multiple groups having significant Facebook presences as of April 2018. Of course, Facebook statistics can be misleading, because social media presence attracts a larger segment of the younger population than the older, and is usually accelerated by frequent photo posts; many organizations conduct outstanding or ongoing activities but do not post as many photographs, i.e., their efforts may go more into organizing the events and less into public relations. Nevertheless, social media presence offers another window into the following of various community groups. Church groups with a Facebook presence have between 155 and 714 followers, while bakeries' followers number between 175 and 1,729. Most organizations have 125–500 followers, with the Hungarian Cultural Center of Northeast Ohio boasting 912 followers, and the various scouting groups having 657–956. The broadest and most diverse of Facebook groups is "Clevelandi Magyar Kozosseg" [*sic*, Cleveland Hungarian Community], started by László Tár and now maintained by Lóránd Csibi and Zsolt Molnár. Its 868 members span most existing social groups, Hungarian churches, and secular organizations in Cleveland. Dwarfing all of these, however, is the Facebook page of Bocskai Rádió, which boasts 3,986 followers as of April 2018. The Hungarian communities of Cleveland are alive and well. Taken as a whole, this shrinking yet still vibrant community, with extended roots significantly shaped by the DP generation, will continue to maintain its Hungarian language and traditions, now and in the future, just as in 1950.

What, then, does it mean to be Hungarian in Cleveland? For many, it means maintaining the Hungarian language, using it in an everyday context with other Cleveland Hungarians, and passing it on to the next generation. It means inviting Hungarian authors, artists, dancers, and musicians to Cleveland. It means publishing books, newspapers, and newsletters in the Hungarian language. For some, it means being involved in Hungarian scouting. For many, it involves cooking and eating Hungarian foods, often at communal events such as church dinners or community festivals. It means listening to Hungarian radio programs. It means getting together with other Cleveland Hungarians, uniting for a common goal. It means participating in recurring traditions and customs, year after year, often with the same group of people, thereby adding predictability and an expectation to the seasons of life. It means passing on to the next generation not only the language but also Hungarian traditions and customs. For many, being Hungarian in Cleveland also means assimiliation and changing neighborhoods. Over the years, it has meant shifting from a geographical entity to a spiritual community, where instead of merely living near each other, members of the community actively travel and commit time to participate in the activities of the community. To be Hungarian in Cleveland is different now than it was in 1950. As the years pass, all grow older, new members arrive and are born, and as each new year dawns, the community continues—which is the reason why I chose to end with a New Year's poem written in Hungarian by local Clevelander Imre Bogárdy. Because throughout the years and even now, just as in 1950, being Hungarian in Cleveland means maintaining language, culture, and traditions in a community setting.

And so it will continue to be.

Bogárdy Imre: Újévi Kívánság[103]

Ismét egy esztendő hanyatlik a sírba,
Nézhetünk utána nevetve, vagy sírva.

Sokan biz örömest búcsúznak el tőle.
Azt várják, hogy különb lesz a követője.

Itt állok magamban is, azt óhajtom itten,
Jobb időket érjünk, mint az elmúlt évben.

Mindenkire áldást, a hazánkban békét,
Az emberek szívében boldog egyetértést.

Ezért fohászkodunk, ezért ver a szívünk,
Adjon az Úr Isten Boldog Új Esztendőt nekünk.

APPENDIX I
Collections of Hungarian Books and Publications in Cleveland

This listing of Cleveland's Hungarian publishing is organized geographically in order to give future researchers an overall picture of where exactly various published Hungarian materials can be found in Cleveland.

The downtown branch of the Cleveland Public Library has an enormous collection of books published in the Hungarian language, officially numbered at 12,000 volumes.[104] This number was verified by visiting the fourth floor shelves open to the public and, using a matrix counting method, an estimated 6,500 volumes were found. These were mostly translations of popular fiction, but also included cookbooks, religion, and history books as well. The Hungarian periodical section includes extensive collections including current editions of the popular magazines *Nők Lapja* [Women's journal], *Kiskegyed* [Your grace], and *Hölgyvilág* [Ladies' world]. Additionally, the fifth floor of the library contains approximately 7,500 volumes of older literature in rarer editions; this collection has restricted access, but a simple conversation with staff members in the foreign literature section allows access. The author personally counted over 240 volumes of Mór Jókai's books alone, as well as complete sets of the famed Révay encyclopedia, and literary works by József Nyírő, Albert Wass, Áron Gábor, and other émigré writers, as well as extensive collections by János Arany, Sándor Petőfi, Géza Gárdonyi, Magda Szabó, László Passuth, and other writers well known in Hungary. Some examples of rare editions found on the Cleveland Public Library's fifth-floor shelves are Pál Balogh's *A népfajok Magyarországon* [Ethnicities in Hungary], published in Budapest in 1902, as well as a twelve-volume collection, *Kossuth összes Munkái* [Complete works of Kossuth], published by Athaenaeum in 1880. The library adds between 50 and 100 Hungarian books to its collection every year; in 2011, for example, it added 43 Hungarian books in its first biannual purchase. These ranged from science to children's to dictionaries to cookbooks to translations of modern popular fiction, and in 2011 included such literary authors as Gyula Krúdy, Kálmán Mikszáth, Magda Szabó, Albert Wass, and the historian Sándor Szakály. In 2016 the purchase included 30 titles, including translations of popular fiction, some science and health books, and contemporary poets and writers like János Lackfi.

A smaller but quite accessible Hungarian library can be found in the Cleveland Hungarian Heritage Society's museum in the Galleria mall. Although not as extensive as the collection of the Cleveland Public Library, the museum's library is conveniently housed in a comfortable room, is neatly organized, and has rare historical collections, especially of émigré literature and the personal papers of Cleveland Hungarians. Perusing the shelves of this smaller library containing about 6,000 volumes, over 65 Hungarian language books published in Cleveland alone can be found, as well as an extensive collection of historical and political books about Hungarian topics, especially the twentieth century, numbering 136 books, all published outside Hungary. Its émigré fiction section has 293 Hungarian books published outside Hungary, including multiple volumes from Albert Wass, József Nyírő, Lajos Füry, István Eszterhás, and Áron Gábor. The publishers range from Cleveland to Canada, Argentina to Australia. Its émigré poetry section contains 215 books, including multiple volumes from József Kovácsy, Tibor Tollas, Ferenc Mózsi, Irén Négyesy, and Péter Hargitai, among others.

Also in the Hungarian Heritage Museum library are mostly complete collections of Hungarian language periodicals published in Cleveland throughout the years. These include *Szabadság* [Freedom], and *Képes Magyar Világhíradó*, also known on its masthead as *Illustrated Hungarian World Review*, editions of *Új Idő: Ismeretterjesztő és irodalmi folyóirat* [New times: a journal of literature and common knowledge], *Őrszem* [Sentry], which morphed into *Nyugati Őrszem* [Western sentry]. The Cleveland Hungarian Heritage Museum's library also holds many back editions of *Erős Vár: Amerikai Magyar Evangéli-kusok Lapja* [Strong Fortress: American Hungarian Lutheran newspaper], as well as many back issues of *Katolikus Magyarok Vasárnapja* [Catholic Hungarians' sunday] and the far-right *Szittyakürt* [Scythian bugle].

In addition, the museum's archives include "Night in Budapest" program booklets from throughout the years and mailing lists dating back to 1935, as well as scrapbooks from 1953–1966, 1980, and 1984–1986 compiled by the Cleveland chapter of the World Federation of Hungarian Veterans (MHBK), including obituaries of prominent Cleveland Hungarian veterans. The museum also holds the records of the Magyar Club of Cleveland from 1924 to 2009, including membership lists, correspondence, official minutes, and event fliers. Another organization whose papers ended up in the museum was the Committee for Hungarian Liberation [*Magyar Felszabadító Bizottság*], with papers from 1956 to 1971. The museum also harbors the manuscript collections of three members of the DP generation who settled in Cleveland. Elemér Homonnay, who died in 1986, was an engineer at General Electric, and he bequeathed his personal correspondence and research activity from the 1930s to the 1980s. Ernest Pereszlényi, who died in 1973, donated his collection of witness statements collected by wartime Hungarian Army command elements regarding confiscated property by Soviet authorities. László Sirchich, who died in 1983, bequeathed personal papers; he edited the periodical *Kettős Járom Alatt* [Under a double yoke] from 1951 to 1966.

Also in the possession of the Cleveland Hungarian Heritage Society, in separate storage, are the audio tapes and film archives of Miklós Kossányi's NBN Studio. These include professional quality three-quarter inch SVHS tapes as well as reel-to-reel audio tapes of Cleveland Hungarian events from the 1960s through the early twenty-first century. Kossányi was very active in Cleveland's Hungarian community, filming balls, picnics, commemorations, and conducting interviews of famous visiting Hungarian personalities. Over 450 films from his estate were donated to the society's museum.

Another part of the Kossányi estate is the personal Hungarian book collection from his home, which numbers close to a thousand and resides in the office of the Fulbright guest professor from Hungary at Cleveland State University. This small but valuable collection includes many volumes of classical

Hungarian literature, as well as significant Hungarian émigré literature and numerous very rare Hungarian books, some published in the United States in the nineteenth century.

The library of the Western Reserve Historical Society in University Circle, which contains many historical artifacts from Cleveland's past, also has a number of Hungarian items in its collection, the most important being a manuscript of Lajos Kossuth's speech given in Cleveland in 1852 with the statesman's own presumable signature. Other highlights of the collection include a complete collection of the *Szabadság* newspaper and many older photographs of Cleveland Hungarian neighborhoods. The *Szabadság* issues from 1988–1994 are on microfilm, and the library also contains earlier Hungarian newspapers that were eventually absorbed by *Szabadság*, including *Amerikai Magyar Világ* [American Hungarian world] and *A jó pásztor* [Good shepherd]. The library also contains many original editions of *Az Újság* [The newspaper] and *Magyar Újság* [Hungarian newspaper], as well as the short-lived youth newspaper *Patria*.

The Western Reserve Historical Society's library also contains the records spanning 1926 to 1962 of the Cleveland Hungarian Aid Society, formed in 1863 by Morris and David Black, Jewish Hungarian immigrants who formed their benevolent society to help new immigrants, assist the needy and sick, bury the dead, and provide benefits to widows and orphans. In 1948, the Society reorganized as a cemetery society, and in the early 1960s its operations were taken over by Park Synagogue. The library also contains family histories of the Rosner and Tykodi families, as well as the personal papers of Manuel Silberger (died 1958), Louis László Balogh (died 1971), Steve Szalai (died 1973), Frank Szappanos (died 1975), and Jack Russell (died 1979), all written in Hungarian.

Additionally, the second through the fiftieth *Krónika*, proceedings of the Hungarian Congress in Cleveland from 1962 to 2011, are scanned and fully available online on the website of the Hungarian Association; they provide insightful snapshots of Hungarian cultural thought in Cleveland and in the diaspora, spanning a half century.

Missing from most local library collections are church congregational anniversary pamphlets, which are often treasure troves of useful historical information, often with pictures and advertising as well. Especially noteworthy is an unpublished exhaustive history of St. Elizabeth church written for the church's 125th anniversary by Nicholas Boros, who plans on using the existing manuscript as the basis for a future Master's thesis.

APPENDIX II
Survey of Scholarship and Extended Theoretical Background

Survey of Scholarship

A great body of literature exists delineating the role of Hungarian-Americans in general. Pioneering historians include Sándor Márki, Eugene Pivány, Charles Feleky, Géza Kende, Edmund Vasváry, and Emil Lengyel, while in Hungary their work was paralleled by Gusztáv Thirring, Andor Löherer, Lóránt Hegedűs, Alajos Kovács, Géza Hoffmann, Iván Nagy, Imre Kovács, Dénes Jánossy, and István Gáll. A burgeoning of Hungarian-American scholarship grew out of the 1960s, including doctoral dissertations by historians P. Bődy, Nándor Dreisziger, M.L. Kovács, Zoltán Kramár, Tamás Szendrey, Steven Béla Várdy, B. Vassady, and F.S. Wagner, in the field of linguistics and literature E. Bakó, Joshua Fishman, A. Kerek, Leslie Könnyű, W. Nemser, and Ágnes Huszár Várdy, in ethnography L. Dégh, M. Hollós, M. Sozan, B. Maday, and A. Vázsonyi, in sociology P. Benkart and A.S. Weinstock, and bibliographies and archival studies compiled by A. as well as M. Boros-Kazai, R. Biro, I. Halász de Beky, L.L. Kovács, A.J. Molnár, and F. Vitéz.

One of the best is the comprehensive book by Julianna Puskás, *Ties That Bind, Ties That Divide: 100 Years of Hungarian Experience in the United States* (2000), which is an extensive study spanning part of the nineteenth and the entire twentieth century. This 444-page sociological and historical study is detailed yet readable, and it provides not only an overview of Hungarian waves of migration, but also firsthand experiences to provide the perspective of ordinary lives.

Miklós Szántó's *Magyarok Amerikában* [Hungarians in America], on the other hand, is not nearly as exhaustive, but nevertheless provides an overall view of Hungarian migration. Published in communist Budapest in 1984, it reviews the successive waves of migration (interwar, post-Second World War refugees from the Displaced Persons camps, and 1956) as disparate and separate, and focuses mostly on the conflicts among them, as well as providing an overview of Hungarian government policies toward its émigrés.

Gábor Tarján's 2003 article in *Magyar Szemle* [Hungarian viewpoint] provides an accurate portrayal of Hungarian-American life, looked at from the perspective of a folk ethnographer. His readable summary details major waves of immigration, addresses language and cultural questions, gives an overview of Hungarian schooling in the United States, and touches on the scouting movement and higher education. In addition, he perceptively characterizes bilingualism, religious and cultural life, the image of Hungary, and dual identities of Hungarians born in the U.S.A., based on his extensive experience living in the Hungarian communities of New Jersey. His conclusions, which question whether Hungarian-American institutions and life can long survive, have with the hindsight of fifteen years been proven wrong, although the general tendencies he described are still accurate.

A fairly recent scholarly work is *Beszédből világ: elemzések, adatok amerikai magyarokról* [Life from speech: analysis and data about American Hungarians], a sociological study compiled by Attila Z. Papp in 2007 and published amidst controversy in 2008.[105] A detailed and objective analysis of modern Hungarian-American communities, the authors conducted 53 extended interviews with leaders of organizations in Hungarian communities in various US cities and provide a useful analysis of the ongoing viability of these communities.

Not peer-reviewed but nevertheless quite useful is the blog written by Dezső Farkas, a marketing researcher born in Hungary but who has lived for over 10 years in New Jersey and California. In 2015 he conducted a three-month online survey of Hungarian-Americans (or American-Hungarians, as the case may be), reaching 47 states. With methodological help and coordination with Attila Z. Papp (who conducted a contemporary parallel study of Hungarians living in the United Kingdom) and an unnamed statistician, the sociological study had almost 2,200 respondents, and its methodology is quite transparent. It was not publicized broadly in "traditional" historical Hungarian-American communities, amassing only 90 responses from New Jersey (with 407 respondents from California, however, 157 from Florida, and 130 from Texas), but it gives useful insights about the recent Hungarian diaspora, and its coverage can be seen as providing many more details than either the 2000 or the 2010 US Census. Its analysis clusters responses about home country, satisfaction, identity, and language proficiency into seven major groups, with attitude as well as demographic portrayals. The study's analysis is quite effective, and paints a recognizable picture of Hungarian-Americans today.

Some quite useful studies were conducted by émigré scholars, most notably by the historian Steven Béla Várdy. Comparable in quality and comprehensiveness to Julianna Puskás's seminal work, his massive *Magyarok az Újvilágban* [Hungarians in the New World] (2000) is written in the Hungarian language. This work encompasses a century and a half of Hungarian-American history, and gives an accurate and detailed portrayal of political, historical, and sociological trends among the Hungarians in the United States. Most of its material has been published in journals before, but it synthesizes very effectively, providing not only insightful analysis, but also trustworthy details proving the general trends.

Somewhat shorter and older, but nevertheless still quite useful is Várdy's *The Hungarian-Americans*, published in 1985. This book addresses not only the successive waves of migration but also gives a comprehensive picture of Hungarian-American history, journalism, publishing, and scholarship. It also includes useful observations about the perpetuation of culture, as well as a case study of the Hungarian Association of Cleveland.

Compiled and written together with his wife, Ágnes Huszár Várdy, *Újvilági küzdelmek: az amerikai magyarok élete és az óhaza* [Struggles of the New World: Hungarian-American lives and the old country] contains 23 articles previously published in Hungarian journals by the Várdys. The themes of the writings range from the past and present of Hungarian-American life to the impact of Lajos Kossuth on America, from religious and social life of Hungarian-Americans to their relationship with Hungary. Another quite useful journal article, albeit now almost 30 years old, was written by the Várdys in 1985. "Hungarian Literary, Linguistic, and Ethnographic Research on Hungarian-Americans: a Historiographical Assessment" does a fine job summarizing Hungarian Studies scholarship up until that point.

Gyula Borbándi's *A magyar emigráció életrajza 1945–1985* [The Story of Hungarian emigration 1945–1985] is comprehensive, objective, and deals mainly with Hungarian émigré literary and political life. Although it discusses Hungarian émigrés worldwide, Hungarian-Americans nevertheless figure prominently in it. Originally published in Bern in 1985, it details three waves of emigration: 1945, 1947, and 1956.

Lesser works also prevail. Leslie Konnyu's 80-page *Hungarians in the United States: an Immigration Study* is a shorter contribution providing a brief background of Hungary's history to the American reader, continuing with phases of Hungarian immigration to the U.S.A., a short chapter on the Americanization of Hungarians, and concluding with a listing of Hungarian contributions to America in language, literature, arts, science-industry, public and military service, cuisine, singing-dancing-acting, and sports.

Joseph Széplaki compiled *The Hungarians in America 1583–1974: A Chronology & Fact Book*. This study provides a useful chronology of dates, offers primary documents and letters of importance, and includes statistics and listings of Hungarian-American institutions, population tables, university language courses, publications, Hungarian collections in American libraries, and Hungarian-named geographic locations in the U.S.A.

Prompted by the visit of Cardinal Joseph Mindszenty to North America, István Török's *Katolikus Magyarok Észak-Amerikában* [Catholic Hungarians in North America] provides a succinct historical as well as a detailed contemporary look at Hungarian Catholic churches, Catholic church organizations, monks, nuns, clergy, Catholic youth organizations, and Catholic publishing in Canada and the United States. Newer and broader in scope is Attila Miklósházy's *A tengeren túli emigráns magyar katolikus egyházi közösségek rövid története Észak- és Dél-amerikában, valamint Ausztráliában* [The short history of émigré Hungarian Catholic Churches across the ocean in

North and South America as well as Australia], published in 2005. On the Protestant front, Zoltán Béky assembled a concise history of the Hungarian Reformed Federation in America, covering 1896 to 1970, titled *Az amerikai magyar református egyesület főbb eseményei* [The Hungarian Reformed Federation's main events].

Also worth mentioning is the modern photographic work of the scholar Gergely Tóth. He travels the world, looking up Hungarian émigré communities in Australia, South America, but mostly in the United States, and Cleveland and its vicinity figures prominently on his website, with recent photographs of places of Hungarian interest. The most recent objective portrayal of Hungarian-Americans is a five-part documentary film produced by the city TV station of Debrecen under the leadership of Tamás Széles and Ferenc Vojtkó, *Üzenem az otthoni hegyeknek* [Message to the mountains at home], completed in 2011. It is not a comprehensive study, but is quite representative, and offers an objective, realistic snapshot of the current state of Hungarian communities in Los Angeles, San Francisco, Cleveland, Boston, New Brunswick, three in Connecticut, and Washington, D.C., along with a short historical introduction to each city.

However, not many scholars have specifically studied Cleveland, although 12 of the 53 interviewees (23 percent) in Attila Z. Papp's work were from the city. Julianna Puskás does have an excellent chapter entitled "The Magyars in Cleveland, 1880–1930" in *Identity, Conflict, and Cooperation: Central Europeans in Cleveland, 1850–1930*, a comprehensive study of six groups of immigrants from Croatia, the Czech lands, Hungary, Poland, Slovakia, and Slovenia. The book provides useful insights about the immigration experience, and Puskás's chapter does trace the development of the Hungarian neighborhoods in the Cleveland area. Most scholars who have explicitly researched Cleveland were Hungarians living there, notably Stephen Erdely, Susan Papp (no relation to Attila Z. Papp), Dr. Ferenc Somogyi, Imre Gál, Alan Attila Szabo, Géza Szentmiklósy Éles, Tibor Bognár, and the scholars John Sabol and Steve Piskor. Let us take a closer look at these works next.

Stephen Erdely published a short article in the January 1964 edition of *Ethnomusicology* entitled "Folksinging of the American Hungarians in Cleveland." He analyzed the traditional song repertoire and the art of folksinging cultivated by Cleveland Hungarians, in particular the 26 active members of the Hungarian American Singing Society, originally formed in 1908 in Cleveland.

Géza Éles Szentmiklósy, who had degrees in law, political science, and history, lived in Cleveland for 27 years and wrote a well-researched treatise on Cleveland's Hungarians titled *Two Hungarian Immigrations: Victims of Misconceptions*. Amply footnoted, the work addresses ethnicity and the melting pot in America, the DP generation, the 1956 generation, and gives a detailed and comprehensive listing of Hungarian organizations active in Cleveland around 1975. The work has a personal slant but is nevertheless a thorough study.

Susan Papp grew up in Cleveland, the child of DP refugees, experiencing its Hungarian life firsthand. Her monograph, *Hungarian Americans and their Communities of Cleveland*, published by the Ethnic Heritage Studies department at Cleveland State University in 1981, is a comprehensive account, devoting one quarter of its contents to an overall history of Hungary, one quarter to Hungarians in America, and over half exclusively to the Hungarian communities of Cleveland. Full of maps and archival photographs, it traces not only the historical development of Cleveland's Hungarian communities but also contains several appendices detailing ethnicity and politics, a case study of building a Hungarian church, and of Hungarian contributions to culture. Although now over 35 years old, it has remained the authoritative English-language study of Cleveland Hungarians. The methodology of the present study differs slightly from that of Susan Papp, but the intent when starting the research was to update and complement her work.

Dr. Ferenc Somogyi was trained in law in pre-Second World War Hungary, was elected to its Parliament in 1939, and emigrated as a refugee of the Second World War, settling in Cleveland in 1951 and taking an active part in its Hungarian intellectual life. His last published work was a history of Hungarians in Cleveland titled *A clevelandi magyarság vázlatos története* [Outline history of Cleveland Hungarians], in 1994. His monograph is also comprehensive, offering a detailed listing of Hungarian organizations in Cleveland from a historical perspective, beginning with Lajos Kossuth's 1852 visit to the city, through the stories of Hungarian oligarchs such as Tivadar Kundtz, chronicling the lives and important facts of each of Cleveland's Hungarian churches as social entities, detailing Cardinal Joseph Mindszenty's visit to Cleveland, and concluding with a very readable listing of active Hungarian organizations in the Cleveland of 1994. Somogyi brought over 40 years of personal experience in Cleveland's Hungarian life to his research, and his work is by far the most exhaustive yet easily readable book on Hungarians in Cleveland published in the Hungarian language. His comprehensive history was chosen as a model for the present study, but in contrast, this study uses the English language to reach a broader audience.

Imre Sári Gál was born and educated in Hungary and came to Cleveland after 1956. He wrote two books about the Hungarians in Cleveland: *Az amerikai Debrecen: képek a clevelandi magyarság életéből* [The American Debrecen: pictures from the life of Hungarian Cleveland], and *Clevelandi Magyar Múzeum: riportok, versek, fényképek a clevelandi magyarság életéből* [Cleveland Hungarian Museum: reports, poems, photos from the life of Hungarian Cleveland]. Both were published in Toronto, the former in 1966 and the latter in 1978. Less scholarly in nature and more of a collection of the author's poems, newspaper articles, and photographs of Hungarian life in Cleveland, these books are valuable treasures with quality interviews, census statistics, detailed histories and descriptions of some businesses and clubs, and accurate listings of all Hungarian organizations in Cleveland, snapshots of Hungarian life in Cleveland in the 1960s and 1970s. The books read like a newspaper, objectively reported yet with a personal interest perspective, and with many photographs, flyers, advertisements, and letterhead samples reproduced to give the reader an impressionistic view of Cleveland's Hungarian life.

Alan Attila Szabo researched Hungarian-American communities of the greater Cleveland area and submitted a cultural anthropology analysis as his Master's thesis at Kent State University in 2001. Drawing on information collected while selling life insurance and determining potential customers' interest in a Hungarian mail order business, he attended hundreds of Hungarian events in Northeast Ohio and assembled a database of 400 individuals and their families, who all defined themselves as Hungarian or of Hungarian descent. He then randomly selected 100 individuals from his database and found similar results to the US Census proportions of Hungarian speakers to Hungarian ancestry. Additionally, he found that of his sample, 10 percent married another Hungarian-American, and those who did, 40 percent had at least one sibling also marry a Hungarian; 10 percent of the offspring of these unions married another Hungarian-American, which points to a standard assimilation process.

Tibor Bognár, on the other hand, did not spend nearly as much time in Cleveland as the previously mentioned authors. A graduate student in media and communications at John Carroll University, he only lived in Cleveland for two years as a member of the Calasanctius Training Program (a nonprofit organization founded by the Buffalo Hungarian ophthalmologist Péter Forgách to train graduate students from Hungary in business and ethical practices), and has since returned to Hungary. His documentary film, self-produced and self-filmed as his master's thesis, is still being taught in graduate media classes at John Carroll University and also in courses at the University of Debrecen. Titled "The Last Hungarian on Buckeye," it uses excellent archival black and white photographs and personal interviews to trace the development and demise of the old Hungarian neighborhood of Buckeye Road, where many Hungarian immigrants arrived and lived. Buckeye Road was the home of at least half a dozen Hungarian churches in a very close-knit neighborhood, where the Hungarian language was so prevalent that local businesses displayed signs stating "We speak English."

The official TV station in Debrecen, Hungary, produced several noteworthy documentary films about Hungarian-American communities, devoting one 25-minute episode exclusively to Cleveland. Additionally, Réka Pigniczky's documentary film *Inkubátor*, with the author's collaboration, also mentions some aspects of Cleveland and its Hungarian community, as does her third film, *Megmaradni* [Heritage]. The latest and most in-depth documentary film about an important aspect of Cleveland's Hungarian community, however, is Réka Pigniczky's two-part series made for Duna World Television and aired in Hungary in early 2014, *Kodály a Cuyahogán* [Kodály on the Cuyahoga]. Devoted to the Hungarian Scout Folk Ensemble's 40th anniversary performance in November of 2013, the documentary gives an in-depth look at the community through interviews and active documentation; the film shows how the community maintains its traditions into the second and third generations.

John Sabol published the most recent book on Cleveland's Buckeye Road neighborhood, titled simply *Cleveland's Buckeye Neighborhood* (2011). The book touches on the Slovak population but focuses mainly on the Hungarian population, using 208 historical pictures, each with a short, solidly-researched descriptive paragraph. The book offers a historical glimpse into the everyday lives of the Hungarians who lived along Buckeye Road in its heyday. Additionally, Steve Piskor's *Gypsy Violins* (2012) has extensive chapters devoted to Cleveland's Gypsy musicians.

The author's previous work can also be added to this category; in 2008 the Hungarian Scout Folk Ensemble published a collection of oral histories of Hungarians in Cleveland, conducted by local teenaged scouts doing ethnographic field work in 14 Hungarian churches within driving distance of Cleveland. Titled *Clevelandben még élnek magyarok? Visszaemlékezések gyűjteménye* [Do Hungarians still live in Cleveland? A collection of oral histories], the book contains some firsthand memories of emigration from Hungary and its surrounding countries but mostly memories of Hungarian traditions in Cleveland, including harvest festival, Easter, Christmas, food, wedding, and Buckeye Road customs. The book is written in Hungarian. In addition, *Cold War to Warm Cooperation – Egy amerikai város magyar katonái 1950–2014*, is a bilingual book mostly of oral histories of those Cleveland Hungarians who served in the US military during the Cold War to the present day. It contains over 250 interviews and photographs, and delves deeper into the military history aspect of Cleveland's Hungarian community, while also offering very personal glimpses into historical events.

Extended Theoretical Background

This study drew on the methodology of Zoltán Fejős in his study of Chicago Hungarians, *A chicagói magyarok két nemzedéke 1890–1940* [Two generations of Chicago Hungarians 1890–1940]. He used personal data to provide important source materials, which allowed him to employ a bottom-up approach to "proceed from the 'lower' level of individual facts towards understanding more general phenomena and processes." Like his study, I also utilized a concept of culture based on an anthropological-ethnographic interpretation, which "provides an interpersonal, interactional and symbolic approach to everyday life and a common knowledge which motivates human activities as an implicit set of values. This set of knowledge is a dynamic construction." Also extremely useful was his observation and warning that "the definition 'Chicago Hungarians' is basically misleading. The study warns us how unreliable it is to use such adjectives in a general sense. Hungarians formed a heterogenous group from the aspect of settlements, social strata, religious affiliation, and culture... [and] it seems important that Hungarians in Chicago were a diaspora within the Hungarian diaspora." The same thing can be said about Cleveland Hungarians. They, too, are heterogenous, with different social circles and areas of interest and levels of participation. Nevertheless, just as in Chicago, it may also be said about Cleveland that "the Hungarian population of differentiated origins could generate a feeling of belonging together on the basis of their common origin, common language, and transplanted customs," and "traditions certainly changed to some extent but did not lose their continuity. Folk habits could also become part of the communities' life within the institutions supported mainly by the continued influence of the old country."[106] In Cleveland's case, however, the influence of the old country, or more specifically, its government, was negligible due to the Cold War and the inherent anticommunism of Cleveland's Hungarians. But the DP generation was able to recreate the prewar Hungarian culture that they left behind as refugees. Folk habits already were, in fact, part of Cleveland Hungarian life, and due to the influx of the DP generation became an even more integral part of their lives.

In terms of assimilation theory, the long prevailing view has been of the American melting pot, in which various ethnicities assimilate and form a quintessentially American culture. In this view, it is only a question of time before immigrants and their succeeding generations lose their ethnic identity and become Americanized. Richard Alba and Victor Nee, on the other hand, reformulated a theory of assimilation. The contemporary alternative to assimilation, they state, is an alternative vision of vigorous ethnic pluralism maintaining ethnic connections in an age of globalization that spawned a substantial body of scholarship known as transnationalism.

Their thesis began with the Chicago School sociological definition of assimilation, continued with the melting pot metaphor, and finally rethought the conceptual foundation of assimilation, arguing that post-Second World War changes in mainstream American society combine with the social capital and networking that immigrants bring with them. They predict, however, that "despite the accuracy of some of the criticisms of the canonical formations of assimilation, [they] believe that there is still a vital core to the concept, which has not lost its utility for illuminating many of the experiences of contemporary immigrants and the new second generation."[107] Contemporary immigration, they argue, has and will have more diverse outcomes than waves of mostly European immigration of the past. Some will assimilate upwards in terms of social mobility, and others downward, depending on what they bring with them and depending on the rigidity of racial, religious, and social boundaries. Indeed, Alba and Nee conclude that

> Assimilation has reshaped the American mainstream in the past, and it will do so again, culturally, institutionally, and demographically. The cultural reshaping of the mainstream that we see as resulting from immigration is not accurately conveyed by the metaphor of the melting pot, which implies that change is largely a process of fusing elements from different cultures into a new, unitary culture. Certainly, there are syncretisms in American culture, but much cultural change appears to occur as the mainstream expands to accommodate cultural alternatives, usually after they have been 'Americanized' to some extent, by shedding their more exotic aspects.[108]

Alba and Nee's reformulation of assimilation is reinforced by Dirk Hoerder in his introduction to the study of six Central European groups, including Hungarians, in their experiences in Cleveland from 1850 to 1930. He writes about a complex process of acculturation, community-building, workplace activity, and family life, that "the life-trajectories of the immigrants and sojourners were more complex that any one-dimensional model of Americanization suggested. They constructed a variety of institutions, social spaces, transoceanic networks, and in the process played a central part in determining the future course of a prototypical American city, Cleveland."[109]

Within the continuum of assimilation, with complete assimilation at one end and bicultural transnationalism at the other end, lie two more frameworks. Herbert Gans formulated an idea of symbolic ethnicity, where the third (sometimes even second) generation refrains from ethnic behavior that requires time or effort or membership in an organization, but rather shows a nostalgic allegiance to culture, a pride in tradition and food, and a historical interest in the symbolic functions of the old country at the time of ancestral departure. This symbolic ethnicity does not need a group setting; it is rather a leisure-time activity that does not interfere with everyday life, much like Irish-Americans taking part in a St. Patrick's Day or Italian-Americans in a Columbus Day parade. Another framework is segmented assimilation. As formulated by Alejandro Portes and Min Zhou, this theory breaks groups of immigrants into segments roughly based on their attachment to their ethnic groups and neighborhoods. One stage of this segmented assimilation of post-1965 immigrants, they observed, is when immigrants "deliberately hold values embedded in their native culture and maintain a tight solidarity within their ethnic community."[110] Although they studied Latino and Asian neighborhoods and communities, Portes and Zhou's theories of segmented assimilation also apply to Cleveland's Hungarians. Their neighborhoods are no longer geographically tight; nevertheless, many members of the community still exhibit a tight solidarity with their community's values.

Elliott Barkan, Hasia Diner, and Alan Kraut refined these concepts even further, using the term "incorporation" instead of "assimilation" to describe the actions taken by individual migrants and their families to bring them closer to the host society, as opposed to assimilation, which also includes the consent and cooperation of those native to a society to accept newcomers. Indeed, "retaining ethnic identity even as they pursue integration into American society has always been a formidable task for newcomers to the United States."[111] Yet this dual process of retaining and incorporating can be accomplished, as the research on Cleveland Hungarians has shown. It is entirely possible to retain language and ethnicity deep into the second and third generations while at the same time being valuable and productive, patriotic members of American society. Barkan, Diner, and Kraut reevaluated old theories on assimilation and reformulated them into a seeming oxymoron that nevertheless makes sense: "Migrants at the turn of the last century and now neither exclusively cling to the traditions of their homeland nor rush to embrace acculturation. They do both. At one and the same time they seek to preserve traditions, which anchor them in the world, and embrace what they see as cultural innovation."[112] So too is it with Cleveland's Hungarians, who are able to both preserve traditions and identity as well as to seamlessly fit into American society successfully and patriotically.

Thus one can draw a continuum of assimilation, with complete assimilation at one end, followed by symbolic ethnicity, then segmented assimilation, and finally biculturalism and transnationalism. However, assimilation and transnationalism are not merely theories, but rather social processes, and they are inextricably intertwined. Furthermore, four generations of at least five different waves of immigration are all together in one community of Cleveland Hungarians, and thus it is hard to apply one theory across all members of a community, especially members who have varying intensity in the strength and proximity of their ties to the community. Some consider themselves Hungarian and take part in the community's life once a year or less frequently, while for others their Cleveland Hungarian identity entails taking part in social activities on an ongoing basis several times per week.

Having said that, despite the seemingly inevitable process of assimilation, i.e., that each succeeding generation tends to maintain its culture and language less and less, an ethnic community such as Cleveland's Hungarian community provides a social means of group identity and vigorous ethnic pluralism, one that enables even second and third generations after original immigration to maintain their language, culture, and traditions, thus adding to and enhancing their city and the American mainstream. Indeed, the community offers an opportunity for language and identity maintenance for first generation immigrants, i.e., those who were born in Hungary or its surrounding countries. An additional yet separate issue is language and identity formation for the second and third generations, i.e., those whose parents or grandparents immigrated but who they themselves were born in the Cleveland area. This is the crucial difference between language and identity maintenance for the first generation, and (in addition to the maintenance) language and identity formation for the second and third generations. The three most important theories for illuminating these two processes, identity maintenance and identity formation, and the main theoretical frameworks used throughout this study are the communication theory of identity of Ewa Urban and Mark Orbe, the microcosm of inherited values by Attila Z. Papp, and the spiritual homeland theory of László Bőjtös.

Ewa Urban and Mark Orbe's work on the identity and communication of immigrants shows that immigrants live in two social worlds, and their identity is transformed into one that is multilocal. Immigrants constantly face the pressure to decide who they are and where their home is, which is related to their cultural worldview and the communication theory of identity (CTI). The CTI advances the understanding of the relationship between communication and identity, according to which communication builds, sustains, and transforms identity, while at the same time identity is expressed through communication. This thought is echoed by Northrop Frye in his work on literary criticism theory in which he refers to the social functions of art, and also by the work of Mihály Hoppál, in which he hypothesized that the reproduction of the symbols of ethnic identity becomes possible and effective in the context of social events.

Attila Z. Papp also summarized Oscar Handlin's view of émigré communities as being uprooted from the old country, as opposed to Rudolph Veccoli's and John Bodnar's idea of communities being transplanted, using a dialectic method to arrive at a hybrid view: Papp's analysis of Hungarian-American community life shows that the "small micro-universes which display certain characteristics of a diaspora, are more accurately hybrids: they are unique community cultures which, however, are built upon inherited values."[113] The local artist George Kozmon, in his curator's statement for a 2013 exhibition of young local Hungarian artists, explained the effect of this community culture built upon inherited values: in contrast with the usual identity politics of contemporary art, which often assumes a negative liability to an individual's ancestry, he highlighted the contributions of an ethnic background in strengthening an individual, adding a dimension of cultural complexity as well as depth and perspective to an artist's work. Echoing Attila Z. Papp's theory, his curator's statement, although intended mainly to clarify the identities of the young artists in relationship to their backgrounds, serves as a useful perspective and can be applied to most members of Cleveland's Hungarian community, whether culturally, linguistically, or in terms of their patriotism and identities:

> The artists in this exhibition all came of age in the greater Cleveland area, with extensive exposure or deep involvement in the Magyar community. They grew up speaking a language that most of their friends didn't speak; their parents came from a country far away, with traditions and customs unfamiliar, finding a way to assimilate into a new context. As a child these things may be a challenge; for a creative adult they're a strength...Art always involves a search. A search to understand the self, to understand one's society, perceptions, context and environment, and the infinitely complex interaction between them all.[114]

It is these strengths and inherited values that the current study attempts to showcase.

Another theoretical framework useful in understanding the Hungarian community of Cleveland is that of a neighborhood shifting from a geographic entity to a purely social entity, kept alive by suburban Hungarian commuters. László Bőjtös, the honorary consul general of Hungary and founding member of the Hungarian Communion of Friends, formulated this theory to the author, saying that in the old days, the community was physical, i.e., an actual geographic neighborhood in which people were bound together by the area in which they lived. Due to the upward mobility aspects of American society, this geographically constricted neighborhood changed to a social or spiritual community, whereby people with a common purpose assemble for events that they consider important. "It is purely a question of belonging, wherever you live in the world," said Bőjtös.[115] This model can be called the spiritual homeland theory. He reiterates this concept in his recollections and analysis of his own post-1956 experiences:

> During these decades, we realized that we were no longer preparing to return home; instead, we were building up a spiritual homeland around us. This homeland is not a function of the political system that happens

to be in power in Hungary; it is a form of our individual and community fate here in the U.S.A., which is nourished by Hungarian intellectual and cultural values. In other words, it is an expression of national identity whereby we, as carriers of Hungarian language, history and culture, are part of the collective Hungarian nation, no matter where we live. Part and parcel of this identity are individual commitment and a principled way of life.[116]

This spiritual homeland concept is especially relevant today, when the Internet facilitates communication and maintenance of ties to other Hungarians worldwide. It is through these three main theoretical frameworks, the Communication Theory of Identity of Urban and Orbe, Attila Z. Papp's microcosm of inherited values, and the spiritual homeland concept of Bőjtös, and using the methodology of Fejős, Balogh, Fülemile, and Tarján that Cleveland's Hungarian community is analyzed here.

APPENDIX III:
Past & Current Church Pastors and Organization Presidents

Churches in the Cleveland Area with Hungarian services

First Hungarian Reformed Church
14530 Alexander Road, Walton Hills
  1891–1894: Gusztáv Jurányi
  1894–1898: Zoltán Harsányi
  1898–1911: Elek Csutoros
  1911–1922: Sándor Tóth
  1923–1947: Dr. József Herczeg
  1947–1983: Dr. István Szabó
  1983-1985: István Nagy
  1986–1989: István Szilágyi
  1989–1996: Ferenc Endrei
  1997–2002: István Géczy
  2003–present: Dr. Csaba Krasznai

St. Elizabeth of Hungary Roman Catholic Church
9016 Buckeye Road, Cleveland
  1892–1907: Károly Böhm
  1907–1923: Gyula Szepessy
  1923–1927: Károly Böhm
  1927–1971: Imre Tanos

1971–1977: Dr. Gyula Záhorszky
1977–1987: Dr. János Nyeste
1987–1988: Richard Orley
1988–2018: András Antal
2018–present: András Mezei

St. Emeric Roman Catholic Church
1860 West 22nd Street, Cleveland

1904: John Hirling
1904–1911: István Soltész
1911–1912: József Szabó
1912–1915: József Péter
1915–1920: János Rátz
1920: József Tóth
1920–1942: József Hartel
1942–1943: Aloysius Bartko
1943–1965: János Mundweil
1965–1975: Ferenc Kárpi
1975–1976: John J. Nyeste
1976–1983: Ferenc Kárpi
1983–1988: Richard Örley
1988–2010, 2012–2013: Sándor Siklódi
2013–2015: Gary Yanus
2015: András Antal
2015–present: András Mezei

West Side Hungarian Reformed Church
15300 Puritas Avenue, Cleveland

1907–1913: Károly Erdei
1913–1926: Elek Csutoros
1926–1935: Ödön Vasvári
1936–1963: Mátyás Daróczy
1963–1990: Áron Elek
1990–2001: Szabolcs Kálmán

2002–2009: Zoltán Kelemen
2009–2010: unfilled
2011–2013: Tamás Bíró
2013–2018: unfilled
2018–present: Dr. Imre László

West Side Lutheran Church
now holding services at 20300 Hilliard Blvd, Rocky River
1933–1955: Gábor Brachna
1955–1956: Aladár Egyed
1956–1991: Imre Juhász
1991–1994: László Lukácsi
1994 – present: Éva Tamásy

Westlake Seventh-Day Adventist Church
2335 Columbia Road, Westlake
1956–1961: András D. Nagy
1961–1963: Károly Daly
1964–1969: Jakab Slezák
1973–1978: István Danyi
1979–2000: Igor Botánsky
2001–2009: Edward Marton
2010–2015: László Hangyás
2015 – present: Dr. Marius Marton

Hungarian Bethany Baptist Church
4124 Stickney Avenue, Cleveland
1959–1973: Emil Bretz
1973–1978: Dr. László Gerzsenyi
1978–1979: Balázs Molnár
1979: Dr. Sándor Haraszti
1979–1982: Dr. Tibor Almási
1982–1986: Dr. Mihály Almási
1986–1990: Dr. Kálmán Mészáros

1990: József Megyesi
1991–1992: Dr. László Fazekas
1992–1998: Béla Zeffer
2000–2015: Dr. Zoltán Pintér
2015–present: Sándor Kulcsár

Hungarian Organizations in the Cleveland Area (in order of their founding)

United Hungarian Societies (exact dates before 1973 lost – presidents listed in order of service)
1902: Lajos Berczel, dr. Elek Csutoros, Ferenc Beck, Miklós Kováchy, Pál Nagy, dr. Henrik Baracs, Lajos Petrásh, Imre Király, György Kemény, István Gobozy, István Körmendy, József Fodor, Gyula Kováchy, István Monoky, Mihály Tóth, János Laskó, István Gobozy, Ferenc Pokorny, András Donó, Sándor Menyhárt
1973–1990: László Kemes
1990–2004: Kathy Kapossy
2004–2012: Jack Kőrössy
2012–2018: Valéria Rátoni-Nagy
2018–present: Endre Szentkiralyi

Hungarian Business and Tradesmen's Club (records unavailable)
1923–present

Hungarian Cultural Garden (records before 2006 lost; dates approximate)
1936: Louis Petrash
1937–1938: Julius Kovachy
1940s: Mrs. John Volosin
1954: Julius Kovachy
1950s, 1960s, 1970s: Lily P. Volosin
1980–1990 : Joseph Krall
1990–2006: Ernest Mihály
2006–present: Carolyn Balogh

Hungarian Association

1952–1992: Dr. János Nádas
1992–1999: Dr. Gyula Nádas
1999–present: Dr. János Nádas, jr.

Hungarian School

1958–1982: Dr. Gábor Papp
1982–1983: Miklós Peller, Zsolt Dömötörffy
1983–1985: Dr. Gábor Papp
1985–1988: Imre Bogárdy
1988–2009: Ödön Szentkirályi
2009–2011: Bea Szentkirályi Tábor
2011–2014: Krisztina Szabadkai Tábor
2014–present: Judit Csia Szentkirályi

Hungarian Cultural Center of Northeastern Ohio

(1904–2001: St. Stephen Dramatic Club and 1975–2001: Geauga County Magyar Club)
2001: Bill Takacs
2001–present: Mary Jane Molnár

Cleveland Hungarian Heritage Society

1985–1987: Dr. János Nyeste
1987: Ottó Friedrich
1987–1994: Dr. Ferenc Somogyi
1994–1997: Elemér Mészáros
1997–2001: Mária Strada Friedrich
2001–2004: István Szappanos
2004–2006: Mária Strada Friedrich
2006–2010: Andrea Vareska Mészáros
2010–2013: László Varga
2013–2016: Éva Szabó
2016–present: Sándor Kézdi

Cleveland Hungarian Development Panel

1990: John Hutchins
1991: George Pogan
1992–1997: Kori Smith
1997–1998: Jay Moldovanyi
1999–2001: István Hargitai
2002–2007: Carolyn Balogh
2007–2012: Mária Megyimóri
2013: Dr. Judit Puskás
2013– present: Elizabeth Papp-Taylor

Hungarian Genealogical Society of Greater Cleveland

1996–2004: Gus Enyedy
2004–2008: Dan Corrigan
2008–2010: Diana Rogers
2010–2012: Mary Uray
2012– present: unfilled

Hungarian Scouts in Cleveland

Scout Troop #14 (Arthur Görgey)

1951–1953: Dr. László Berkes
1953–1955: Vilmos Bárdossy
1955–1956: Dénes Dietrich
1956–1957: Ferenc Beodray
1957–1958: Gyula Dolesch
1958–1961: Dr. Gábor Papp
1961–1963: Lothár Stieberth
1963–1965: Béla Megay
1965–1967: Ferenc Beodray
1967–1969: Béla Megay
1969–1971: Gyula Dolesch
1971–1981: Viktor Falk

1981–1991: Levente Szabolcs
1991–1996: Endre Szentkirályi
1996–2004: Andreas Tábor
2004–2007: Pál Strada
2007–2009: Péter Hokky
2009–2012: Tamás Csajka
2012–2013: Endre Szentkirályi
2013–2015: Dr. István Turoczi
2015–present: Tamás Csajka

Scout Troop #22 (György Bessenyei)
1951–1952: Dr. Ede Chászár
1952–1953: Zoltán Bócsay
1953–1956: István Szappanos
1956–1958: Dénes Koltaváry
1958–1966: Dr. György Vareska
1966–1968: László Zala
1968–1970: László Riedl
1970–1980: Viktor Simonyi
1980–1986: Zsolt Gregora
1986–1991: Mihály Horváth
1991–1995: Ernő Kálnoky
1995–1998: János Szigeti
1998–present: György Kovács

Girl Scout Troop #34 (Ilona Zrínyi)
1952–1962: Melinda Dolesch Gaydán
1962–1969: Erzsébet Mód Borosdy
1969–1984: Klára Thurner
1984–1988: Krisztina Szabadkai Tábor
1988–1994: Judit Csia Szentkirályi
1994–1997: Zsuzsi Patay Linder
1997–2000: Andrea Szabolcs
2000–2005: Gabriella Ormay Nádas

2005–2011: Eszter Pigniczky
2011–2013: Krisztina Szentkirályi
2013–2014: Ida Lieszkovszky Hargitai
2014–present: Ilona Balássy Strober

Girl Scout Troop #33 (Erzsébet Szilágyi)

1957–1958: Dr. Ágnes Huszár Várdy
1958–1960: Ágnes Bodnár
1960–1962: Márta Tarnay Szabó
1962–1963: Dr. Ágnes Huszár Várdy
1963–1964: Emőke Hargittay Csipke
1964–1969: Mária Strada Friedrich
1969–1970: Paula Payrits Riedl
1970–1971: Emőke Hargittay Csipke
1971–1976: Mária Strada Friedrich
1976–1982: Andrea Vareska Mészáros
1982–1983: Zsuzsanna Győri
1983–1986: Klára Bócsay Toth
1986–1989: Helga Nagy Gyermán
1989–1991: Judit Gráber Horváth
1991–1997: Valéria Szőke Rátoni–Nagy
1997–1999: Judit Torma
1999–present: Valéria Szőke Rátoni–Nagy

District Commissioners (responsible for all Cleveland-area scout troops, as well as Chicago, Buffalo, Pittsburgh)

1955–1959: Gyula Borosdy
1959–1960: Dr. György Remes
1960–1963: Gyula Dolesch
1963–1964: István Tarján
1964–1966: István Szappanos
1966–1991: Balázs Bedy
1991–2010: Mihály Horváth

2010–2017: Andrea Vareska Mészáros

2017– present: Krisztina Nádas

American Hungarian Friends of Scouting

1958–1960: Gusztáv Szabó

1960–1962: Dénes Dietrich

1962–1964: Gyula Borosdy

1964–1966: Dr. György Remes

1966–1986: Balázs Bedy

1986–1991: Mária Strada Friedrich

1991–2010: József Györky

2010–2016: Bea Szentkirályi Tábor

2016– present: Mihály Horváth

Hungarian Scout Folk Ensemble

1973–1976: András and Magdi Temesváry

1977–1980: Krisztina Szabadkai Tábor and Mihály Ádám

1980: Krisztina Szabadkai Tábor

1981–1986: Zsuzsi Virágh Globits and István Gráber

1986–1987: Judit Gráber Horváth and Károly Szélpál

1987–1991: Eszti Fricke Kovács and Péter Balássy

1991–1993: Ilona Balássy Strobel and József Földesi

1993–1995: Ilona Balássy Strobel

1995–1997: Emily Jálics Rauchert and Marika Megyimóri and András Strada

1997–1998: Eszti Pigniczky and András Strada

1998–2000: Eszti Pigniczky and Lehel Horváth

2000–2004: Eszti Pigniczky

2004–2006: Ilona Gulden Solomon and Béla Halácsy

2006–2007: Kristen Slattery and Béla Halácsy

2007–2012: Kristen Slattery and Hajnal Tábor Eppley and Mátyás Tábor

2012–2014: Zsófia Szélpál and Anna Tábor and Mátyás Tábor

2014–2016: Zsófia Szélpál and Mátyás Tábor

2016–2018: Andrea Horváth Nádas and Mátyás Tábor

2018–present: Emese Chmielewski and Bendegúz Pigniczky

APPENDIX IV
Survey Instruments Used for Research

SURVEY = HUNGARIANS IN CLEVELAND [online + paper]

1. I was born in   [*circle one answer*]
   · the greater Cleveland area
   · USA (outside the Cleveland area)
   · Hungary
   · Romania
   · Ukraine
   · Serbia or Yugoslavia
   · Slovakia or Czechoslovakia
   · in or near a refugee camp (Displaced Persons)
   · other (please specify) _____

2. I have lived in the Cleveland area   [*circle one answer*]
   · all of my life
   · since before 1948
   · since my arrival 1949–1955 (Displaced Persons wave)
   · since my arrival as a result of the 1956 Revolution
   · since before 1989
   · since after 1989
   · other (please specify) _____

3. How often do I meet other Hungarians (not including family) from the Cleveland area?   [*circle one answer*]
   · never
   · yearly or less frequently
   · almost monthly
   · at least monthly
   · weekly or more often

4. My Hungarian language skills (understanding spoken Hungarian) are [*circle one answer*]
   · practically nonexistent (I only recognize a few words)
   · weak
   · medium (I can understand a basic conversation in Hungarian)
   · strong (I understand practically everything I hear)

5. My Hungarian speaking skills are   [*circle one answer*]
   · practically nonexistent (I can only say a few words)
   · weak
   · medium (I can express myself in simple situations)
   · strong (I am comfortable speaking Hungarian)

6. My Hungarian reading skills are   [*circle one answer*]
   · practically nonexistent
   · weak (I can recognize that a text is Hungarian but can make out very little meaning)
   · medium (I can read basic texts but nothing too complicated)
   · strong (I can comfortably read most Hungarian texts)

7. Of which Hungarian organization am I currently a dues-paying member? [*circle all that apply*]
   · none
   · I attend events and functions but do not belong to any organization
   · a Hungarian church
   · Cleveland Hungarian Heritage Society (museum)

- Hungarian Cultural Center of Northeast Ohio
- William Penn Association, Branch 14
- Hungarian Cultural Garden
- Cleveland Hungarian Development Panel
- Hungarian Business and Tradesmen's Club
- Hungarian Genealogical Society of Greater Cleveland
- American Hungarian Friends of Scouting
- Hungarian Scout Troops, 14, 22, 33, or 34
- I was once a member of Csardas Dance Ensemble
- I was once a member of MHBK
- I was once a member of CMAC
- I was once a member of the Cleveland Magyar Club
- I was and/or am a member of MBK (Itt-Ott)
- I was once a member of the Cleveland Hungarian Scouts
- My child currently attends one of Cleveland's Hungarian schools
- My child is currently a member of a Cleveland Hungarian scout troop
- Other (please specify) _____

8. Demographics [*circle one choice*]: my age is
   under 15   16–20   21–29   30–39   40–49   50–69   70+
   My ZIP code is _____

9. My spouse/partner/significant other   [*circle one choice*]
   - is also Hungarian
   - is not Hungarian
   - N/A (I am single)

Thank you for taking this survey. The results will be used by Endre Szentkiralyi in a forthcoming book he is completing about Hungarians in Cleveland.

SURVEY = POLITICAL INVOLVEMENT OF HUNGARIANS IN CLEVELAND [online + paper]

1. In the 1950s and/or the 1960s my political tendency in US elections was to vote
   · always Democratic
   · mostly Democratic
   · slight tendency towards the Democrats
   · nor real pattern; more of an issues voter
   · slight tendency towards the Republicans
   · mostly Republican
   · always Republican
   · I was a US citizen but did not vote
   · I was not yet a US citizen
   · Other (please specify) _____

2. In the 1970s and/or the 1980s my political tendency in US elections was to vote
   · always Democratic
   · mostly Democratic
   · slight tendency towards the Democrats
   · nor real pattern; more of an issues voter
   · slight tendency towards the Republicans
   · mostly Republican
   · always Republican
   · I was a US citizen but did not vote
   · I was not yet a US citizen
   · Other (please specify) _____

3. In the 1990s my political tendency in US elections was to vote
   · always Democratic
   · mostly Democratic
   · slight tendency towards the Democrats
   · nor real pattern; more of an issues voter

- slight tendency towards the Republicans
- mostly Republican
- always Republican
- I was a US citizen but did not vote
- I was not yet a US citizen
- Other (please specify) _____

4. In the early 2000s my political tendency in US elections was to vote
   - always Democratic
   - mostly Democratic
   - slight tendency towards the Democrats
   - nor real pattern; more of an issues voter
   - slight tendency towards the Republicans
   - mostly Republican
   - always Republican
   - I was a US citizen but did not vote
   - I was not yet a US citizen
   - Other (please specify) _____

5. In the 2016 US election my political tendency was to vote
   - always Democratic
   - mostly Democratic
   - slight tendency towards the Democrats
   - nor real pattern; more of an issues voter
   - slight tendency towards the Republicans
   - mostly Republican
   - always Republican
   - I am a US citizen but did not vote
   - I am not yet a US citizen
   - If you wish, list whom you voted for President (Clinton, Trump, etc)
   - _____

6. Did you ever take part in any political demonstrations regarding Hungarian issues?   [*Check all that apply*]
   · Against Soviet oppression in 1956 (in Hungary)
   · Against Soviet oppression in 1956 (in Cleveland and/or USA)
   · Against the return of St. Stephen's Holy Crown in 1977
   · Against the closing of St. Emeric church in 2009/2010
   · Other (please specify) _____

7. Dual Hungarian citizenship and participation in Hungarian elections [*circle one choice*]
   · I am a dual US/Hungarian citizen and vote in Hungarian elections
   · I am a dual US/Hungarian citizen but do NOT vote in Hungarian elections
   · I am not a dual citizen

   · If a dual citizen and voted in Hungarian elections, please list the years you voted: _____

8. Demographic information   [*Circle all that apply*]
   · I was born in the United States
   · I was born in Hungary or outside the United States
   · I served in the US military

9. Demographics [*circle one choice*]: my age is
   under 18   18–20   21–29   30–39   40–49   50–69   70+
   My ZIP code is _____

Thank you for taking this survey. The results will be used by Endre Szentkiralyi in a forthcoming book he is completing about Hungarians in Cleveland.

QUALITATIVE QUESTIONS
(administered to 18 persons in small-group interview sessions)

Name, age, birthplace. City of residence, level of education, occupation. Purpose of study.
For ease in transcribing the recordings, please say your name before you answer each question

When did your parents come to America and why?

As you were growing up, how much English or Hungarian was spoken in your household? Describe the language habits of the people living with you.

What percentage of your parents' friends/social acquaintances spoke Hungarian?

Did your parents take you to Cleveland Hungarian community events (church, picnics, school, scouts, etc)? How often?

Did they take you to more or less Hungarian events as you grew older?

Did you ever have negative emotions attached to you or your family speaking Hungarian?

Have you ever been to Hungary? How often, for how long?

How did that impact your language skills? How did that impact your identity (who you are)?

Did you ever have negative emotions attached to being an American visiting Hungary?

How often do you speak Hungarian nowadays?

How often do you read or write Hungarian?

Describe your own fluency in Hungarian (if your fluency in English is 100 percent, would your Hungarian be 40, 60, 80, 90 percent?) speaking, reading, writing

Describe the Hungarian proficiency of your relatives.

What do you think the reasons are for their language proficiency?

What percentage of your friends speak Hungarian? Why do you think this is so?

Describe the Hungarian proficiency of your friends.

What do you think the reasons are for their language proficiency?

Do you consider yourself American or Hungarian? Why?

Describe your spouse's attitude to your Hungarian identity and language use. Reasons why?

Do you plan on speaking Hungarian to your own children? Why or why not?

Did the subject of Hungarian language use with eventual kids come up before marriage or before children?

Any other thoughts about factors impacting Hungarian language maintenance here in Cleveland?

Thanks for taking part in this research.

STATEMENT OF INFORMANT CONSENT
(for small-group interview sessions)

PROJECT TITLE: Hungarian language use in the USA

RESEARCHER: Endre Szentkiralyi, independent researcher

PURPOSE: This is a research study. Its purpose is to gain a deeper under-standing of the factors impacting second-language maintenance in an ethnic community (i.e., Hungarian in the USA). I am inviting people of Hungari-an ancestry who grew up in the Cleveland area to talk about and share their experiences of growing up Hungarian in the USA, reflecting upon their own and their family's language use and degree of ethnic identity. Participants will be asked to take part in a one-time group discussion that should not take longer than 1–2 hours during the fall of 2010 / spring of 2017.

PROCEDURES: If you agree to participate, we will set up a group discus-sion with other participants. In order to help me with the write-up, I will re-cord the discussions. Should you wish to look at or comment on the tran-scripts or the report in its draft or finalized forms, you may do so.

VOLUNTARY PARTICIPATION: All participation is voluntary. You may choose not to answer any of the questions during the group discussion. You may also withdraw from further participation at any time. If, after the inter-views, you decide that you would rather not have your comments published, you have the right to retract permission provided you contact me before the study results go to press.

RISKS: There are no foreseeable risks to participating in this study.

BENEFITS: There are no personal benefits for taking part in this research and you will not be compensated in any way. Nevertheless, I do hope that those who read the results of these interviews will benefit by understanding more about the dynamics of ethnic language maintenance in the USA.

CONFIDENTIALITY: Recorded material and notes from this project will be maintained and kept confidential. However, the research results (including but not limited to the University of Debrecen, Hungarian Studies Review, and Helena History Press) will be published / has been published) in my forthcoming book about the language, culture, and traditions of Cleveland Hungarians, and my kept records pertaining to the research may contain personal identifiers. Except during review, analysis, and editing for publication, the recordings and notes will be secured in my home. You have the option to decide whether you want to be identified or named in the reports or publications of this study.

QUESTIONS: If you have questions about this study, please contact me.

INFORMANT CONSENT

By initialing in one of the spaces provided below, please verify that you either

_____ A) want to be credited as a source in reports and publications from this project (your name will be used)

or

_____ B) do not want to be identified as a source in reports and publications from this project (you will remain anonymous).

I, _____ (informant's name), hereby certify that I have been told by Endre Szentkiralyi about his research on Hungarian language use in the USA.

I was told about the purposes and procedures to be followed and the nature of my participation. I have had ample help and time to consider the possible risks and benefits to me and others from the research. I have also been told the extent to which any records which may identify me will be kept confidential.

I understand that I have the right to ask questions at any time and that I can contact the researcher, Endre Szentkiralyi for answers about the research and my rights.

I understand that my participation is voluntary, that I may refuse to participate or withdraw my consent and stop taking part at any time before publication without penalty.

AUDIORECORDING AGREEMENT: Please initial in the space below to verify that you understand that our group discussions will be recorded:

_____

SIGNATURE OF INFORMANT: _____
DATE: _____

RESEARCHER'S STATEMENT: I have discussed the above points with the informant or his/her legally authorized representative. It is my opinion that the subject understands the risks, benefits, and obligations involved in participating in this project.

Researcher's name (printed): _____

Signature of researcher: _____

Bibliography

Audiovisual Materials

"Azt mondják hogy tavasz nyílik" [They say spring blooms]. LP Record, SG-1011. B & F Record Company, Cleveland, date unknown.

Bognár, Tibor. "The Last Hungarian on Buckeye." Masters thesis: John Carroll University, 2004. DVD, 55 mins.

Like Bubbles in the Wine (Dennis Goulden, director; Jon Boynton, writer, producer), episode in the documentary series *Montage*, WKYC-TV. Accessed online via library.csuohio.edu/speccoll/collections/montage.html.

Pigniczky, Réka. *Inkubátor*. 56Films: Budapest, 2010. DVD, 83 min.

———. *Kodály a Cuyahogán* [Kodály on the Cuyahoga]. Duna World Television: Budapest, 2014. Two-part series, 2 x 26 min.

———. *Megmaradni* [Heritage]. 56Films: Budapest, 2012. DVD, 65 min.

Széles, Tamás and Ferenc Vojtkó, eds. *Üzenem az otthoni hegyeknek...* [Message to the Mountains at Home]. Debrecen Városi Televízió Kft: Debrecen, 2011. DVD, 125 mins.

Published & Primary Sources and Private Manuscripts

Alba, Richard and Victor Nee. *Remaking the American Mainstream: Assimilation and Contemporary Immigration*. Cambridge, MA: Harvard University Press, 2003.

Alszeghy, Zsolt, Sándor Sík and József Teichert. *Magyar nyelvtan*. Cleveland: Kossuth Publishing, 1958.

Balogh, Balázs. "Lifestyle, Identity, and Visions of the Future of Generations of Hungarian-American Communities in Western Pennsylvania." *Hungarian Heritage* 11, nos. 1–2 (2010): 19–33.

Balogh, Judith Petres and Nora Hegedus Sztaray. *School of a Different Kind: the story and history of a Hungarian school in postwar Germany during 1947–1951*. North Charleston, SC: CreateSpace Independent Publishing, 2015.

Bán, Oszkár. *A Hajsza Végén* [At the end of the pursuit]. Montreal: Magyar Hírlap, 1968.

——. *Zsidó versek* [Jewish poems]. Cleveland: Classic Printing, 1977.

Barkan, Elliott, Hasia Diner, and Alan Kraut, eds. *From Arrival to Incorporation: Migrants to the U.S. in a Global Era*. New York: New York University Press, 2008.

Bartha, Csilla. "Adalékok a detroiti magyar közösség nyelvállapotához" [Contributions to the study of the linguistic situation of the Hungarian community in Detroit], *Magyar Nyelv* 2 (1989): 230–235.

——. "Nyelvhasználat és identitás-szimbólumok a detroiti magyar közösségben" [Language use and symbols of identity in a Hungarian community of Detroit], Első Magyar Alkalmazott Nyelvészeti Konferencia, Nyíregyháza [First Conference on Hungarian Applied Linguistics], (May 3–4, 1991) II. 532–536.

Béky, Zoltán. *Az amerikai magyar református egyesület történetének főbb eseményei* [Major events from the history of the American Hungarian Reformed Federation]. Ligonier, PA: Bethlen Freedom Press, 1970.

Béldy, Béla, ed. *Első Magyar Találkozó Krónikája* (November 24–26, 1961) [Chronicle of the first Hungarian Congress]. Cleveland: Árpád Könyvkiadó, 1962.

B. Kovács, Fréda. *A halhatatlan harcos* [The undying warrior]. Second edition, reprint of Budapest edition. Cleveland: Hungarian School Care Club, 1972.

Bócsay, Zoltán. *Vázlatos Magyar Történelem* [Outline of Hungarian history]. Cleveland: Magyar Cserkészszövetség, 1984.

Bodnar, John. *The Transplanted: A History of Immigrants in Urban America*. Bloomington: Indiana University Press, 1985.

Bodolai, Zoltán and Endre Csapó. *The Unmaking of Peace: The Fragmentation and Subsequent Destruction of Central Europe After World War One by the Peace Treaty of Trianon*. Cleveland: Árpád Publishing Company, 1984.

Bolváry, Pál and Ernő Kálnoky. *Magyar Földrajz* [Hungarian geography]. Cleveland: Magyar Iskola kiadása, 1979.

Bonutti, Karl B. and George J. Prpic. *Selected Ethnic Communities of Cleveland: a Socio-Economic Study*. Cleveland: The Cleveland Urban Observatory, 1974.

Borbándi, Gyula. *A magyar emigráció életrajza 1945–1985* [The story of the Hungarian emigration 1945–1985]. Budapest: Európa Kiadó, 1989.

Catholic Hungarians' Sunday 90th Anniversary Album. Youngstown, OH: Catholic Publishing Company, 1974.

Cizmic, Ivan, Ivan Miletic, and George Prpic. *From the Adriatic to Lake Erie: A History of Croatians in Greater Cleveland*. Eastlake, OH: American Croatian Lodge, Inc., and Zagreb: Institute of Social Sciences, 2000.

Deme, Károly. *Harctéri naplóm: a m.kir. 20. könnyű hadosztály egészségügyi oszlop harctéri naplója* [My combat diary: the Hungarian Royal 20th light division medical unit's combat diary]. Youngstown, OH: Dora Deme, 1984.

Dobolyi, Árpád. *Hungarian Monument*. Cleveland: Sunset Memorial Park Association, 1998.

Ébresztő [Awake]. Cleveland: Hungarian Bethany Baptist Church, October 2012.

Eiben, Christopher. *Tori in Amerika: the Story of Theodor Kundtz.* City N/A: Ewald E. Kundtz, Jr., 1994.

Erdely, Stephen. "Folksinging of the American Hungarians in Cleveland." *Ethnomusicology* 8, no. 1 (January 1964): 14–25.

Értavy Baráth, Kata. *Történelem: kitünő* [History: outstanding]. Cleveland: Kárpát Publishing, 1966.

Eszenyi, László. *Hiven Mindhalálig: Az Amerikai Függetlenségi Háború Magyar Hősének, Fabricy Kováts Mihály Huszárezredesnek Élete és Hősi Halála* [True to Death: the life and death of the hero of the American Revolutionary War, Hussar Colonel Michael Fabriczy Kovats]. Washington, DC: Amerikai Magyar Református Egyesület, 1975.

Eszterhás, István. *A bíboros és a rendőr* [The cardinal and the cop]. Cleveland Heights, OH: self-published (printed by Classic Printing), 1985.

———. *A hézag* [The rift]. Cleveland Heights, OH: self-published (printed by Classic Printing), 1983.

———. *Kováts Mihály hajóra száll* [Michael Kováts boards a ship]. Cleveland Heights, OH: self-published (printed by Classic Printing), 1980.

———. *Száműzött a szabadság igájában* [Exiled in freedom's yoke]. Cleveland Heights, OH: Alpha Publications, 1978.

Fai-Podlipnik, Judith. "One Goal, Many Paths: Internal and External Struggles of the Hungarian Émigrés." In *Anti-Communist Minorities in the U.S. - Political Activism of Ethnic Refugees,* edited by Ieva Zake, 87–107. New York: Palgrave Macmillan, 2009.

Farkas, Dezső. "Amerikai magyar vagy magyar amerikai? Az újkori amerikai honfoglaló magyarok regionális jellemzői" Available at http://prehryfarkas.hu/category/amerikai-magyar-vagy-magyar-amerikai/. Site accessed December 30, 2016.

Fejős, Zoltán. *A chicagói magyarok két nemzedéke 1890–1940* [Two generations of Chicago Hungarians 1890–1940]. Budapest: Közép-Európai Intézet, 1993.

Fekete, István ifj. *Ítéletidő* [Judgment time]. Cleveland: Árpád Könyvkiadó Vállalat, 1979.

Fishman, Joshua. *Hungarian Language Maintenance in the United States.* Bloomington, IN: Indiana University, 1966.

Fodor, Mónika. "My Slice of Americana: Hungarian-Americans Construct Their Ethno-Cultural Identities in Narratives." Unpublished dissertation, University of Pécs, 2007.

Frank, Tibor. *Double Exile: Migrations of Jewish-Hungarian Professionals through Germany to the United States, 1919–1945.* Oxford: Peter Lang, 2009.

———. "Imre Kovács and Cold War Émigré Politics in the United States (1947–1980)." In *The Inauguration of Organized Political Warfare: Cold War Organizations sponsored by the National Committee for a Free Europe,* edited by Katalin Kádár Lynn, 309–322. Saint Helena, CA: Helena History Press, 2013.

Fricke, Valér. "A Fricke család emlékeiből." Cleveland: 1981, unpublished manuscript.

Füry, Lajos. *Árva Magyar János* [Hungarian John, orphan]. Cleveland: publisher unknown, 1957.

Gábor, Áron. *Az embertől keletre* [East of man]. Munich: XX. Század, 1967.

———. *Ázsia peremén* [On the fringe of Asia]. Munich, Los Angeles: XX. Század, 1974.

———. *East of Man.* Toronto: Weller Publishing, 1975.

———. *Évszázados emberek* [Centenarians]. Munich, Los Angeles: XX. Század, 1971.

———. *Szögletes szabadság* [Freedom framed]. Munich, Los Angeles: XX. Század, 1968.

———. *Túl a Sztálin vonalon* [Beyond the Stalin line]. Budapest: Stádium, 1941 (second edition, Toronto: Weller Publishing, 1975).

———. *Túlélés* [Survival]. Munich, Los Angeles, Sydney: XX. Század, 1978.

———. *Wohin Amerikaner?* [Whereto, American?] Munich: Südwest Verlag, 1970.

Gál Sári, Imre. *Clevelandi Magyar Múzeum: riportok, versek, fényképek a clevelandi magyarság életéből* [Cleveland Hungarian Museum: reports, poems, photos from the life of Hungarian Cleveland]. Toronto: Amerikai Magyar Írók, 1978.

Gál Sári, Imre. *Az amerikai Debrecen: Képek clevelandi magyarság életéből* [The American Debrecen: pictures of Cleveland Hungarian life]. Toronto: Patria Publishing, 1966.

Gans, Herbert J, "Symbolic ethnicity: the future of ethnic groups and cultures in America." *Ethnic and Racial Studies* 2, no. 1 (January 1979): 1–20.

Gárdosi, Rita. "A clevelandi magyar nyelvoktatás múltja és jelene" [The past and present of Hungarian language instruction in Cleveland]. *THL2* 51, no. 2 (2014): 58–67.

Gerzsenyi, László. *A clevelandi magyar baptista misszió 100 éve* [100 years of the Cleveland Hungarian Baptist mission]. Budapest: Északamerikai baptista szövetség, 1999.

Glant, Tibor. *A Szent Korona amerikai kalandja és hazatérése* [The American adventure and homecoming of the Saint Crown]. Debrecen: Debreceni Egyetemi Kiadó, 2018.

Graber, Richard. *Csárdás Dance Company: a History.* City N/A: Lulu Publishing Services, 2015.

Hajdu, Tibor. "Emigrációs hullám a forradalmak után – 1919" [Wave of emigration after the revolutions – 1919]. *Rubicon* 19 (2008): 36–42.

Hajdú-Németh, Gergely. "Az amerikai magyarság intézményei jövője" [The future of American Hungarian institutions]. *ITT-OTT Kalendárium.* Ada, OH: Magyar Baráti Közösség, 2012: 111–121.

Hammack, David and Diane L. and John J. Grabowski, eds. *Identity, Conflict, and Cooperation: Central Europeans in Cleveland, 1850–1930.* Cleveland: Western Reserve Historical Society, 2002.

Handlin, Oscar. *The Uprooted.* Boston: Little, Brown, 1953.

Hatoss, Aniko. "Community-level approaches in language planning: the case of Hungarian in Australia." In *Language Planning in Local Contexts,* edited by Anthony J. Liddroat and Richard R. Baldauf Jr, 55–74. Clevedon, UK: Multilingual Matters, 2008.

Hoerder, Dirk, "From Ethnic to Interethnic History: an Introduction." In *Identity, Conflict, and Cooperation: Central Europeans in Cleveland, 1850–1930*, edited by David Hammack, and Diane L. and John J. Grabowski, 8. Cleveland: Western Reserve Historical Society, 2002.

Hoppál, Mihály. "Tradition and Ethnic Symbols in an American Hungarian Community." *Hungarian Heritage* 11, nos. 1–2 (2010): 34–58.

Hungarian Aid Society Records, 1926–1962. Minutes, annual reports, cemetery records, legal documents, correspondence. Cleveland: Western Reserve Historical Association.

Hungarian Scout Folk Ensemble. *Regös Emlékkönyv* (15th Anniversary Performance program booklet). Fairview Park, OH: October 15, 1988.

———. *20th Anniversary Performance* (program booklet). Parma, OH: November 13, 1993.

———. *Szülőhazám, Te szép ország!* [My Native Land, You Beautiful Country] (30th Anniversary Performance program booklet). Lakewood, OH: November 15, 2003.

———. *Egyszer esik esztendőben* [Once in a Year] (35th Anniversary Performance program booklet). Lakewood, OH: November 15, 2008.

Huseby-Darvas, Éva. "Should We Leave or Stay? Notes on Recent Hungarian Outmigration." *AHEA: E-journal of the American Hungarian Educators Association* 5 (2012): http://ahea.net/e-journal/volume-5-2012.

Jacobson, Matthew Frye. *Roots Too: White Ethnic Revival in Post-Civil Rights America*. Cambridge, MA: Harvard University Press, 2006.

Jeszenszky, Géza. "A magyar emigrációk jelentősége" [The significance of Hungarian emigrations]. *Rubicon* 19, no. 181 (2008): 4–11.

Kádár Lynn, Katalin ed. *The Inauguration of Organized Political Warfare: Cold War Organizations sponsored by the National Committee for a Free Europe*, St. Helena, Helena History Press, 2013

Kálnoky, Ernő. *Magyar Néprajz* [Hungarian Folklore]. Cleveland: 1977, no publisher listed, but contains note regarding Hungarian-American parents photocopying manuscript, with professional printing by Ottó Friedrich, Zsolt Gregora, and Viktor Simonyi.

Kárpi, Ferenc A. *Bőhm Károly: Élet- és korrajza 1885–1907* [The life and times of Károly Bőhm 1885–1907]. Cleveland: Classic Printing Corporation, 1991.

Kerecsendi Kiss, Márton. *Hetedhétország* [A land far away]. Toronto: Weller Publishing, 1976.

———. *Rőzseparázs* [Kindling coals]. Toronto: Orpheus Publishing, 1963.

Király, Imre, ed. *Emléklapok a Petőfi szobor leleplezési ünnepélyéről* [Memories of the unveiling ceremony for the Petőfi statue]. Cleveland: Egyesült Magyar Egyletek, 1930.

Klelmencic, Matjaz. *Slovenes in Cleveland: The Creation of a New Nation and a New World Community Slovenia and the Slovenes of Cleveland*. Novo Mesta, 1995.

Konnyu, Leslie. *A History of American Hungarian Literature 1583–1987*. St. Louis,

MO: American Hungarian Review, 1988. An earlier Hungarian version was published as: László Könnyű. *Az amerikai magyar irodalom története*. New York: Amerikai Magyar Írók Munkaközössége, 1961.

——. *Hungarians in the United States: an Immigration Study*. St. Louis, MO: American Hungarian Review, 1967.

Kovács, Ilona. *Az Amerikai Közkönyvtárak Magyar Gyűjteményeinek Szerepe az Asszimiláció és az Identitás Megőrzésének Kettős Folyamatában 1890–1940* [The role of American public libraries in the dual processes of assimilation and identity maintenance 1890–1940]. Budapest: Országos Széchenyi Könyvtár, 1997.

——, ed. *Search for American Values: Contributions of Hungarian Americans to American Values, an American-Hungarian Bi-national Symposium*, a publication detailing 10 lectures held in Budapest December 12–14, 1983. Budapest: Országos Széchenyi Könyvtár, 1990.

Kovács, Ilona, August J. Molnár, Katherine Marothy Hames, Patricia L. Fazekas, and Margaret Papai, eds. *The Hungarian Legacy in America: the history of the American Hungarian Foundation, the first fifty years: 1955–2005*. New Brunswick, NJ: American Hungarian Foundation, 2007.

Kovácsy, József. *Arctalan titánok* [Faceless titans]. Cleveland: Árpád Publishing, 1997.

——. *Elsodort forgácsok* [Shavings drifting away]. Cleveland: self-published, 1987.

——. *Idegen emlőkön* [On foreign teats]. Cleveland: self-published, 1988.

——. *Kettős kereszten* [On a double cross]. Cleveland: Árpád Publishing, 1992.

——. *Magtalan aratás* [Seedless harvest]. Cleveland: Árpád Publishing, 1990.

——. *Magunk rabságában* [In our own slavery]. Cleveland: Árpád Publishing, 1995.

Lauer, Andrea and Edith Lauer, eds. *56 Stories: Personal Recollections of the 1956 Hungarian Revolution, A Hungarian American Perspective*. Atlanta: Lauer Learning, 2006.

Lázár, George. "The Forgotten Generation: Immigration to the US between 1959–1989." Lecture given at the American Hungarian Educators Association conference at the University of Maryland, April 29, 2016.

Levy, Donald. *A Report on the Location of Ethnic Groups in Greater Cleveland*. Cleveland: Institute of Urban Studies, 1972.

Mac Thòmais St.-Hilaire, Aonghas. "Segmented Assimilation." *Encyclopedia of American Immigration*, ed. James Ciment. Armonk, NY: Sharpe Reference, 2001.

Magyar, József. *Kincsesláda* [Treasure chest]. Cleveland: Árpád könyvkiadó, date unknown.

Magyar Református Egyház és a Lorántffy Otthon Jubileumi Évkönyve [Hungarian Reformed Church and the Lorántffy Home's Jubilee Yearbook]: *1914–1994, 1974–1994*. Akron: compiled by church leadership and the jubilee committee, 1995.

Maslow, Abraham. „A theory of human motivation." *Psychological Review* 50, no. 4 (July 1943): 370–396.

Mátyás, Dénes. "Magyar nyelv és kultúra a Clevelandi Állami Egyetemen: az újraindult magyaroktatás első két éve (2014–2016) [Hungarian language and culture at Cleveland State University: the first two years of Hungarian instruction's new beginnings 2014–2015]." Hungarológiai Évkönyv 17 [Yearbook of Hungarology] 1 (2016): 28–38.

Mécs, László. *Vissza a csendbe* [Back to the silence]. Cleveland: Classic Printing Corporation, 1976.

Miklósházy, Attila. *A tengeren túli emigráns magyar katolikus egyházi közösségek rövid története Észak- és Dél-Amerikában, valamint Ausztráliában* [The history of Hungarian Catholic émigré church communities in North and South America, as well as in Australia]. Toronto: publisher unknown but assumed to be the émigré Hungarian Bishopric, 2005.

Mindszenty Choir 25th Anniversary 1972–1997 (program booklet). Cleveland, OH: 1997.

Mindszenty, Joseph. *Memoirs*. New York: MacMillan, 1974.

Mindszenty József Biboros Érsek-Prímás Úr Látogatása 1974 Tavaszán Cleveland Egyházmegyében [The visit of Cardinal Mindszenty to the Cleveland Diocese in 1974]. Cleveland: Kárpát Publishing, 1975.

Nádas, Gyula, ed. *A XL. Magyar Találkozó Krónikája*. Cleveland: Árpád Könyvkiadó, 2001.

Némethy Kesserű, Judit. *Szabadságom lett a börtönöm: az argentínai magyar emigráció története 1948–1968* [My freedom became my jail: the history of the Hungarian émigré community in Argentina 1948–1968]. Budapest: A Magyar Nyelv és Kultúra Nemzetközi Társasága, 2003.

Nyirő, József. *A sibói bölény* [The buffalo of Sibő]. Cleveland: Kossuth Publishing, 1954.

Oláh, Krisztina. "A Plan to Address the Communication Challenges of the Hungarian Community of Cleveland." Masters thesis: John Carroll University, 2012.

Pap, Michael S, ed. *Ethnic Communities of Cleveland*. Cleveland: Institute for Soviet & East European Studies at John Carroll University, 1973.

Papp, Attila Z. *Beszédből világ: elemzések, adatok amerikai magyarokról* [World from words: analysis and data about American Hungarians]. Budapest: Hungarian Institute of International Affairs, 2008.

Papp, Gábor. "Bad Kreuznach, Romilly, Mailly le Camp." Cleveland: undated but with a reference to 1991, unpublished manuscript.

Papp, Susan. *Hungarian Americans and their Communities of Cleveland*. Cleveland: Cleveland State University, 1981.

Patria 1, no. 1 (Spring 1974).

Patrias, Carmela. *Hungarians in Canada*. Ottawa: Canadian Historical Society, 1999.

Peller, Miklós. "Éjszakai Menekülésem a Vasfüggönyön át" [My nighttime flight across the Iron Curtain]. Cleveland: 1997, unpublished manuscript.

Pintz, Katalin, "New Brunswick, N.J. as a Magyar Ethnic Island," *Hungarian Studies Review* 38, nos. 1–2 (2011): 83–120.

Piskor, Steve. *Gypsy Violins: Hungarian/Slovak Gypsies in America*. Cleveland: Saroma Publishing, 2012.

Pohárnok, Jenő, ed. *Séta betűországban* [A walk in letterland]. Cleveland: Árpád Publishing and Kossuth Könyvkiadóvállalat, date unknown.

————. *Szép magyar világ* [Beautiful Hungarian world]. Cleveland: Árpád Könyvkiadó, no date listed, but a reprint of edition published 22 years earlier.

Puskás, Julianna. *Ties That Bind, Ties That Divide: 100 Years of Hungarian Experience in the United States*. New York: Holmes and Meier, 2000.

Rodis, Themistocles and Manuel Vasilakes. *Greek Americans in Cleveland: Immigration and Assimilation since 1870*. Cleveland: Hellenic Preservation Society of Northeast Ohio, 2008.

Rubin, Herbert J and Irene S. *Qualitative Interviewing: the Art of Hearing Data*. Thousand Oaks, CA: Sage Publications, 2005.

Sabol, John. *Cleveland's Buckeye Neighborhood*. Charleston, SC: Arcadia Publishing, 2011.

St. Elizabeth of Hungary Parish 125th Anniversary Commemorative Book. Cleveland: St. Elizabeth Church, 2017.

Sherith Jacob Congregation Records, 1905, 1932–1971. Minutes of congregational meetings, correspondence, financial statements, publications. Cleveland: Western Reserve Historical Association.

Simontsits, Attila, and Károly Kövendy. *Harcunk 1920–1945* [Our battle 1920–1945]. Toronto: Sovereign Press, 1975.

Simontsits, Attila. *The Last Battle for St. Stephen's Crown*. Cleveland: Weller Publishing, 1983.

Somogyi, Ferenc. *A clevelandi magyarság vázlatos története* [Outline history of Cleveland Hungarians]. Berea, OH: Institute of Hungarology, 1994.

————. *Emlékkönyv az Egyesült Magyar Alap húszévi működéséről 1968–1988* [Yearbook of 20 years of the United Hungarian Fund]. Cleveland: Egyesült Magyar Alap, 1989.

————. *Irodalomtörténet* [History of literature]. Cleveland: Árpád Könyvkiadó, date unknown.

————. *Küldetés: a magyarság története* [Calling/mission: the history of Hungarians]. Cleveland: Kárpát Könyvkiadó, 1978.

————. *Magyar Nyelv és irodalom 1825-ig* [Hungarian language and literature to 1825]. Cleveland: Kárpát Publishing, 1975.

————. *Magyar Nyelv és irodalom 1825-től 1925-ig: Hagyományok* [Hungarian language and literature from 1825 to 1925: traditions]. Cleveland: Kárpát Publishing, 1977.

————. *A Magyar Társaság három évtizedének vázlatos története* [Outline history of Cleveland Hungarians]. Cleveland: Magyar Társaság, 1983.

————. *Szent István: a magyar nemzeti élet központjában* [St. Stephen: in the Midst of the Life of Hungary]. Cleveland: Árpád Könyvkiadóvállalat, 1970.

————, ed. *A X. Magyar Találkozó Krónikája* [The chronicle of the 10th Hungarian Congress]. Cleveland: Árpád Könyvkiadó, 1971.

————, ed. *A XX. Magyar Találkozó Krónikája* [The chronicle of the 20th Hungarian Congress]. Cleveland: Árpád Könyvkiadó, 1981.

————, ed. *Emlékkönyv: A Clevelandi Magyar Nyelvoktatás 1958–1978: An Album of the 20 years of the West Side Hungarian School.* Cleveland: Hungarian School Care Club, 1978.

———, and János Nádas, eds. *A XXX. Magyar Találkozó Krónikája* [The chronicle of the 30th Hungarian Congress]. Cleveland: Árpád Könyvkiadó, 1991.

Somogyi, Lél, ed. *A XLIX. és L. Magyar Találkozók Krónikája* [Chronicle of the 49th and 50th Hungarian Congresses]. Cleveland: Árpád Könyvkiadó, 2011.

———, ed. *Siker a balsorsban: Somogyi Ferenc munkássága* [Triumph in adversity: the work of Ferenc Somogyi]. Cleveland: Institute of Hungarology, 1992.

Stone, Gregory. "Ethnicity, Class, and Politics among Czechs in Cleveland, 1870–1940." Unpublished doctoral dissertation, Rutgers University, 1993.

Strada, Hanna. "Nagymama Naplója" [Grandmother's diary]. Lakewood: Strada family descendants, 2008.

Szabó, Alan Attila. "Hungarian Immigrants in Northeastern Ohio: Ethno-Cultural Contact and Assimilation." Masters thesis: Kent State University, 2001.

Szappanos, István. "Immigration after the Second World War (1945–1955)." Session III of "In Search of a New Home," a lecture series at the Cleveland Hungarian Heritage Museum, January 14, 2006, unpublished manuscript.

Szántó, Miklós. *Magyarok Amerikában* [Hungarians in America]. Budapest: Gondolat Könyvkiadó, 1984.

Szegedy-Maszák, Mihály, "Values in Contemporary Hungarian Literature," Search for American Values: Contributions of Hungarian Americans to American Values, an American-Hungarian Bi-national Symposium (a publication detailing 10 lectures held in Budapest December 12–14, 1983. Budapest: Országos Széchenyi Könyvtár, 1990.

Szentkirályi, Endre, ed. *Clevelandben még élnek magyarok? Visszaemlékezések gyűjteménye* [Do Hungarians still live in Cleveland? A collection of oral histories]. Cleveland: Hungarian Scout Folk Ensemble, 2008.

———. *Cold War to Warm Cooperation – the Military Service of Cleveland Hungarians: Egy amerikai város magyar katonái 1950–2014.* Budapest: Zrínyi Publishing, 2014.

———. "No Passport? Can't Go Home!" *Hungarian Quarterly* 51, no. 99 (Autumn 2010): 139–145.

Szentkirályi, Ödön. "Csengőfrász 1951: a Szentkirályi család története." [Doorbell-terror 1951: the story of the Szentkirályi family]. Cleveland: 2000, unpublished manuscript.

Szemtanú (pseudonym of István Csia). *Zarándok az Úr pitvarában* [Pilgrimage in the Lord's anteroom]. Cleveland: József H. Csia, 1978.

Szentmiklósy Éles, Géza. *Fabricy Kováts Mihály Almanach.* Cleveland: Clevelandi Kováts Emlékbizottság, 1979.

Szentmiklósy Éles, Géza. *Two Hungarian Immigrations: Victims of Misconceptions.* Cleveland: publisher N/A, 1975.

Széplaki, Joseph. *The Hungarians in America 1583–1974: A Chronology & Fact Book.* Dobbs Ferry, NY: Oceana Publications, 1975.

Tarján, Gábor. "Nemzedékváltás az amerikai magyarságnál [Generational shift among Hungarian Americans]." *Magyar Szemle* 12, no. 4 (2003). www.magyarszemle.hu /cikk/nemzedekvaltas_az_amerikai_magyarsagnal. Accessed online March 9, 2013.

Török, István. *Katolikus Magyarok Észak-Amerikában* [Catholic Hungarians in North America]. Youngstown, OH: Katolikus Magyarok Vasárnapja, 1978.

Tóth, Gergely. www.magyarnegyed.com. Accessed online October 21, 2017.

Tóth-Kurucz Mária. *Daloló Öregamerikások* [Singing oldtimers]. Cleveland: Néprajzi Kiskönyvtár, 1976.

Urban, Ewa L. and Mark Orbe. "Resisting the notion of a 'typical' immigrant experience: a thematic analysis of communication, identity gaps, and cultural worldviews." 2009 National Communication Association Conference Program, February 5, 2009.

Várdy, Ágnes Huszár. "Magyar énekek idegenben: Kemény György költészete. Van-e amerikai magyar irodalom?" [Hungarian songs abroad. The poetry of György Kemény. Does American-Hungarian literature exist?] Pittsburgh: 2011, unpublished manuscript.

Várdy, Steven Béla. "Clevelandi magyarok emlékeznek." [Cleveland Hungrians remember]. Review of *Clevelandben még élnek magyarok?* In *Amerikai Magyar Népszava Szabadság* [American Hungarian People's Voice & Freedom], volume N/A (February 20, 2009).

———. *Hungarian Historiography and the Geistesgeschichte School.* Cleveland: Árpád Academy, 1974.

———. "Hungarians in America's Ethnic Politics." In *America's Ethnic Politics*, edited by Joseph S. Roucek and Bernard Eisenberg, 171–196. Westport, CT: Greenwood Press. 1982.

———. "The Hungarians (Magyars) in the United States." *Ethnic Forum: Journal of Ethnic Studies and Ethnic Bibliography* 10 (1990): 63–79.

———. *The Hungarian-Americans.* Boston: Twayne Publishers, 1985.

———. "Hungarian Americans and the Mother Country: Relations with Hungary Through the Twentieth Century." In *Studi Finno-Ugrici* (Naples, Italy: Universita Degli Studi di Napoli) 4 (2005): 207–225.

———. "Hungarian National Consciousness and the Question of Dual and Multiple Identity." *Hungarian Studies Review* 20 (1993): 53–70.

———. "Kettős és többes kötődés kérdése Magyarországon" [The question of dual and multiple ties to Hungary]. In *Régi és új peregrináció Magyarok külföldön, külföldiek Magyarországon* [Old and new peregrination Hungarians abroad, foreigners in Hungary], edited by Imre Békési, József Jankovics, László Kósa, and Judit Nyerges, 925–937. Budapest: Nemzetközi Magyar Filológiai Társaság (1993).

———. *Magyarok az Újvilágban* [Hungarians in the New World]. Budapest: Magyar Nyelv és Kultúra Nemzetközi Társasága, 2000.

———. "Professor Ferenc Somogyi: Man, Scholar, and Publicist." In *Triumph in Adversity*, edited by Steven Béla Várdy and Ágnes Huszár Várdy, 1–13. New York: Columbia University Press, 1988.

————. "A Traditional Historian's View of Hungarian History: Ferenc Somogyi's History of Hungary." *Canadian-American Review of Hungarian Studies* 4 (1977): 59–65.

————. "Trianon in Interwar Hungarian Historiography." In *War and Society in East Central Europe*, edited by Béla K. Király and Gunther Erich Rothenberg, 361–389. New York: Columbia University Press, 1982.

Várdy, Steven Béla and Ágnes Huszár Várdy. "Hungarian Literary, Linguistic, and Ethnographic Research on Hungarian-Americans: a Historiographical Assessment." *Hungarian Studies* (Budapest) 1 (1985): 77–122.

————. "Research in Hungarian-American History and Culture: Achievements and Prospects." In *The Folk Tales of Hungary*, edited by Walter W. Kolar and Ágnes H. Várdy, 67–124. Pittsburgh, PA: Duquesne University Tamburitzans Institute for Folk Arts, 1981.

————, eds. *Triumph in Adversity*. New York: Columbia University Press, 1988.

————. *Újvilági küzdelmek: az amerikai magyarság élete és az óhaza* [Struggles in the New World: the life of American Hungarians and the old country]. Budapest: Mundus Magyar Egyetemi Kiadó, 2005.

Vasady-Nagy, Andor. *Cleveland és környéke magyarvonatkozású vállalkozásainak címtára és kézi telefonkönyve: Hungarian Business Directory*. Cleveland: Rajkai Enterprises, Inc, 1967.

Veccoli, Rudolph. "The Contadini in Chicago: A Critic of the Uprooted." *The Journal of American History* 51 (1964): 404–417.

Wass, Albert. *A költő és a macska* [The poet and the cat]. Cleveland: Hazánk, 1989.

Waxman, Sharon. "In a Screenwriter's Art, Echoes of His Father's Secret." *New York Times*, March 18, 2004.

West Side Hungarian Reformed Church. *Congregational Yearbook*. (Pastoral and organizational reports) Cleveland: 2011.

Zake, Ieva. *Anti-Communist Minorities in the U.S. – Political Activism of Ethnic Refugees*. New York: Palgrave Macmillan, 2009.

Interviews

Antal, András, personal interview, October 1, 2011.

Balogh, Carolyn, email correspondence, July 30, 2012 and October 30, 2017.

Bartus, László, email correspondence, July 25, 2012.

Basa, Enikő, email correspondence, March 17, 2013.

Bernhardt, Béla, email correspondence, April 11, 2011, and personal interview, March 31, 2012.

Berta, Erika, telephone conversation, August 23, 2012.

Bíró, Zoltán, handwritten correspondence, February 10, 2012.

Bócsay Tóth, Klára, email correspondence, March 26, 2013.

Bodnár, Lajos, email correspondence, July 18, 2011.

Botyánszky, Igor, personal interview, October 3, 2010.

Bőjtös, László, email correspondence, August 2, 2012.

Chmielewski, Emese, personal interview, June 29, 2017.

Chmielewski, Erika, personal interview, June 29, 2017.

Csatáry, George, personal interview, June 2010, and email correspondence, November 20, 2012.

Csia, Éva, personal interview, March 25, 2012.

Csia, Pál, personal interview, March 25, 2012.

Dévai, Samantha (pseudonym), personal interview, October 17, 2010.

Dömötörffy, Zsolt, telephone conversation, May 3, 2018.

Duna, Andrew, personal interview, September 2017.

Dunay, Sofi, personal interview, September 2017.

Enyedy, Gustav, telephone conversation, October 13, 2010.

Falk, Nicholas, personal interview, November 16, 2017.

Fazekas, Robert, personal interview, April 29, 2018.

Feigenbaum, Maria, telephone conversations on July 26, 2011 and June 21, 2012.

Graber, Ann, personal interview, October 15, 2017.

Gulden, Julianna, email correspondence, March 25, 2013.

Gulden Kaschl, Katalin, email correspondence, March 25, 2013.

Gulden, Tamás, email correspondence, September 17, 2012.

Gyékényesi, Sarolta, email correspondence, July 23, 2017.

Harmat, Ákos, last president of CMAC, telephone conversation, March 21, 2012.

Hartmann, Charles, telephone conversation, July 29, 2011.

Hegedeos, Kálmán, email correspondence, October 5 and November 19, 2012.

Hegyi, Jennifer, personal interview, October 17, 2010.

Horváth, Mihály, email correspondence, November 2, 2012.

Huszti, Elizabeth, personal interview, April 24, 2012.

Kádár, Dániel, email correspondence, May 1, 2012.

Karetka, Livia, personal interview, June 5, 2017.

Kita, Bob, personal interview, February 4, 2017.

Kobus, Matt, personal interview, October 18, 2010.

Kohuth, Shirley, church secretary of H. Presbyterian Church in Youngstown, letter to the author, July 15, 2010.

Kovács, Gábor, personal interview, October 18, 2010.

Krasznai, Bea, email correspondence, October 31, 2017.

Krasznai, Csaba, email correspondence, August 3, 2011 and October 30, 2017.

Kucinich, Dennis, telephone conversation, June 14, 2011.

Lázár, Andrea, email correspondence, November 19, 2017.

Lehmann, Paul, email correspondence, October 31, 2017.

Leitgeb, Sándor, email correspondence, September 16, 2012.

Linder, Susan, personal interview, October 15, 2010.

Mahovlich, Walt, personal interview, December 27, 2016 and email correspondence, November 17, 2017.

Markovic, Milos, personal interview, July 20, 2010.

Mészáros, Andrea, personal interview, April 15, 2012.
Mihály, Ernest, personal interview, February 26, 2012 and July 20, 2017.
Molnár, Mary Jane, email correspondence, October 31, 2017.
Muhoray, George, personal interview, August 14, 2010.
Nádas, Gabriella, personal interview, March 25, 2012.
Osváth-Nagy, Judith, email correspondence, March 26, 2013.
Pál, Gergő, personal interview, June 29, 2017.
Papp, Klára, email correspondence, June 23, 2012.
Papp-Taylor, Elizabeth, email correspondence, November 12, 2017.
Patay, Karl, personal interview, October 15, 2010.
Patay, Péter, personal interview, March 22, 2013.
Piskor, Steve, telephone interview, November 18, 2017.
Poecze, Joseph, email correspondence, March 29, 2012.
Ponti, György, personal interview, April 14, 2013.
Radva, Éva, personal interview, July 12, 2017.
Ramsey, Megan, personal interview, October 18, 2010.
Rátoni-Nagy, Valéria, personal interview, June 12, 1998.
Repic, Nick, email correspondence, June 23, 2013.
Riczo, John, telephone conversation, February 23, 2012.
Robinson, Margaret, organizer of the Hungarian group, telephone conversation, July 18, 2011.
Rózsahegyi, Ida, personal interview, January 15, 2012.
Sárosi, Richard, telephone interview, March 19, 2012.
Siklódi, Sándor, email correspondence, July 26, 2011.
Soltay, István, personal interview and email correspondence, May 19-21, 2013.
Somogyi, Lél, email correspondence, January 2012.
St. John, Chuck, personal interview, July 28, 2011, and email correspondence, June 23, 2013.
Sundem, Sándor, personal interview, September 2017.
Szabó, Éva, email correspondence, November 26, 2017.
Szénásy, Ildikó, telephone conversation, September 22, 2012.
Szentkirályi, Paul, email correspondence, October 28, 2012.
Tabor, Krisztina the elder, personal interview, June 5, 2017.
Tabor, Krisztina the younger, personal interview, June 29, 2017.
Thompson, Robert, telephone conversation, March 15, 2012.
Tóth, Gergő, personal interview, November 26, 2012.
Uray, Marylou, telephone conversation, October 13, 2010.
Varjas, Vivian, personal interview, October 17, 2010.
Zamiska, Mark, email correspondence, June 23, 2013.

Endnotes

1   Referring to entities outside of Hungary. For more detail about Hungarian scouts in Cleveland and worldwide, see Chapter Three.

2   For a more detailed explanation of each type of assimilation, see the second half of Appendix II: Survey of Scholarship and Extended Theoretical Background.

3   See Appendix II: Extended Theoretical Background for a more thorough discussion.

4   One organization was inadvertently left off the possible response choices of the sociological survey, the Hungarian Association, but its history and current status are described in Chapter Three.

5   See Rodis and Vasilakes, also Cizmic, Miletic, and Prpic's work, Klelmencic's monograph, and Stone's dissertation.

6   US Census population estimate of 385,809 as of July 1, 2016.

7   See map of Cuyahoga and adjoining counties on the front endpaper.

8   Julianna Puskás, *Ties That Bind, Ties That Divide: 100 Years of Hungarian Experience in the United States* (New York: Homes and Meier, 2000), 21–22.

9   Steven Béla Várdy, *The Hungarian-Americans* (Boston: Twayne Publishers, 1985), 91.

10 Puskás, *Ties That Bind*, 200.

11 Ibid., 262–264.

12 Carmela Patrias, *Hungarians in Canada* (Ottawa: Canadian Historical Society, 1999), 20.

13 Ferenc Somogyi, *A clevelandi magyarság vázlatos története* (Berea, OH: Institute of Hungarology, 1994), 64.

14 István Szappanos, from an unpublished lecture given at the Cleveland Hungarian Heritage Museum on January 14, 2006, emailed to the author on September 24, 2012.

15 Susan Papp, *Hungarian Americans and their Communities of Cleveland* (Cleveland: Cleveland State University, 1981), 274–276.

16 Borbándi, *A magyar emigráció életrajza 1945–1985* (Budapest: Európa Kiadó, 1989), 474–475.

17 George Lázár, "The Forgotten Generation: Immigration to the U.S. between 1959–1989." Lecture given at the American Hungarian Educators Association conference at the University of Maryland, April 29, 2016.

18 Abraham Maslow, "A theory of human motivation." *Psychological Review.* 50 (4): 370–396.

19 Lázár, "Forgotten Generation" lecture.

20 Entry/Exit Overstay Report Fiscal Year 2015. United States Department of Homeland Security.

21 See Map of Hungarian Ancestry in Pictures & Illustrations.

22 See Chapter Three for detailed descriptions of what these organizations do.

23 See Membership and Mailing Lists table, along with Geographical Breakdown of Two Representative Mailing Lists. Also see the number of Facebook followers for various churches, businesses, and organizations, found in the Conclusion under the heading Outlook for the Future.

24 See Geographical Breakdown table at the end of this chapter.

25 Thanks to Tibor Purger for urging the author to devise a novel way of estimating the Hungarian population of Cleveland.

26 Karl B. Bonutti and George J. Prpic, *Selected Ethnic Communities of Cleveland: a Socio-Economic Study* (Cleveland: The Cleveland Urban Observatory, 1974), 44.

27 See films *Like Bubbles in the Wine* and *Last Hungarian on Buckeye.*

28 Film, *Like Bubbles in the Wine.*

29 The translation is difficult: literally, "On the Warpath: News from Comrades," but *Hadak Útján* additionally means the Milky Way, mythologically the path of ancient Hungarian warriors, and *bajtárs* has none of the communist connotations that the word "comrade" has acquired.

30 Including József and Béla Csorba, Frank Frendl, László Harmat, Ferenc Ilkanich, Miklós Jánosi, István Luczek, János Molnár, and Árpád Nagy. Kálmán Elek and József Lendvay lived on the property and were its caretakers.

31 For a more detailed history of Csárdás, see Richard Graber's history (2015). Although its prologue and epilogue are fiction, the rest of the book is an accurate memoir.

32 Hommonay's personal papers are housed in the Cleveland Hungarian Heritage Society library.

33 See the ethnographic fieldwork done by teenaged members of the Hungarian Scout Folk Ensemble, published in 2008 in an oral history collection edited by the author, *Clevelandben még élnek magyarok?*

34 Imre Király, *Emléklapok a Petőfi szobor leleplezési ünnepélyéről* (Cleveland: Egyesült Magyar Egyletek, 1930), 49–50.

35 Balázs Balogh, "Lifestyle, Identity, and Visions of the Future of Generations of Hungarian-American Communities of Western Pennsylvania," *Hungarian Heritage* 11, nos. 1–2 (2010): 26–27.

36 Mihály Hoppál, "Tradition and Ethnic Symbols in an American Hungarian Community," *Hungarian Heritage* 11, nos. 1–2 (2010): 55.

37 Hoppál, "Tradition and Ethnic Symbols," 53, from which the next two quotes stem as well.

38 See *Cold War to Warm Cooperation*, which details over 250 individual life stories of the military service of Cleveland Hungarians from 1950 to 2014.

39 Over 3,000 people attended the Scout Picnic in September 2017, a record number.

40 Walter Mahovlich, personal interview.

41 Civic subsidiaries of the Hungarian Association included the World Federation of Hungarian Engineers and Architects, the Transylvanian World Federation, the United Hungarian Fund, the Organization of American Hungarian Libraries, the Free Hungarian Journalists Association, the American Hungarian Catholic Priests Association, the Occidental Society, and the Hungarian-American Physicians organization. AHEA was organized at a 1974 meeting of the Hungarian Association, with bylaws ordained at a 1975 meeting, but shortly thereafter became independent, with incorporation in Maryland in 1976, and tax-exempt status attained in 1977.

42 Mihály Szegedy-Maszák, "Values in Contemporary Hungarian Literature," in Search for American Values: Contributions of Hungarian Americans to American Values, an American-Hungarian Bi-national Symposium, a publication detailing 10 lectures held in Budapest December 12–14, 1983. (Budapest: Országos Széchenyi Könyvtár, 1990), 51.

43 Ibid.

44 From the introduction, presumably by Béla Béldy, editor, *Első Magyar Találkozó Krónikája* (Cleveland: Árpád Könyvkiadó, 1962), 11–12. "Nem veszitek észre, hogy mi mindig csak Cleveland-re gondolunk, amikor csinálni akarunk valamit? Hogy valami érthetetlen megadással beletörődünk a clevelandi közönyfüggöny-be és nem igyekszünk áttörni a kis lokális klikkek aknamezőin, hogy érintkezést teremthessünk többi magyar testvéreinkkel?" The translation into English in the text body is the author's, as are all of the following.

45 For a more detailed description of the organizations's history and activities, see Chapter Two, under the heading Physical Landscape.

46 Incorporated in 1994 as a 501(c) 3.

47 Susan Papp, *Hungarian Americans*, 279.

48 Andor Vasady-Nagy, *Cleveland és környéke magyarvonatkozású vállalkozásainak címtára és kézi telefonkönyve: Hungarian Business Directory* (Cleveland: Rajkai Enterprises, Inc, 1967).

49 Imre Sári Gál, *Az amerikai Debrecen: Képek clevelandi magyarság életéből* (Toronto: Patria Publishing, 1966), 79.

50 The author took part in each anniversary performance from 1988 on, and thus had each program booklet. The information detailing Hungarian businesses in Cleveland in the rest of the chapter are all firsthand experiences gleaned from personal contacts.

51 Michael Harrison, who learned his trade from Farkas and later bought the business.

52 While in high school, the author served and washed dishes for her catering business, as did many Hungarian immigrants.

53 Although many scholars prefer the nomenclature Roma to describe the Romani people, this particular group preferred to call themselves Gypsies.

54 The orchestra's composition varied in number and included George Petty, Sándor Leitgeb, John Markovics, Miki Molnár, Denis Wendt, Gil Yachon, László Vince, and Lajos Boday, along with occasional special guests like István Mózsi, László Roósz and Béla Baráth.

55 The 25th anniversary performance was held at the West Side Hungarian Reformed Church, with 22 people singing with the choir in addition to the 22 regular Mindszenty Choir members. The Mindszenty Choir's conductors included Endre Alapi, Ildikó Búza Ormay, Mihály Almási, Emőke Tapolyai, Fr. Sándor Siklódi, Klára Seefeld, Miklós Peller, and Zsuzsa Kálmán, while its presidents were Ervin Hollósy, Kálmán Elek, and Ellie Mihály.

56 The artists were Krisztina Lázár, János Nádas, Peter Tábor, and Krisztina Walter. Additionally, in March of 2013, George Kozmon curated a similar exhibition of contemporary art entitled "Hungarian Rhapsody: a celebration of Hungarian American Culture" at a suburban Cleveland community center, with artwork by the aforementioned young artists, as well as additional works by Dave Szekeres and Judy Takacs. Over 300 people were in attendance at its opening, with a dance performance by the Hungarian Scout Folk Ensemble, as the author personally witnessed.

57 They included Zsolt Gyombolai, Mihály Bodor, Ádám Török-Dancsó, Krisztina Pethő, and Bertold Illés hosted and mentored by the Cleveland Hungarian Heritage Society, and Tünde Tálas hosted and mentored by Bocskai Rádió.

58 Aniko Hatoss, "Community-level approaches in language planning: the case of Hungarian in Australia," in *Language planning in local contexts* (Clevedon, UK: Multilingual Matters, 2008), 55–74. The exception is non-profit status for tax-exempt purposes.

59 See Steven Béla Várdy's "Hungarians in America's Ethnic Politics," in *America's Ethnic Politics*, ed. Joseph Roucek & Bernard Eisenberg (Westport, CT: Greenwood Press, 1982). Two additional comprehensive works detailing the crown are also worthwhile, one by Attila Simontsits, *The Last Battle for St. Stephen's Crown* (Cleveland: Weller Publishing, 1983), and the other by Tibor Glant, *A Szent Korona amerikai kalandja és hazatérése* (Debrecen, Hungary: Debreceni Egyetemi Kiadó, 2018).

60 Other dignitaries specifically visiting Cleveland's Hungarian community included Prime Minister Viktor Orbán in October 2004 and President Pál Schmitt in September 2011. While these visits did draw crowds of several hundreds, they were nowhere near the size of the crowds that Reverend Tőkés or Cardinal Mindszenty attracted.

61 Judith Fai-Podlipnik, "One Goal, Many Paths: Internal and External Struggles of the Hungarian Émigrés" in *Anti-Communist Minorities in the United States – Political Activism of Ethnic Refugees*, ed. Ieva Zake (New York: Palgrave Macmillan, 2009), 100.

62 In a letter to Imre Kovács on October 21, 1952, as quoted by Tibor Frank in "Imre Kovács and Cold War Émigré Politics," 314.

63 Ieva Zake, *Anti-Communist Minorities in the United States – Political Activism of Ethnic Refugees* (New York: Palgrove Macmillan, 2009), from the preface.

64 Inventory spreadsheet provided by Julius Nádas to the author on September 9, 2012.

65 The author's father.

66 Ágnes Huszár Várdy, in an unpublished manuscript presented at the Hungarian Congress in Cleveland on November 26, 2011, which she was kind enough to lend the author.

67 *Nyugodt lehetsz elvtárs* [Rest assured, comrade] won a literary award in Rome in 1958. Novels written in Cleveland include *A besugó és az apostol* [The informer and the apostle], *Magyar disputa* [Hungarian argument], *Mendő Szabó Mari néni komendál* [Mrs. Szabó commends], *Ünneplő halál okából* [Commemoration on account of a death], a double edition including *Vérző karcolatok* [Bleeding vignettes] and *Kétszer radikális Gyuri* [Twice radical Georgie], *Döbrönte kürtje* [Döbrönte's horn], *Atlanti szaletli* [Atlantic gazebo], *Száműzött a szabadság igájában* [Exiled in freedom's yoke], *Kováts Mihály hajóra száll* [Michael Kováts boards a ship], *Eltékozolt fiak* [Wasted sons], *A hézag* [The rift], and *A bíboros és a rendőr* [The cardinal and the cop].Translations of the titles are the author's, and many of the jacket covers of these books contain artwork by George Kozmon.

68 All translations are mine, unless otherwise noted.

69 Original: "A szülőföldjén! Amit igen fontos hangoztatni, mert ma a párt nagyon hajtja a 'szülőföld' használatát a 'haza' kifejezés helyett, különösen idegenben élő honfitársaink irányában, akiket a szocialista hazába nem akarunk befogadni, de kis ideig engedünk lébecolni a szülőföldön. Ezt én ügyesnek tartom, jól kispekulálták: a pártban, a sok nyugatosnak haza nuku, de a szülőföldre minden fasiszta, félfasiszta, vagy fasisztagyanus magyar jöhet valutával vakációzni – túristaként..." in István Eszterhás, *A hézag*, 16.

70 Ibid., 338.

71 Joe Eszterhas as quoted by Sharon Waxman in "In a Screenwriter's Art, Echoes of His Father's Secret," *New York Times*, March 18, 2004. Accessed electronically on April 22, 2013.

72 A longer version of this section appeared as: "No Passport? Can't Go Home: The Novels of Áron Gábor," *Hungarian Quarterly* 51, no. 99 (Autumn 2010). All quoted passages are my own translations.

73 Recorded by Miklós Kossányi during the Hungarian Congress held in Cleveland in November 1968. After Kossányi's death, his archives were for a while temporarily housed in Cleveland State University's library. The video and sound archives are as of this writing being stored by the Cleveland Hungarian Heritage Society, with a portion previously shipped to the Széchenyi library in Budapest. They include original recordings of Albert Wass, Zita Szeleczky, Magda Szabó, and other notable Hungarian authors who visited Cleveland.

74 The original Hungarian, as the author transcribed it from the voice recording: "Nem csak azért, hogy elszörnyűlködtessen, hanem azért is, hogy megerősítsen

bennünket abban a kitartásunkban, hogy mindnyájan szószólók legyünk a magyar ügyekben és a Vasfüggöny mögé zárt embermillióknak."

75 The original Hungarian comments, as recorded by Miklós Kossányi and as the author transcribed them: "Engedjék meg, hogy elmondjam amit Wass Albert barátom és mélyen tisztelt költő oly szépen mondott, egy-két szóval kiegészítsek, hogy a magyarság, amit Önök, független attól hogy melyik generáció és emigrációs korosztályok, amit Önök itt Amerikában létesítettek, amelyeket Önök létesítettek társadalmi csúcson, azon az emigrációban egyik nép se produlkált. Nagyon büszke vagyok erre, és nagyon kérem, jegyezzenek meg ezzel valamit: adósok. Annak a felismerésével és tudatával adósok, hogy ezt, hogy ennek a sikernek az eredeteit, amely otthonról hozták… onnan amiből egy ezer éves történelem fölépül, Önök ennek a történelemnek a tényezőit mentették át ide, s ezek a tényezők Önöknek szellemi kulcsot, társadalmi rangot emeltek, kérem, ne felejtsék ezt… Necsak ide gyűljenek össze, a Magyar Találkozókra, és beszéljünk egymásnak, és mondjuk el itt az igazságot, hanem Önök politizáljanak, hölgyeim és uraim, éljenek azzal az alkotmányban adott joggal amit egy szabad Amerika biztosít Önöknek, és hirdessék, hogy odaát Európában nemcsak egy nép, hanem Európa is veszedelemben forog. Mondják azt, amit közvetve vagy közvetlenül tudnak a kommunizmusról, mondják el azt, hogy odaát dráma van…"

76 Robert Fazekas unearthed a time capsule from 1954 when the church and school buildings were sold in 2018.

77 Ferenc Somogyi, *Emlékkönyv*, 16–17. A reproduction of the original letter to parents announcing the formation of the school can be found in this source. Written in Gábor Papp's characteristically frank style, it tells parents to "shove a clean notebook and a reading book into your child's hands [and] arrange carpools" [Tehát szerdán nyomjunk a gyermek kezébe egy tiszta füzetet és egy olvasókönyvet. A szülők szervezzék meg a gyermekek szállítását].

78 The author's sister-in-law. After Gábor Papp, the school was directed by Imre Bogárdy, then Ödön Szentkirályi (the author's father), then Bea Tábor (the author's sister), then Krisztina Tábor (Bea's sister-in-law), and now Judy Szentkirályi. Cleveland is indeed a Hungarian village.

79 An earlier, shorter version of this chapter was published in *Hungarian Studies Review* 40, no. 1 (Spring 2013).

80 Katalin Pintz, "New Brunswick, N.J. as a Magyar Ethnic Island," *Hungarian Studies Review* 38, nos. 1–2 (2011): 86.

81 Ibid.

82 Ibid, 89.

83 Herbert J. and Irene S. Rubin, *Qualitative Interviewing: the Art of Hearing Data* (Thousand Oaks, CA: Sage Publications, 2005), 4.

84 Ibid., 238.

85 ÓV is the abbreviation for *Őrsvezetőképző tábor*, the scout leadership training camp for patrol leaders aged 14 and above, which teaches them small-group leadership skills.

86 Mónika Fodor, "My Slice of Americana: Hungarian-Americans Construct Their Ethno-Cultural Identities in Narratives." Unpublished dissertation, University of Pécs, 2007.

87 For further explanation of peer orientation vis-à-vis parental upbringing, see Gordon Neufeld and Gabor Maté, *Hold On to Your Kids: Why Parents Need to Matter More than Peers* (New York: Ballantine Books, 2005). The book devotes an entire chapter to recreating an attachment village, which is what Hungarian scouting in Cleveland already seems to do as told by the subjects of this study.

88 Mónika Fodor, "My Slice of Americana," 91.

89 Joshua Fishman, *Hungarian Language Maintenance in the United States* (Bloomington, IN: Indiana State University, 1966).

90 István Szappanos, from an unpublished lecture given at the Cleveland Hungarian Heritage Museum on January 14, 2006, emailed to the author on September 24, 2012.

91 see Miklós Szántó, *Magyarok Amerikában* (Budapest: Gondolat Könyvkiadó, 1984).

92 Gyula Borbándi, *A magyar emigráció életrajza 1945–1985* (Bern: Európai Protestáns Magyar Szabadegyetem, 1985), 474–475.

93 These include Balázs Bedy, the Reverend Béla Bernhardt, Viktor Falk, József Györky, and János Nádas.

94 These include János Nádas, Gabriella Ormay Nádas, Zsolt Dömötörffy, Ilona Simon Erőssy, Panni Nádas Ludányi, Ildikó Falk Peller, Márta Pereszlényi Pintér, Valéria Rátoni Nagy, and Lél Somogyi.

95 DP members included Gyula Borosdy, Gyula Dolesch, István Szappanos, Balázs Bedy, Mihály Horváth, Andrea Vareska Mészáros, and Krisztina Nádas.

96 For Troop #22, these included its founder Ede Chászár, Zoltán Bócsay, István Szappanos, Dr. György Vareska, László Zala, Zsolt Gregora, Mihály Horváth, and Ernő Kálnoky. For girl scout Troop #33, its founders Dr. Ágnes Huszár Várdy and Mária Strada Friedrich, Ágnes Bodnár, Andrea Vareska Mészáros, Klára Bócsay Tóth, and Valéria Rátoni Nagy. For girl scout Troop #34, its founder Melinda Dolesch Gaydán, Erzsébet Mód Borosdy, Klára Thurner, Krisztina Szabadkai Tábor, Judy Csia Szentkirályi, Andrea Szabolcs, Gabriella Ormay Nádas, and Krisztina Szentkirályi. For Troop #14, DP or descendant scoutmasters included László Berkes, Vilmos Bárdossy, Dénes Dietrich, Ferenc Beodray, Gyula Dolesch, Gábor Papp, Lothár Stieberth, Béla Megay, Viktor Falk, Levente Szabolcs, Andreas Tábor, Pál Strada, and Peter Hokky

97 Joseph Széplaki, *The Hungarians in America 1583–1974: A Chronology & Fact Book* (Dobbs Ferry, NY: Oceana Publications, 1975), vii.

98 Joshua Fishman, *Hungarian Language Maintenance.*

99 Steven Béla Várdy, *The Hungarian-Americans,* 42–43.

100 Dirk Hoerder, "From Ethnic to Interethnic History: an Introduction," in *Identity, Conflict, and Cooperation, Identity, Conflict, and Cooperation: Central Europeans in Cleveland, 1850–1930,* David Hammack and Diane L. and John J. Grabowski, eds. (Cleveland: Western Reserve Historical Society, 2002), 7.

101 Attila Z. Papp, *Beszédből világ: elemzések, adatok amerikai magyarokról* (Budapest: Hungarian Institute of International Affairs, 2008), 442–443, 452–453.

102 Krisztina Oláh, "A Plan to Address the Communication Challenges of the Hungarian Community of Cleveland," Masters thesis: John Carroll University, 2012.

103 Imre Bogárdy: New Year's Wish
Once more a year passes into the grave
We can gaze after it laughing or crying.
Many may happily bid it farewell
They hope, the next one will be different.
I stand here also alone, and what I wish
Is that we see better days than the last year.
Blessings on everyone, peace in the homes,
Happy understanding in all men's hearts,
This is what we pray for, this is why our hearts beat,
Let God grant us a happy New Year.

104 Milos Markovic, manager of the Cleveland Public Library Foreign Literature section, in discussion with the author, July 2010. This is the same number listed in: Ilona Kovács, "Hungarian Immigrants in the United States and Hungarian Studies," in *Search for American Values: Contributions of Hungarian Americans to American Values: American-Hungarian Bi-national Symposium* (Budapest: Országos Széchenyi Könyvtár, 1990), 81. In the twentieth century, thousands of those Hungarian books resided in the Carnegie branch of the Cleveland Public Library at Lorain and Fulton Avenues on the West side, but these books have since been moved to the downtown main branch.

105 Attila Z. Papp, ed., *Beszédből Világ* (Budapest: Hungarian Institute of International Affairs, 2008). Originally commissioned by the Hungarian government institution HTMH (Határon Túli Magyarok Hivatala: Institute for Hungarians Beyond Hungary's Borders) and contracted to the Teleki László Intézet (a foreign policy research institute), funding for its research was unexpectedly rescinded part way through the project, then reinstated, and upon initial publication by the Hungarian Institute for International Affairs (Magyar Külügyi Intézet), political controversy led to the temporary confiscation of published copies, a situation which was eventually resolved, leading to the eventual uninhibited distribution of the study.

106 Zoltán Fejős, *A chicagói magyarok két nemzedéke 1890–1940* (Budapest: Közép-Európai Intézet, 1993), 290–295.

107 Richard Alba and Victor Nee, *Remaking the American Mainstream* (Cambridge, MA: Harvard University Press, 2003), 9.

108 Ibid, 282.

109 Dirk Hoerder, "From Ethnic to Interethnic History: an Introduction," in *Identity, Conflict, and Cooperation*, eds. Hammack and Grabowski, 8.

110 As summarized by Aonghas Mac Thòmais St.-Hilaire in "Segmented Assimilation," *Encyclopedia of Immigration*, ed. James Ciment (Armonk, NY: Sharpe Reference, 2001), 460–467.

111 Elliott Barkan, Hasia Diner, and Alan Kraut, *From Arrival to Incorporation*, (New York: New York University Press, 2008), 25.

112 Ibid, 10.

113 Attila Z. Papp, *Beszédből világ*, 450.

114 George Kozmon, in his curator's statement for "Hungarian Rhapsody," a display of six Hungarian-American artists at the Beachwood Arts Council, March 2013.

115 László Bőjtös, in multiple conversations with the author, also confirmed in an email on October 31, 2012, and clarified again personally on November 4, 2012. "A területi egységbe zárt közösség ma már nem mehet, különösen az amerikai világban, ahol mindegyik generáció feljebb akar menni. Ez ma már csupán hovatartozás kérdése, bárhol élsz a világban," were his exact words; the translation is my own.

116 László Bőjtös, in *56 Stories*, ed. Andrea and Edith Lauer (Atlanta, GA: Lauer Learning, 2006). Accessed online October 31, 2012, at www.freedomfighter56. com/en_stories_bojtos_l.html.

Index

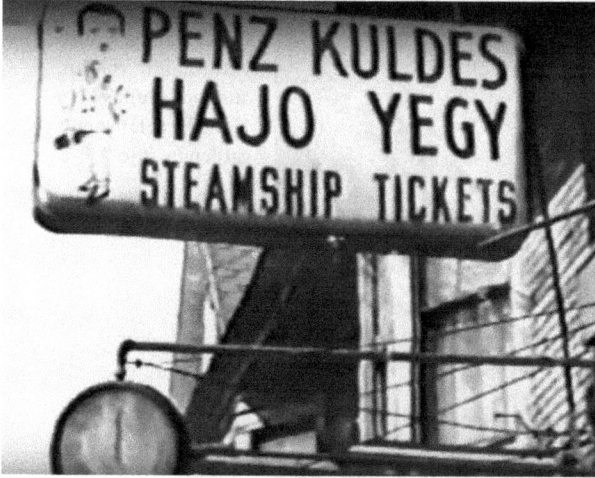

Hungarian sign on Buckeye road

Still from "The Last Hungarian on Buckeye," movie made by Tibor Bognár

Hungarian immigrants celebrating the sunflower harvest in Cleveland, 1913
https://commons.wikimedia.org/w/index.php?curid=2986854

265

Hungarian Cultural Garden. Judge Louis Petrash, Lily Volosin, and Judge Julius M. Kovachy at far end of garden in 1950

Cleveland Public Library / Photograph Collection

Hungarian refugees at William Penn Hall soup kitchen, 8637 Buckeye Rd in 1957
Cleveland Public Library / Photograph Collection

MHBK (The Collegial Society of Military Veterans) Ball, ca 1953
Cleveland Hungarian Heritage Society

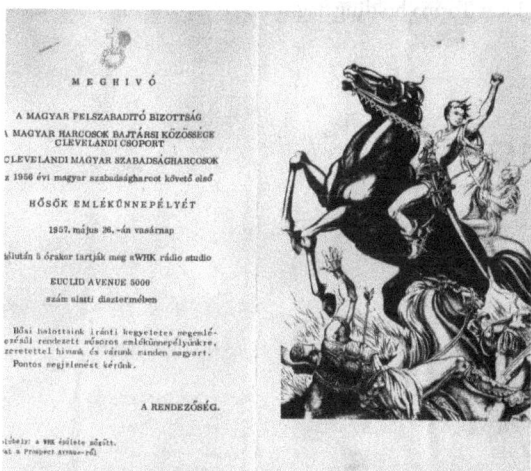

First commemoration of the 1956 Revolution
in Cleveland in 1957
Cleveland Hungarian Heritage Society

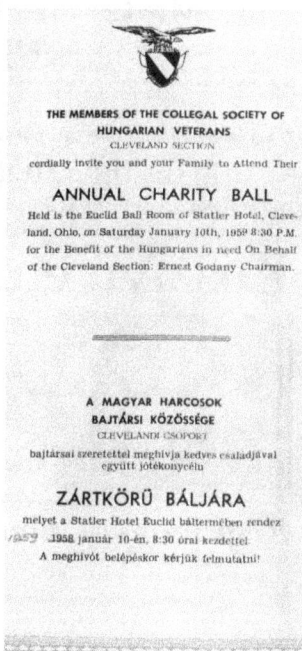

MHBK (The Collegial Society of Military Veterans) Ball
invitation from 1959
Cleveland Hungarian Heritage Society

Girl Scout Troop 33 at Scout Picnic. Judit Torma holding flag, Valéria Szőke behind her, Nóra Kovács at corner, 1960's
Girl Scout Troop 33

Kőszívű ember fiai
[The Heartless Man's sons] at the Capitol Theater in Cleveland, ca. 1966

268

Soccer team of the Cleveland Magyar Athletic Club in 1973
Ödön Szentkirályi

Night in Budapest program
booklet from 1968
Cleveland Hungarian Heritage Society

Cardinal Mindszenty in Cleveland in 1974
Pictures from the album "Mindszenty József Bíboros Érsek-prímás Úr Látogatása 1974 Tavaszán Cleveland Egyházmegyében," Kárpát Publishing, 1975

St. Nicholas and the bogeyman (krampusz) at scouts, 1993
Joseph Földesi

1995 The author's big fat Hungarian wedding, front L to R: Roxanne Samay, Chilla Gáspár, Enikő Kiss, Erzsi Hajdú-Németh, Réka Pigniczky, Eszti Pigniczky, the author, Emi Lengyel, Andrea Vajtay, Katica Avvakumovits, Aliz Demecs, Adriana Vera, back row L to R: Andrew Udvarnoki, Zsolt Szentkirályi, Gábor Szórád, Pál Szentkirályi, Géza Pál Balássy, Károly Hokky, Károly Szélpál, Árpád László Kovács, Dániel Szendrey, István Tábor jr
From the author's collection

Székely kapu [carved wooden gate] at the Hungarian Cultural Center of Northeast Ohio club grounds
Hungarian Cultural Center of Northeastern Ohio

Templomőrző [guardians of the church] group lobbies Representative Dennis Kucinich, L to R Kucinich, Éva Szabó, Kati Fördös, Edit Juhász, Márta Fördös, Hanna Geréby, 2009
Joseph Földesi

Demonstration against closing
St. Emeric church, 2010
Joseph Földesi

St. Elizabeth dancers at the Hungarian Cultural Center of Northeast Ohio, Hiram picnic
L to R Renee and Steve Spisak, Szuszi Juhasz, Mary Slater, Elizabeth Gulyas Lewis, Edith
Karacsony, Denise and Tim Gordon, Gayle Thompson, Andy Toth, 2015
Elizabeth Gulyas Lewis for the Hungarian Cultural Center of Northeast Ohio

St. Elizabeth dancers at Hungarian Cultural Gardens L to R Andy Toth, Mary Ann Draves,
Carolyn Biro, Gayle Thompson, Elizabeth Gulyas Lewis, Edith Karacsony, Szuszi Juhasz,
Steve Spisak, 2016
Elizabeth Gulyas Lewis

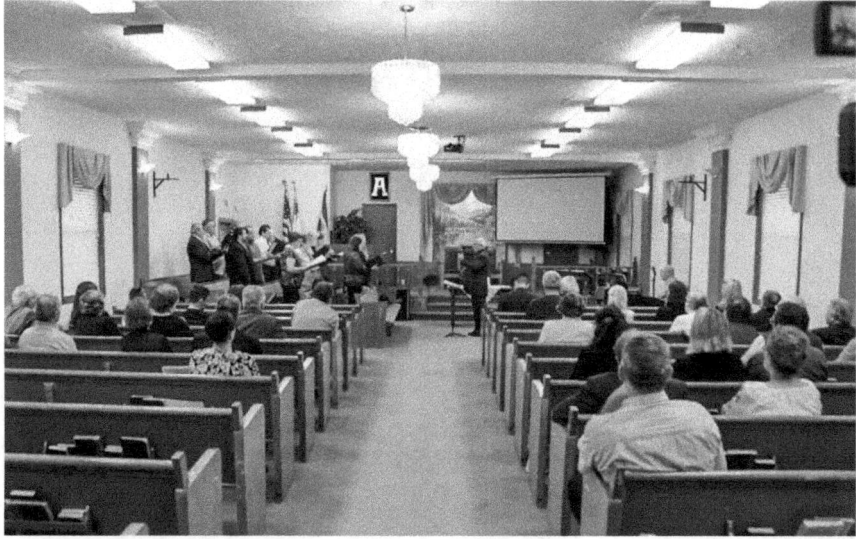

Hungarian Seventh Day Adventist Church choir, 2017
Bocskai Rádió

Hungarian Bethany Baptist Church interior, 2017
Bocskai Rádió

Hungarian School class, 2017
Bocskai Rádió

Monument entitled "Freedom Is Not Free". Erected to honor the Hungarian Freedom Fighters who fought against Soviet oppression beginning on 23 October 1956 and lasting through 10 November 1956. Front of monument states "The crack in the Berlin Wall began with a hole in a flag in Budapest!"

SammyJL27 - Own work, CC BY-SA 4.0, https://commons.wikimedia. org/w/index.php?curid=62083342

Scouts in summer camp in 1993
Péter Balássy for Hungarian Scout Troop 14

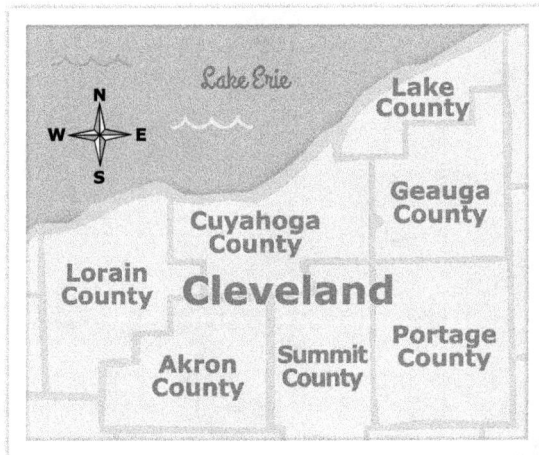

9 781943 596102